Mary Celeste

Mary Celeste:

THE GREATEST MYSTERY OF THE SEA

Paul Begg

PEARSON
Longman

Harlow, England • London • New York • Boston • San Francisco • Toronto
Sydney • Tokyo • Singapore • Hong Kong • Seoul • Taipei • New Delhi
Cape Town • Madrid • Mexico City • Amsterdam • Munich • Paris • Milan

PEARSON EDUCATION LIMITED

Edinburgh Gate
Harlow CM20 2JE
United Kingdom
Tel: +44 (0)1279 623623
Fax: +44 (0)1279 431059
Website: www.pearsoned.co.uk

First edition published in Great Britain in 2005

© Pearson Education Limited 2005

The right of Paul Begg to be identified as author of this work has been
asserted by him in accordance with the Copyright, Designs and Patents Act 1988.

ISBN 0 582 78422 0

British Library Cataloguing in Publication Data
A CIP catalogue record for this book can be obtained from the British Library

Library of Congress Cataloging in Publication Data
Begg, Paul.
    Mary Celeste : the greatest mystery of the sea / Paul Begg.
        p. cm.
    ISBN 0–582–78422–0
    1. Mary Celeste (Brig) I. Title.

  G530.M37B44 2005
  910′.9163′3—dc22

                          2004051486

10 9 8 7 6 5 4 3 2 1
09 08 07 06 05

Set by 35 in 9.5/14pt Melior
Printed by Biddles Ltd., Kings Lynn

The Publishers' policy is to use paper manufactured from sustainable forests.

Contents

List of maps and illustrations

Acknowledgements

We are grateful to the following for permission to reproduce copyright material:

The Peabody Essex Museum for plates 1, 2, 5, 6, 9, 10, 12, 13, 14, 15, 16 and 17; New Bedford Whaling Museum for plate 4; Reynolds DeWalt for plates 3 and 8; and HarperCollins Inc. for plates 7 and 11.

We are also grateful to Reynolds DeWalt Printing Inc. for permission to reproduce an extract from *Rose Cottage* by Oliver Cobb, 1968.

In some instances we have been unable to trace the owners of copyright material, and we would appreciate any information that would enable us to do so.

For Paul Fitzgibbon

CHAPTER 1

◆ ◆ ◆ ◆ ◆ ◆ ◆ ◆ ◆ ◆ ◆ ◆ ◆ ◆

The ocean wanderer

At about 1.00 p.m. on Thursday, 5 December 1872, sea time, a sailor named John Johnson was at the wheel of the brigantine *Dei Gratia* when he sighted a vessel about six miles off the port bow. The state of the stranger's sails caught his attention and suggested to him that there was something wrong. He called to the second mate, John Wright, and pointed the ship out to him. The *Dei Gratia*'s skipper, Captain Morehouse, who was coming on deck from below, also saw the stranger and scanned her through his glass (telescope). With the greater clarity this provided it was obvious that something was indeed wrong. The two vessels were sailing towards each other and as they closed the distance, Captain Morehouse ordered *Dei Gratia*'s boat be readied to take some of his men across to the ship to render whatever assistance they could.

The two ships came within hailing distance, but there seemed to be no life aboard the stranger. It was decided to lower the boat and for *Dei Gratia*'s mate, Oliver Deveau, to take two men, Second Mate John Wright and seaman John Johnson, over to investigate. They accordingly piled into the small boat and rowed over to the stranger.

It was now mid-afternoon. On the stranger's boards they could see her name painted, *Mary Celeste*, but had no cause to imagine as they clambered over the side and dropped to her deck that they were about to enter the history books as participants in the greatest of all maritime mysteries. The only sounds that greeted them aboard *Mary Celeste* were those normally encountered aboard a ship, otherwise she was strangely silent.

Mary Celeste was deserted.

In the months to come Captain Morehouse, Mate Deveau and the crew of *Dei Gratia* would be suspected of piracy, of having boarded *Mary Celeste* and slaughtering everyone on board. Other thinkers speculated that they had colluded with the crew of *Mary Celeste* in a scam in which they first took them to land and then claimed the salvage reward with the intention of splitting it between them. The captain and crew of *Mary Celeste* would fare even worse, being accused of almost everything from murderous religious fanaticism through most seafaring crimes imaginable to rank stupidity.

Over the years a myth would also grow up around *Mary Celeste*, ensuring that she would pass into the common language to describe any strangely deserted place. This myth entailed a minor name change – *Mary Celeste* is more often than not called *Marie Celeste* – and the story of her discovery and the mysterious disappearance of all those aboard her is immeasurably enhanced In the popular imagination by details such as all the lifeboats being found secure in place on board, half-eaten meals and cups of warm coffee left on the galley table, and the aroma of fresh tobacco smoke lingering in the Captain's cabin, where a cat is supposed to have been found sleeping peacefully on a bed.

Disappointingly, none of this is true.

The disappearance of the crew from *Mary Celeste* is a real, genuine and impenetrable mystery, but even real, genuine and impenetrable mysteries attract embellishments like a magnet attracts iron filings. I have no idea why this happens, why it is that people take a good mystery and try to make it even more mysterious, but it is a sad fact that a really good mystery, enjoyably taxing to the imagination, seems far less interesting when stripped of these embellishments. Happily, that is not the case with *Mary Celeste*.

True, the story is far less excitingly mysterious than the half-eaten meals, warm mugs of tea and the lingering aroma of fresh tobacco smoke make it seem, but instead of such things leading to wild and supernatural theories such as the terrified crew being snatched one by one from the deck of the vessel by the tentacles of a massive octopus or of being beamed aboard a flying saucer in a Close Encounter of the Third Kind to join other abductees such as the captain and crew of the *Cyclops* or the pilots and navigators of Flight 19, we are confronted with the need for prosaic explanations of the 'closed room' kind. Aficionados of detective fiction will be familiar with this type of crime story: a person is murdered inside a room from which there is no apparent means of access or egress except through a door that is locked from the inside. How did the murderer escape the room? The death of Julia Stoner in Conan Doyle's Sherlock Holmes mystery 'The Speckled Band' is just such a closed room mystery.

In the case of *Mary Celeste* we are confronted with a ship that appears to have been abandoned – or which somebody wanted it to be believed had been abandoned: the only 'lifeboat', a small yawl lashed to the main hatch, was missing and a piece of railing nearby had been removed to facilitate launching, and some of the ship's papers and instruments were missing. Those aboard *Mary Celeste* appear therefore to have launched the small boat, climbed in and, it must be assumed, drifted away from *Mary Celeste* until it had eventually capsized and everyone aboard been drowned. But *Mary Celeste* was a perfectly seaworthy ship. She was not sinking or taking on water, and she was fully provisioned. There is no apparent reason why she should have been abandoned.

Why would the highly capable, honest and experienced captain and crew desert in mid-ocean a perfectly seaworthy and well-provisioned ship?

This was a question that would exercise the mind of a man named Frederick Solly Flood, who had the very grand-sounding title of Her Majesty's Advocate-General and Proctor for the Queen in Her Office of Admiralty, and Attorney-General for Gibraltar. *Mary Celeste* was brought into Gibraltar by a small skeleton crew put aboard by *Dei Gratia* – a feat of seamanship – and Captain Morehouse claimed the ship and her cargo as salvage, expecting that he and his men would each receive a just and reasonable reward for the danger and risks they had undergone in saving the vessel.

Under maritime law a proportion of the value of a ship and her cargo can be claimed by those through whose labour and skill the ship and cargo were saved. The amount is usually based on the danger and skill involved in bringing the ship or cargo into safe harbour, or more often from recovering goods from a sunken vessel, as was the case, for example, when nearly £5,000,000 of gold bullion was recovered from the White Star liner *Laurentic*, sunk off Ireland in 1917, or the recovery of five tons of gold and ten tons of silver from the P&O liner *Egypt* from the Bay of Biscay in 1930.

However, whilst claiming salvage is not uncommon, finding a perfectly seaworthy and well-provisioned ship at sea is, so it was not unreasonable for foul play to have occurred to suspicious minds; thus it was that the story of *Mary Celeste* turned from a maritime mystery into a murder mystery, complete with assorted and disputed clues, among them a supposedly bloodstained sword.

The fact is that *Mary Celeste* is more than a perplexing maritime mystery – more, even, than an unusual and exciting murder mystery. It veers into the occult too. *Mary Celeste* has been discussed as a jinxed ship, a ship marked out by fate to bring disaster and misery to everyone associated with her.

Jinxes are things of the imagination, but if ever there were a story that could persuade of their reality, it is the story of *Mary Celeste*. Misfortune dogged *Mary Celeste* from the death of her young first captain during her maiden voyage to her own end when she was deliberately run aground and destroyed in an insurance scam; those involved were caught and brought to trial but a legal technicality allowed them to walk from court free men. The jinx reached from the ship's watery grave, however, and each of the conspirators apparently died in unpleasant circumstances and trouble befell almost everyone else associated with the case. The jinx may have continued even to this very day, as a well-publicised discovery of *Mary Celeste*'s remains may not have discovered the *Celeste* at all.

A jinx may also have doomed Captain Benjamin Briggs, the vanished skipper of *Mary Celeste*. All but one of his brothers and his sister died at sea and his seafaring father was struck by lightning as he stood in the doorway of his home!

Naturally over the years many people have tried to explain what happened aboard *Mary Celeste*. Some have written their theories and explanations as fiction in short stories and novels, some have presented their fiction as fact, and from time to time the story has been at the centre of heated controversy. *Mary Celeste* has also featured on postage stamps and provided material for various radio shows, including the all-time classic *Goon Show*. It even provided the plot for an early offering from the famous Hammer film studios, *Phantom Ship*, starring Bela Lugosi.

Mary Celeste was a brigantine, a two-masted vessel, square-rigged on the foremast and fore and aft rigged on the mainmast – strictly speaking a

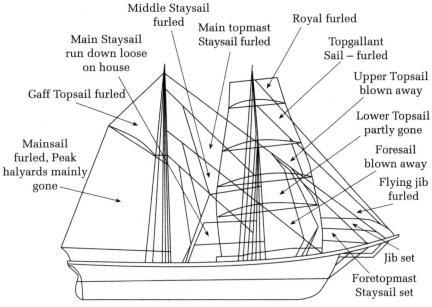

Middle Staysail
furled

Main topmast
Staysail furled

Royal furled

Main Staysail
run down loose
on house

Topgallant
Sail – furled

Upper Topsail
blown away

Gaff Topsail furled

Lower Topsail
partly gone

Mainsail
furled, Peak
halyards mainly
gone

Foresail
blown away

Flying jib
furled

Jib set

Foretopmast
Staysail set

Approximate layout of *Mary Celeste's* deck

hermaphrodite brig. The difference was that the square-rigged sails were
set to take the wind on the same side of the sail (in other words, the sails
took the wind from behind), whereas fore-and-aft sail could take the
wind either side of the sail, depending on the direction of the wind. *Mary
Celeste* was 103 feet long, 25.7 feet broad. Moving from bow to stern,
there was the windlass, the forehatch, immediately under which was a
new hawser, and beyond the forehatch was the foremast. Immediately
abaft the foremast was the forward deck house. It was 13 feet square
and six feet above the deck, made of thin planking painted white, and
consisted of three rooms divided fore and aft (lengthways), two on the
port[1] (left) and one, the galley, on the starboard. The two cabins were
the fore-cabin, entered through a sliding wooden door facing the bow of
the ship and which was the crew's quarters, sleeping four, measuring 9 feet
6 inches broad and 6-feet 9-inches long, and aft was the Second Mate's
room, about 6 feet 9 inches square. The Second Mate's cabin was entered
through a door on the port side. The starboard or right-hand side room
was the galley, containing the steward's bunk. There was a scuttle hatch
overhead in the galley. The sills of the doors to these cabins were about a
foot in height. The cabins had four windows, two on either side. On the

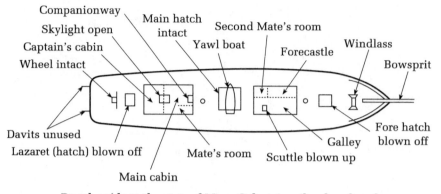

Companionway
Main hatch
intact
Second Mate's room
Skylight open
Captain's cabin
Yawl boat
Windlass
Wheel intact
Forecastle
Bowsprit

Davits unused
Fore hatch
blown off
Lazaret (hatch) blown off
Galley
Mate's room
Scuttle blown up
Main cabin

Rough guide to the state of *Mary Celeste's* sails when found

port side the windows were covered by a thin sliding shutter, the after window on the starboard side was uncovered.

Beyond the forward house was the main hatch with a small boat, a yawl, on it. Then the pumps just in front of the mainmast and abaft the mainmast was the main deck house, 14 feet wide, 18 feet long, and again made of thin, white-painted planking. It consisted of four rooms and was entered through a hatch, where a sliding door opened onto the companion-way. There was a pantry on the port side of the main cabin, entered by a door with a sill about $1^1/_2$ inches above the level of the lower deck or floor of the cabin. On the floor of the pantry there were various packets and boxes, among them a bag of sugar, a bag containing two or three pounds of tea, a barrel containing flour and a box containing dried herrings; also some rice, a nutmeg, some kidney beans, and several pots of preserved fruits and other provisions in tins covered with paper.

The main deck house also housed the Chief Mate's cabin. Here various articles of clothing and other things were stowed under the bed, including the vessel's ensign and her private signal 'W. T.'.

A fore-cabin or saloon was furnished with a table, two bench seats, a sideboard and stove. Beyond this communal room was the Captain's cabin, lighted by petroleum lamps. Mrs Brigg's melodeon was in the centre against a partition. Next to it were a number of mostly religious books. There was a little child's highchair and a medicine chest containing bottles and various medical preparations in good condition. There was also a sword in a scabbard, about which much would be made when

Mary Celeste was minutely examined in Gibraltar because it appeared to have been smeared with blood and afterwards wiped clean.

On the port side of the Captain's cabin was a water-closet. Near the door, opposite a partly uncovered window was a bag used to deposit dirty laundry. A skylight consisting of six panes of glass gave light and air to both the main and the Captain's cabins.

Aft of the main deck house was the lazaret hatch, the cover of which was secured by an iron bar and led into the after hold used to store provisions. It contained barrels of stores and other provisions, including a barrel of Stockholm tar – an insoluble tar known commercially as either Stockholm or wood tar which had various uses but was used by boat-builders as a caulking agent. Beyond the hatch was the ship's wheel.

The technical aspects of the sails, though important, are complicated and in general it is sufficient to know that on 24 November *Mary Celeste* had met a strong westerly that had grown stronger through the day and as night fell turned into a moderate gale accompanied by heavy rain. By about 5 a.m., 25 November, the western end of Santa Maria in the Azores was sighted. By 8 a.m. it was noted in the log: 'Eastern Point bears SSW, 6 miles distant.' The weather had improved.

Meeting fair sailing weather, the captain had set the sails for a strong, fair wind coming from the starboard (right) quarter – then something had happened . . .

Notes and references

1   Port and starboard, left and right: viewing the ship from the aft or rear,
    a steering oar, the forerunner of the vertical rudder, was always on the
    right-hand side, which came to be called the steer-board and was in time
    contracted to starboard. Because the steering oar made it difficult to berth a
    vessel on the right-hand side, it was almost always berthed on the left-hand
    side and it was loaded or laded from the left-hand side, which became
    known as lading-board, ladeboard and eventually larboard. It came to be
    called port because starboard and larboard could be misheard and confused
    for one another. The left-hand side was referred to as the port side before
    the 1600s, being mentioned as an apparently established term in Sir Henry
    Mainwaring's *Seaman's Dictionary*, the first authoritative work on
    seamanship, published in 1625; port became the official name for
    left-hand side in 1844.

CHAPTER 2

Spencer's Island

The Maritimes. For anyone even slightly acquainted with the old days of sailing under sail – the days of wooden ships and iron men – the words almost taste of salt spray. They refer to the provinces of Canada noted for shipbuilding – New Brunswick, Prince Edward Island and Nova Scotia. The area's shipbuilding history stretches back to 1606 when two small boats are known to have been built at Port Royal, Nova Scotia, but the industry didn't begin to develop until the government actively supported and encouraged it in the 1750s. By the 19th century the coast-line was lined by shipbuilding yards. Nearly 6,000 vessels were built in New Brunswick between 1820 and 1880, while 2,300 were built in Prince Edward Island. By the middle of the 19th century, when the industry was on the tip of a decline, there were 176,000 tons of registered shipping in Nova Scotia alone.

The province of Nova Scotia lies off the coast of New Brunswick, Canada, and the United States state of Maine. Its name means New Scotland and was bestowed by the Scots who first settled there. To all intents and purposes it is an island, just a bit smaller than Ireland, being 360 miles long (575 kilometres) and on average 80 miles wide (130 kilometres). It is separated from the mainland by the Bay of Fundy, at the top of which is the Minas Basin where the tides usually rise and fall more than 33 feet (10 metres) every $12^{1}/_{2}$ hours, the highest tides in the world.

On the upper arms of Minas Basin is a pretty little village bearing the odd name of Spencer's Island. The name was taken from a little island about two miles distant which the native Indians called Wochuk,

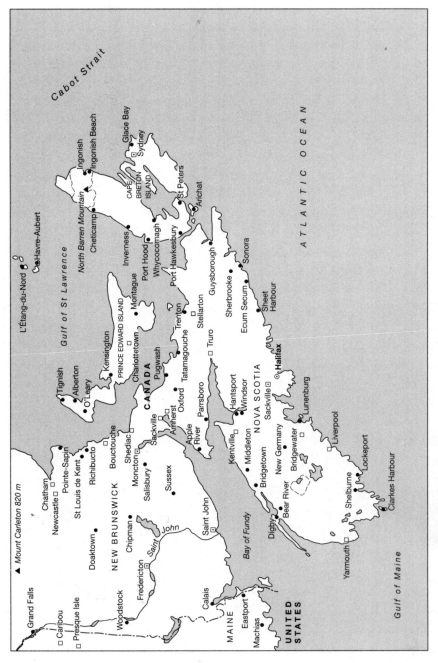

MAP 1 ◆ *Nova Scotia showing the Bay of Fundy*

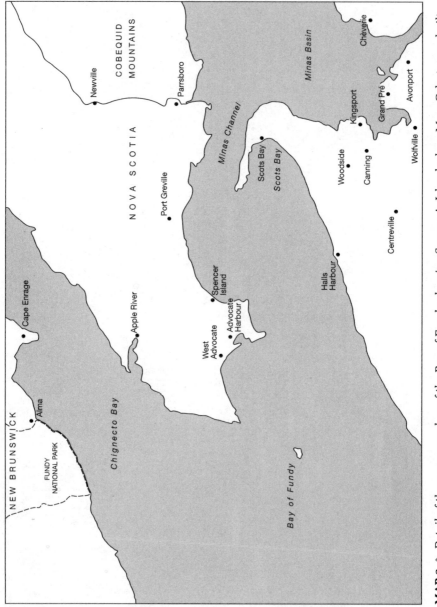

MAP 2 ◆ *Detail of the upper reaches of the Bay of Fundy showing Spencer's Island where Mary Celeste was built*

meaning small kettle or pot, but which was named Spencer's Island, either after a man named Spencer who died aboard a ship and was buried there, or alternatively in honour of Lord Spencer. Whatever the origin of the name, it was certainly known by that name when Nathaniel Blackmore drew a chart of the area in 1714–15.

It is claimed that the first person to settle at Spencer's Island was a British army officer named Robert Spicer, who built a home there about 1778 for his wife, Priscilla, and their baby son, Robert. In due course Robert married a lady named Hannah Loomer and their sons, Isaac and Jacob, inherited the lands their father and grandfather had acquired, becoming the largest landowners in the area.

Mary Celeste was the first vessel built at Spencer's Island and a stone cairn located there records:

Nearby the world's most famous mystery ship, the Mary Celeste, *a brigantine was built and launched in 1861. Was first named the* Amazon. *In 1868 she was driven ashore in a storm and after being repaired was renamed the* Mary Celeste. *In December 1872 she was discovered at sea with all sail set and everything in order but not a person was on board or ever found.*

Mary Celeste was built by a man named Joshua Dewis. Born 1815 in the little village of Economy, Nova Scotia, and the son of a farmer, Dewis knew that the easiest and quickest way for the farmers based around the coastal towns and villages to deliver their produce to market was by boat, and so it was that he went into the boat-building business, starting with small craft and graduating about 1845 into larger boat building with a schooner. Sometime later – we don't know when – he moved to West Advocate, about seven miles from Spencer's Island, where he purchased about one thousand acres that included a farm and a lot of trees. Looking for a suitable place to start a full-scale boat-building business, his eyes settled on Spencer's Island, which had a beach and extensive woodland owned by Isaac and Jacob Spicer. The latter was Dewis's brother-in-law, their wives, Naomi and Mary, being sisters, the daughters of a farmer of Advocate named George Reid.[1]

This was a sparsely populated area. In the whole of the Advocate polling district, which included the area around Spencer's Island, there were 181 families, consisting of 1,074 persons, about the same as some small English villages. There was a wide range of occupations, all catering for the needs of the residents: carpenter, clockmaker, cooper, doctor, farmers and farm labourers, seamstress, shoemaker, teacher, and assorted occupations to do with the sea. Joshua Dewis was honest and industrious and he soon put together a consortium of friends, family, and local businessmen in a shipbuilding venture. He hired a team of reliable and able workers, and by the autumn of 1860 he had laid the keel of the first of some thirty ships that would be built at the yards, albeit no other would be built there by Dewis himself.

No sawmill seems to have existed at Spencer's Island so all the timber must have been worked by hand. The timber would have been cut in a sawpit, a deep pit over which the timber was laid. One man stood in the pit, a second stood on top, and between them they worked a long saw. It wasn't easy work, the man on top being bent back-breakingly forward, the man in the pit standing with his arms upraised and no doubt doing what he could to shield his eyes and nose from the falling sawdust. Once cut, the wood would have been finished with a limited number of tools, probably no more than a saw, broad axe and adze.

The shipyard itself was very rough and ready and typical of the majority that lined the coastal regions of the Maritimes. It lacked almost all the niceties of the larger shipyards and seems to have consisted of little else beyond a few small buildings used as workrooms and store-rooms for equipment, fittings and supplies. There would have been a wood-fired steambox where wood was softened for bending, and a forge for ironworking. There was a cookhouse where food for the workers was prepared. This had previously been the local store run by Daniel Cox and his brother-in-law W.H. Payzant. Tradition says that the first school in Spencer's Island was established in an upstairs room there in 1848.

Joshua Dewis set about building his first ship, the first ship to be built at Spencer's Island, and on 18 May 1861 it was launched. We don't know why, but Dewis christened the vessel *Amazon*. A writer named Clara Dennis visited Spencer's Island in the 1930s and in her book *More About Nova Scotia* recalled an interview with the eldest son of Jacob Spicer, Captain George Spicer, who had served for two years as second mate aboard *Amazon*. Gazing down on what had been the shipyards he said:

*[Amazon] was launched down here on the beach just beside the mill,
on a day in May. She was 184 tons burden, and was named the* Amazon.
*Those men are making hay now on the spot where the builder got timber
for the* Amazon *seventy-five years ago . . .*[2]

It isn't known whether the launch attracted many spectators. In later
years launches often attracted huge crowds from all the neighbouring
districts and there was a lively party atmosphere. It isn't likely to have
happened in the case of *Amazon* but it is highly likely that the locals
would have come along as much out of curiosity as to celebrate the
launching of the ship and the maiden venture of the new shipyard.

It has been claimed that the launch did not take place without
complications. It is said that *Amazon* stuck on the ways. George S. Bryan
in his book *Mary Celeste in Fancy and in Fact* attributes this story to
Robert Dewis, who was aboard, but does not say where and when Dewis
said it. He also cites an article by Allan Kelly in the New York *Evening
Post* for 15 October 1904 which asserted, 'Being built of green timber. She
stuck on the ways and was floated only at great expense.' The story was
repeated several times and in 1937 Dr John W. Dewis stated on the
authority of his brother Robert:

*The craft seemed possessed of the devil to begin with, but where she got
it I don't know. I am sure it couldn't have been from any of our good
people.*[3]

By the 20th century the ship was quickly acquiring all the trappings of
myth and it is possible that Dr Dewis simply got caught up in the desire
to represent the ship as jinxed. Captain George Spicer, also present at the
launching, all his life vehemently denied the story that any misfortune
was suffered by the vessel when she was launched.

On 10 June 1861 *Amazon* was registered at Parrsboro, a town some
25 miles away and the nearest port of registry. She is described in the
records as 99.3 feet in length, 25.5 feet in breadth and her depth was
11.7 feet. Her gross tonnage was 198.42 tons. She had one deck. There
were two masts, the foremast being square-rigged and the mainmast,
fore-and-aft or schooner-rigged. There were fore and aft cabins and a
square stern. *Amazon* was carvel built (meaning that the planks were
flush, rather than overlapping or clinker or clinched built) with a wooden

framework of birch, beech and maple up to light load-line, spruce to the rails, and pine in the cabins.

The owners were

16/64 shares	*Joshua Dewis of Parrsboro, Shipwright*
12/64 shares	*William Henry Bigelow of Parrsboro, Daniel Cox and William Henry Payzant of Cornwallis, merchants*[4]
8/64 shares	*George Reid of Parrsboro, farmer*
8/64 shares	*Isaac Spicer of Parrsboro, farmer*
8/64 shares	*Jacob Spicer of Parrsboro, farmer*
8/64 shares	*William Thompson of Economy, Mariner, superintended the rigging*
4/64 shares	*Robert McLellan of Economy, Mariner*

There seems to be some slight confusion about what happened next. The late Charles Edey Fay, probably the world's leading authority on the mystery, says *Amazon*'s first trip shortly after registration was from Spencer's Island to Windsor, a port further up Minas Basin, where she was supposed to take on a load of plaster for New York.[5] Other sources say *Amazon* sailed up the Bay of Fundy to Five Islands to load lumber for London. Captain Spicer recalled:

> *I sailed with the* Amazon *to Five Islands where she was to be loaded with deals for London. . . . There was nothing unusual about the ship; she went along very well. I did not get any farther than Five Islands, that time, however, for I took sick and had to return home. The* Amazon *herself got no further than Quaco, near St John, New Brunswick. Captain McLellan took ill and they sailed back here.*[6]

All sources agree that the young, recently married skipper and part-owner Robert McLellan fell ill. He apparently saw *Amazon* through loading, but according to Captain Spicer *Amazon* got no further than Quaco, near St John, when McLellan developed pneumonia and the mate headed *Amazon* back to Spencer's Island. Captain Spicer remembered:

> *The Captain was brought up to our house where he passed away. He was sick only a few days. He was just a young man. We took his remains over to his home in Economy. I remember his young wife came down to the shore to see what was in the boat.*[7]

McLellan died on 19 June 1861. His four sixty-fourths interest in the vessel was granted by the Probate Court to his widow, Mary Ann McLellan, on 29 October 1862 and she eventually took possession on 11 January 1864, immediately transferring them to W.H. Payzant, Daniel Cox and William H. Bigelow.

In the meantime command of *Amazon* had been entrusted to Captain John Nutting Parker, of Walton, Nova Scotia, who would be her skipper for two years before moving to take command of the brig *W.H. Bigelow* in 1863. Parker completed McLelland's voyage to London, but according to Robert Dewis:

> *We started on the voyage again (after McLellan's death) and for some reason I cannot recall we put into Eastport, Maine. On the way out of port we ran into some fish weirs in the Narrows and then lay for some days before we finally proceeded on our course across the Atlantic.*
> *We got to London, discharged the cargo and loaded another for Lisbon. On the way down the channel we ran into an English brig in the Strait of Dover and sunk her quickly, the crew climbing on board with us and all being saved. We put into Dover and landed our shipwrecks, repaired damages and resumed our voyage.*[8]

She traded among the coastal ports, the West Indies and went once to Marseilles, where she was painted, the inscription reading 'Amazon of Parrsboro, J.N. Parker, Commander, entering Marseilles Nov'b'r. 1861.'

In 1863 Captain William Thompson took charge of *Amazon*. According to Captain Spicer:

> *I sailed as mate in the* Amazon. *We went to the West Indies, England and the Mediterranean – what we call the foreign trade. Not a thing unusual happened. We finally brought a load of corn from Baltimore to Halifax – Halifax imported corn then – and I came home to see the folks after a voyage of two years and three months in the* Amazon. *A week later, the* Amazon *had gone to Cow Bay, Cape Breton, to load coal for New York. There came a gale o' wind and she went ashore.*[9]

As Spicer recalled, in the early autumn of 1867 *Amazon* brought a cargo of corn from Baltimore to Halifax, where Spicer left the ship. *Amazon* unloaded her cargo and sailed on from Cow Bay. According to Robert Dewis, *Amazon* was anchored in the harbour when a sudden gale swept her onto the shore. As far as the surviving records indicate, the *Amazon*'s owners abandoned their interest in the ship or sold her as a wreck, presumably because her insurers had a reason not to pay up and the owners either couldn't afford to refloat or repair her. Ownership passed to a man named Alexander McBean, who seems to have managed to pull the vessel off the rocks and refloat her. The petition for change of ownership still exists and whilst full of legal gobbledygook is nevertheless an interesting document. It is dated 'Halifax, 14th of October, A.D. 1867':

> *To His Excellency, Lieutenant-General Sir William Fenwick Williams of Kars, Baronet, Knight Commander of the Most Honourable Order of Bath, etc., etc., etc.,*
>
> *The petition of Alexander McBean humbly sheweth that your petitioner is the purchaser of the brigantine* Amazon *which was registered in the name of William Henry Bigelow and others the Port of Parrsboro in the Province of Nova Scotia on the 10th day of June A.D., 1861 as appears by the certificate of Registry herewith transmitted. That the said brigantine was afterward wrecked and stranded at Big Glace Bay in the County of Cape Breton in the aforesaid Province and sold by one William Thompson, under and by virtue of a Power of Attorney for the owners, to your petitioner as appears by the power of attorney and bill of sale herewith transmitted. That your petitioner having purchased the brigantine* Amazon *is desirous of procuring a transfer of her certificate of registry to his own name and prays that she may be registered at the Port of Halifax in said province in the name of Alexander McBean of Big Glace Bay in the County of Cape Breton, that being the name and address your petitioner.*

The change was sanctioned the following day:

> *It appears that the owners of the brigantine* Amazon *by power of attorney which, although not in accordance with the Registry Act, seems to be genuine and to have been regularly executed, authorized one William Thompson to sell and convey, said vessel then stranded at Glace Bay. It also appears that said vessel was sold and conveyed by said William Thompson to one Alexander McBean, the petitioner. This appears to have been a bona fide sale.*
>
> *I am therefore of the opinion that an order may be granted at once for the registry of said vessel at the Port of Halifax in the name of said*

Alexander McBean, the original name and number of said vessel being retained.

In the curious way that fate has of dealing its cards, Gen. Sir William Fenwick Williams (1800–1883) was a native Nova Scotian, having been born in Annapolis Royal, and became a distinguished British soldier, being appointed administrator of Canada on 12 October 1860 and holding the post until 22 January 1861, during the absence of the governor-general Sir Edmund Head. He became administrator of Nova Scotia in 1865 and it was during his time in office that the re-registration of *Amazon* came under his jurisdiction. In 1870 he was appointed governor-general of Gibraltar, a post he held until 1876, so it was during his time that *Mary Celeste* was brought into Gibraltar and into the annals of mystery. It is to be doubted that he ever knew how often his path had crossed that of the ocean wanderer.

We know very little about the new owner of *Amazon*, Alexander McBean, but the record shows that he quickly sold the vessel to a man named John Howard Beatty, whereupon the ship's history again falls into obscurity and we don't hear of her again until November 1868, when she was put up for auction in New York and bought for $1,750 by Captain Richard W. Haines.

The amount paid by Haines suggests that *Amazon* was probably in poor condition but, as estate agents notoriously say about houses, offering great potential. The potential must indeed have been great because Haines proceeded to spend a further $8,825 on repairs.

Haines then sought an American registration and on 22 December 1868 the Collector of Customs at New York obtained the authority of the Secretary of the Treasury to grant it. The formal transfer took place on the last day of the year, 31 December 1868, and the vessel was re-christened *Mary Celeste*. Nobody knows why this name was chosen and some sources say that it has no known origin or derivation. This isn't true, however, as Gallileo's illegitimate daughter was named Marie Celeste and there was also a renowned nun of that name. Whether or not Captain Haines named his ship after one of these women or whether he had some reason of his own is not known. It has been suggested that the intended name was 'Mary Sellars' and that somehow a mistake was made, but this is highly unlikely.

Haines did not retain possession of the vessel for very long. On the same day that Haines received US registration he sold a one-eighth interest to Sylvester Goodwin of New York and less than a year later, in October 1869, he sold his interest in the vessel altogether. His reasons for doing so are unknown. It may be that he had intended all along to sell the ship at a profit or possibly the years of economic depression following the American Civil War were bad for business and, as has been claimed by some sources, the vessel was seized when Haines fell into debt. Whatever the reasons, on 13 October 1869 James H. Winchester bought six-eighths and Daniel T. Samson bought a one-eighth share. Sylvester Goodwin retained his one-eighth.

Mary Celeste received a new captain named Walter S. Johnson, who may not have commanded the vessel for very long because the following January a man named Rufus W. Fowler, who hailed from a place called Searsport, bought a two-eighth share from James H. Winchester. As it was common for the skipper of a vessel to have a financial investment in it, albeit a small one, it is possible that Fowler replaced Johnson as skipper.

James H. Winchester had been a seagoing captain but like so many skippers in those dangerous days of sailing ships when voyages could take a man away from home for months and sometimes a year or more, he had taken the opportunity in 1867 to start a business on land, first as a ships' chandler then in partnership with others as a ships' broker with ships available to carry freight or for charter. Advertisements from the period mention his vessels, which included *Thomas Jefferson*, *Anna M. Knight*, *Gipsy Queen* and *Fanny Keating*.

Under Winchester *Mary Celeste* continued her West Indies run and there is no record that she encountered any problems during that time, but the relentlessness of rapidly plying between ports reveals itself in the fact that the vessel quickly began to show signs of wear and tear. Repairs soon became essential, so Winchester brought the vessel into dock and took the opportunity to undertake some enlargements. The work cost $10,000, a significant sum of money, and when the work was completed *Mary Celeste* was to all intents and purposes a new ship. She now had two decks, her length was increased to 103 feet, her breadth to 25.7 feet and her depth to 16.2 feet. Her total tonnage was increased to 282.28. She was brigantine rigged, although for easier handling her single topsail was divided into upper and lower. She also had a new skipper, an eight twenty-fourths share having been bought by Captain Benjamin Spooner Briggs on 29 October 1872. The owners now were:

James H. Winchester   *12/24*
Benjamin S. Briggs   *8/24*
Sylvester Goodwin   *2/24*
Daniel T. Samson   *2/24*

Notes and references

1   Their connections would become even more complicated when Isaac Spicer's daughter, Emily Jane, married Dewis's son, Robert.

2   Clara Dennis, *More About Nova Scotia. My Own, My Native Land*, Toronto: The Ryerson Press, 1937, p. 63.

3   George S. Bryan, *Mystery Ship, the Mary Celeste in Fancy and in Fact*, Philadelphia: J.B. Lippincott, 1942, p. 18.

4   Clara Dennis (op. cit.) tells how the Payzants came from Jersey in 1753 and settled on an island in Mahone Bay on the Atlantic Coast of Nova Scotia. Louis Phillipe Paisant (1698–1756), (the son of Antoine Paisant, of Caen, Calvados, France), was killed by MicMac Indians in May 1756 in Coveys Island, Lunenburg County, Nova Scotia. According to Clara Dennis, his wife (Anne née Noget) and children were rounded up and taken away by the Indians, Anne being separated from her children and eventually making it to the protection of the French Commandant at Quebec, who ordered the return of the children, one of whom, John, became pastor of Liverpool, Nova Scotia, and remained so for 41 years.

5   Charles Edey Fay, *The Story of the 'Mary Celeste'*, New York: Dover Publications, 1988, p. 49.

6   Clara Dennis, op. cit., p. 63.

7   Stanley Spicer, *The Saga of the Mary Celeste*, Hantsport, Nova Scotia: Lancelot Press, 1933, pp. 23–4.

8   Ibid.

9   Clara Dennis, op. cit., p. 64.

CHAPTER 3

. . . .

Benjamin Spooner Briggs

The new captain of *Mary Celeste* and the man destined to sail into poster-ity by vanishing from aboard his ship was Benjamin Spooner Briggs. Born at Wareham, Massachusetts, on 24 April 1835, he was the third of six children born to Captain Nathan Briggs and his wife Sophia (née Cobb). There were five sons and one daughter, Maria, all the sons except one, James, going to sea, two becoming master mariners at an early age. Maria also went to sea, having married a sea-captain named Joseph D. Gibbs, and would die aboard his ship.

The Briggs family were long-standing residents in the Wareham area having lived there since Clement Briggs arrived from England aboard the brig *Fortune* in November 1621. Nathan Briggs was born in 1799, went to sea as so many young men did, and by the age of 21 years was the skipper of his own vessel, a schooner named *Betsy & Jane*. His long-time sweet-heart was Maria Cobb and the couple had married on 14 August 1827. He soon after went to sea and returned from the voyage to find her dying. He remained a widower for eighteen months before finding happiness with Maria's sister, Sophia. He would spend most of his life at sea and command several vessels, mostly involved with the cotton trade from Southern ports to Liverpool.

From his surviving letters and sea journals Nathan Briggs seems to have been something of a poet and a philosopher and although he was a kind and affectionate family man, aboard ship he was a strict disciplin-arian. In his book *Rose Cottage*, Dr Oliver W. Cobb said that Nathan Briggs:

. . . navigated his ship with great care. There was no slacking with him. He did not order his sailors about or talk to them. All his orders were given to his mates and they were held responsible for the execution of the same. When the Captain walked the quarter-deck, no sailor ever thought of passing on the weather-side. If going to or from the wheel, they always went on the lee side, or if a sailor had work to do on the weather side, he would, in passing, touch his cap in salute and pass to leeward, never going between the Captain and the wind.[1]

This strict discipline at sea extended even to his sons and other relatives and when they shipped under him and he treated them like strangers. Dr Cobb recalled:

He was a Spartan father when it came to having his sons on shipboard. They had to do the regular work of sailors, take their trick at the wheel, stand watch, help reef and furl sails . . . The Captain expected his boy to be the first man aloft in an emergency. In addition to this, the boy had regular lessons to study and to recite to the Captain; navigation, geography, history, literature. There was no idleness on these voyages.[2]

Nathan Briggs was rigidly teetotal on land and at sea and abstinence from alcohol when aboard ship was one rule about which he was especially strict. In 1834 when he embarked on his first voyage in command of the schooner *Betsy & Jane* he had 'No grog will be allowed on board' written into the articles of agreement. He was a little ahead of a trend in this but by 1840 abstinence from alcohol had become fairly standard aboard merchant vessels. It was something Benjamin Briggs adopted himself, and which in years to come would contribute to his image as a strict religious puritan.

In about 1839 the family suffered a severe financial setback when Nathan Briggs invested heavily in a business venture in Wareham which failed. He lost everything, including the family home, and Sophie was forced to take four of her children, including four-year-old Benjamin, back to live with her father, Reverend Oliver Cobb, pastor of the Congregational Church at Marion, Massachusetts. It must have been a disaster for all concerned at the time and their distress is easily imagined, but by all accounts the five years they had to live with Rev. Cobb were happy and contented years. Meantime Nathan Briggs worked hard and managed to regain his fortunes to such an extent that in 1844 he was able to move his family into a newly built home, 'Rose Cottage', about a mile from Rev. Cobb at Sippican Village, which in future years would achieve a degree of fame when in 1886 Henry James based the village of Marmion in *The Bostonians* on it.

At home Captain Nathan Briggs maintained a relaxed discipline; he regarded education very highly and manners and deportment no less so. Sophia, the daughter of a pastor, was also a powerful influence on the children and ensured that they all read their Bible. Benjamin became particularly religious, read his Bible regularly, knew it thoroughly, and also attended prayer meetings.

Benjamin grew up to be a responsible and respectable man who according to J. Franklin Briggs, in a letter to the great *Mary Celeste* historian Charles Edey Fay, 'spoke in a quiet tone of voice, and with an inclination to reticence',[3] and from childhood his sweetheart was his cousin Sarah Elizabeth Cobb, seven years his junior. J. Franklin Briggs recalled that 'Benjamin and Sarah had been boy and girl sweethearts. It was a love match, and they always remained deeply devoted to each other.' They married on 9 September 1862 at Marion, Massachusetts, the wedding being performed by Sarah's father, the Reverend Leander Cobb.

By this time Benjamin Briggs was already an experienced seaman and a master mariner who had already commanded the brig *Sea Foam* and was now the captain of the schooner *Forest King*, on which he and Sarah honeymooned in the Mediterranean. He would later take command of the barque *Arthur*, his brother Oliver taking over command of *Forest King*. Sarah often accompanied him on his voyages, as she would when he captained *Mary Celeste* to Gibraltar. The couple would have two children, Arthur Stanley, born on 20 September 1865, the baby accompanying them the following year on a voyage to Marseilles, and Sophia Matilda, born on 31 October 1870, who was destined to disappear with everyone else aboard *Mary Celeste*.

Sarah loved music and owned a melodeon which she took on their voyages, as was the case when she went aboard *Mary Celeste*. She was blessed with an excellent singing voice and she and Benjamin would often sing together, their choice of music being religious, which would contribute to later speculation that Benjamin was a religious fanatic. The evidence, such as it is, indicates that whilst Benjamin was indeed deeply religious, this was far from an uncommon characteristic of the time and there is no suggestion of fanaticism about him. In fact he seems to have had a good, solid reputation and in future years was well known and respected by the United States Consul to Gibraltar, where Benjamin had joined a Masonic Lodge. Consul Sprague said that Briggs 'bore the highest character for seamanship and correctness' and in a letter to N.W. Bingham, Treasury Department Agent at Boston dated 3 April 1873, Sprague wrote that he had known Briggs for many years and that 'he always bore a good character as a Christian, and as an intelligent and active shipmaster.'[4]

By the 1870s Benjamin and his brother Oliver had tired of the sea and wanted to settle down to a normal life with their families ashore. The brothers considered combining their money in a small business. As related by Dr Oliver W. Cobb in his account of his family, *Rose Cottage*, Benjamin and Oliver wanted to take care of their growing families and planned to buy a hardware business in New Bedford, but at the last minute they recalled their father's disastrous business venture and reluctantly abandoned the idea. Oliver Briggs, who had bought some land and intended to buy a house, instead invested his money in a vessel named *Julia A. Hallock*, using his capital to undertake substantial repairs. Benjamin in 1872 invested his hardware store share in an interest in *Mary Celeste*.

It is curious to note that Oliver Briggs was a victim of misfortune, having lost James H. Winchester's schooner *Thomas Jefferson* in a storm off Cape Hatteras and another vessel, *Royal Charles*, in ice during a return voyage from Rotterdam. He was destined to have no luck with *Julia A. Hallock* either and would be drowned during a voyage aboard her about the same time as Benjamin disappeared.

As a new shareholder in *Mary Celeste* and about to take her on her first voyage after a thorough refit, Captain Benjamin Briggs left his home in Marion, Massachusetts, for New York on or about 19 October 1872. *Mary Celeste* was at pier 44, East River, at the foot of Rutgers Street, and here Captain Briggs attended to all the arrangements for sailing and supervised the loading of *Mary Celeste*'s cargo of 1,700 barrels of alcohol valued at $37,000, being shipped to Genoa by Meissner, Ackermann and Co., importers of 48 Beaver Street. As Captain Briggs explained on Sunday, 3 November 1872 in a letter to his mother,[5] the work of preparing *Mary Celeste* for the voyage was 'tedious, perplexing, and very tiresome', but he had quickly settled down to it. The daily grind had improved for him on 27 October when he was joined by Sarah Briggs and daughter Sophia Matilda, although Sophia, suffering a bad cold, was miserable. Time aboard can't have been much fun for Sophia and, Matilda as they were effectively trapped on the ship, and according to a letter written by Benjamin, Sarah found it particularly confining 'On account of the horse disease the horse cars have not been running on this side of the city, so we have not been able to go and make any calls as we were so far away from anyone to go on foot . . .'.

The 'horse disease' was an epidemic of distemper known as the 'Great Epizootic' which spread across the eastern United States at the end of 1872 and killed thousands of horses. The cities were reliant on horses not merely to transport people from one part of town to another but also and more importantly to deliver goods. The epidemic therefore paralysed the city and businesses suffered, some collapsing, and on top of that there was considerable anxiety about fire because the fire engines were horse-drawn. Six days after Benjamin wrote to his mother about the 'horse disease', on 9 November, a terrible fire devastated Boston, in which 776 buildings were destroyed and fourteen people, all but three being firemen, were killed.

The epidemic made travelling almost impossible, confining the Briggs to the ship and to pier 50, to which *Mary Celeste* had been moved. They managed to get out once when Sarah's brother, Rev. William H. Cobb, and his wife visited and took them 'on a ride up to Central Park'. This was a special trip, more important than it might seem because it was the first urban landscaped park in the United States and therefore even more of a tourist attraction than it is today. Central Park was laid out on an 840-acre site that occupied a $2^1/_2$-mile span of rocky, swampy land in central Manhattan. It was believed unsuitable for commercial building, but some 1,600 people lived there, most of them in dilapidated and disease-ridden shantytowns, one of the best remembered being Seneca Village, a singularly multi-ethnic community with 264 residents, three churches, several cemeteries and a school. The area was also the location of a number of 'noxious industries' such as soap and candle factories and a bone-boiling plant. The City of New York had invited plans for a new park to be created there and had eventually accepted one submitted by Frederick Law Olmsted (1822–1903) and London-born Calvert

Vaux (1824–95). The city legislature in 1853 passed a bill authorising the purchase of the land by right of eminent domain and the residents were ordered to vacate their homes and workplaces by 1 August 1856. Construction began the following year, and by the 1860s Central Park had become the playground of the wealthy. Its paths became crowded with luxurious carriages as the rich came to promenade, attend concerts, and enjoy assorted entertainments such as the famous carousel which opened in 1871, driven by a blind mule and a horse in a treadmill in an underground pit. Sophia was perhaps taken to see it. The trip out was enjoyed and welcome, and Captain Briggs wrote happily to his mother that 'Sophia behaved splendid and seem to enjoy the ride as much as any of us'.

Otherwise Sarah got on with sewing – she had had her sewing machine shipped aboard – and the couple seem to have spent what little free time they had singing. 'We enjoy our melodeon and have some good sings,' wrote Benjamin to his mother, adding that Sophia missed her brother Arthur, who had been left with his grandmother to go to school, 'and wants to see him in the Album which by the way is a favorite book of hers. She knows your picture in both albums and points and says Gamma Bis, She seems real smart . . .'.[6] Fortunately Sophia had recovered from her cold and now had 'a first rate appetite for hash and bread and butter.' Captain Briggs evidently had an interest in and concern about food, mentioning it twice in his letter, observing that his own 'appetite keeps good and I hope I shan't lose any flesh'.

Loading was completed before darkness on Saturday, 2 November, and Briggs planned to set sail the following Tuesday. He visited the New York office of the United States Shipping Commissioner on Monday and signed the 'Articles of Agreement' and the Atlantic Mutual Insurance Company accepted liability for $3,400 on the vessel's freight. (Of the five American insurance companies with an interest in *Mary Celeste*, Atlantic Mutual, which had been granted its charter on 11 April 1842 and for almost 100 years were exclusively marine insurers, is the only one to remain in business.) Some accounts claim that on the evening before *Mary Celeste* set sail Captain Briggs and his wife had dinner with an old friend, Captain Morehouse of the *Dei Gratia*, at the Astor House, between Vesey and Barclay Streets on Broadway, for many years considered the finest hotel in the United States.[7] However, there is no evidence that the two men knew each other and one would expect to find reference to their friendship in the documents had they done so.

Mary Celeste left pier 50 on the East River on the morning of Tuesday, 5 November, but the weather almost immediately turned bad and Sarah wrote to her mother-in-law, 'it was strong head wind, and B. said it looked so thick & nasty ahead we shouldn't gain much if we were beating & banging about.'[8] *Mary Celeste* therefore sought shelter until 7 November, when the weather became favourable and she finally set out to sea – and into the annals of maritime mystery.

For those who consider such things as jinxes and predetermined misfortune to be realities, and old-time seafarers were famous for their superstitions, perhaps the mystery of *Mary Celeste* owes as much as anything to the meeting of a strangely doomed ship and an equally doomed family. *Mary Celeste*, as we have seen, suffered misfortune from the day she was launched, but the Briggs family, or at least that generation of it, seem equally dogged by disaster. Benjamin vanished at sea, his brother Oliver was lost at sea when his ship went down, two brothers, Nathan and Zenas, died at sea of yellow fever, his sister Maria was drowned when her husband's ship on which she was travelling was run down by a steamer near Cape Fear, and his father, Captain Nathan Briggs, was killed when he was struck by lightning as he stood in the doorway of his home.[9]

Notes and references

1   Oliver W. Cobb, *Rose Cottage*, New Bedford, MA: Reynolds-DeWalt Publishers, 1968, pp. 37–8.

2   Ibid., p. 38.

3   Charles Edey Fay, *The Story of the 'Mary Celeste'*, New York: Dover Publications, 1988, p. 22.

4   Ibid., p. 22.

5   Ibid., pp. 5–9.

6   Ibid.

7   That Captains Briggs and Morehouse knew one another is stated by J.G. Lockhart in his book *A Great Sea Mystery. The True Story of the 'Mary Celeste'* (London: Phillip Allen and Co., 1927) and is claimed on the authority of a letter to Lockhart from Mrs Morehouse. It is repeated in other books, notably George S. Bryan's *Mystery Ship, the Mary Celeste in Fancy*

and in Fact (Philadelphia: J.B. Lippincott, 1942). One should not doubt the authority of Mrs Morehouse, but in this case it seems almost inconceivable that such a friendship, had it existed, would not have been mentioned during the salvage hearing or have afterwards been independently confirmed by Captain Briggs's family.

8   Charles Edey Fay, op. cit., pp. 11–16.

9   The only brother not to die at sea was James, who had taken a job on land.

CHAPTER 4

The crew

The mystery of why a captain and crew would desert a perfectly seaworthy ship is such that they have become something of the focal point for theorists and they have been credited with many and varied crimes and to be as black and evil a bunch of scum as to be found in the worst harbour-side bars. There are no sins of which the crew of *Mary Celeste* were incapable – thugs, drunks, villains so vile they would contaminate a gallows, their names and number have been changed according to whim and the demands of theory alike.

In reality the owner and captain of *Mary Celeste* were highly reputable and would appear to have attracted crew of the highest calibre and beyond reproach. Captain Briggs wrote to his mother of both his ship and the men he had hired aboard: 'Our vessel is in beautiful trim and I hope we shall have a fine passage but I have never been in her before and can't say how she'll sail,' he explained, adding of the crew, 'We seem to have a very good mate and steward and I hope I shall have a pleasant voyage.'

Sarah Briggs also expressed satisfaction, writing of the crew to her mother-in-law just before *Mary Celeste* put to sea, 'Benj. thinks we have got a pretty peaceable set this time all around if they continue as they have begun. Can't tell yet how smart they are.'

There were seven crewmen consisting of the first and second mate, a steward and four seamen. Their names were:

Albert G. Richardson, first mate
Andrew Gilling, second mate

Edward William Head, steward and cook
Volkert Lorenzen, seaman
Boz[1] Lorenzen, seaman
Arian Martens (also variously given as Arian Harbens,
Arian Hardens, Adrian Martens, Arian Mardens), seaman
Gottlieb Goodschaad (or Goodschaal) seaman

Beyond their good reputations, we know precious little about any of these men.

Albert G. Richardson was the son of Theodore and Elizabeth Richardson and the brother of a sea-captain named Lyman Richardson. He was born in Charlestown, Massachusetts, but at some point had moved to Stockton Springs, Maine, which by 1870 was a still significant but declining ship-building and outfitting town. He had served in the Civil War, enlisting on 27 February 1864 at Belfast, Maine, in Captain Baker's Independent Company for Coast Defences, later designated Company A, Coast Guard Infantry, Maine Volunteers. He was honourably discharged on 25 May 1865 at Portland.

We know that he was 5ft 8in tall, had blue eyes, brown hair and a light complexion. Richardson was related to James H. Winchester, *Mary Celeste*'s principal owner, being married to his wife's niece, Fannie. He had sailed for J.H. Winchester & Co. for about two years and had previously sailed under Captain Briggs. The *New York Sunday World*, 24 January 1886, quoted James H. Winchester as saying that Richardson was 'a man of excellent character' and Dr Oliver W. Cobb recalled to author Charles Edey Fay that he had heard Captain Briggs express his good fortune at having Richardson as first mate on *Mary Celeste*.[2]

We know that his wife Fannie N. Richardson never remarried after her husband's disappearance and that she lived to the advanced age of 99 years, dying on 29 April 1937 at 1962 Brown Street, Brooklyn, New York.

The second mate was Andrew Gilling. He was born in New York, was 5ft 8in tall, had light-coloured hair and a light complexion. He was living at 19 Thames Street, New York, which would appear to have been a lodging house of some kind for seamen as the four ordinary crew aboard *Mary Celeste* also lived there. Although born in New York, the pastor of the parish of Kathy, Samso, Denmark, wrote to the Royal Danish Consul at Gibraltar on 8 July 1873 on behalf of 'the bereaved and sorrowful mother' of Andrew Gilling and seeking any news of his fate and how she should go about having her son's effects returned to her.

Edward William Head was the cook and steward aboard *Mary Celeste*. Born in New York, he was 23 years old, 5ft 8in tall, and had light hair and complexion. He was described by Captain Winchester in the *New York Sunday World* as coming from Williamsburg 'where he was respected by all who knew him'. His wife, Emma J. Head, would later write to the US Consul in Gibraltar requesting the return of her husband's effects.

We know next to nothing about the four crew members except that they all came from Germany. Volkert and Boz Lorenzen are believed to have been brothers. Volkert was 29 years old, 5ft 9in tall, with light hair and complexion. Boz was 25 years old, also with light hair and complexion. Arian Martens was the eldest of the crew, being 35 years old. He was 5ft 8in, had light hair and complexion. The last member of the crew was Gottlieb Goodschaad or Goodschaal. He was also the youngest, being 23 years old. He had light hair and light complexion. On 24 March 1873 T.A. Nickelsen wrote to the US Consul in Gibraltar from Utersum on the Isle of Fohr, then part of Prussia,

> *DEAR SIR: March 24, 1873.*
> *Please excuse me of writing these few lines of information regarding two sailors (brothers) belonging to the American Brig* Mary Celeste, *their mother and their wives wish to know in which condition the ship has been found, whether the boats were gone or not, whether the log-book has been found on board or not, so as to find out on what day they have left the ship, and further do they like to know whether any signs of disturbance have been found on board. I know three of the sailors personally and know them to be peaceable and first-class sailors. Please favor us with an answer and let us know your opinion why they left said Brig.*
> *I remain, Yours, truly, T.A. NICKELSEN* [3]

Utersum is on the western coast of Föhr, one of the North Friesian Islands in the North Sea, but protected from its full force and known today as the green island because of its fields, meadows and pastureland. T.A. Nickelsen was referring to the brothers Volkert and Boz Lorenzen and Arian Martens. Volkert and Boz both had wives. Volkert Lorenzen also had a daughter, Ida, who in 1937 wrote to the author George S. Bryan in the hope of obtaining some information about the fate of her father.

Arian Martens was also married and when he disappeared his wife was pregnant with their second daughter, Clara, who died on 5 December 1936. There was an elder daughter, but nothing is known about her except that she married and had a son, Heinrich. Martens also had two brothers, Karl and Arnold, and a sister, Caroline (who married a man named Gerhard Matzen), all of whom were living in New York at the time of *Mary Celeste*'s fateful voyage.

It is reasonable to assume that Captain Briggs, experienced mariner that he was, would exercise more than ordinary care in the selection of a crew for a voyage on which his wife and two-year-old daughter were to accompany him, and nothing is or was known about any of those aboard the ship to suggest that they were not responsible, capable and honest men.

Notes and references

1   George S. Bryan in his book *Mystery Ship, the Mary Celeste in Fancy and in Fact* (Philadelphia: J.B. Lippincott, 1942), says he had the names verified by D. Lorensen, mayor of Utersum, and that a daughter of Volkert was living there in 1937, as was a niece of Arian Martens.

2   Charles Edey Fay, op. cit., p. 26.

3   Ibid., p. 30.

CHAPTER 5

The voyage

W̲e know very little about the last voyage of *Mary Celeste*, her log
being among the items taken by the abandoning crew (we have only
the log slate on which several notes were made the day the crew vanished),
but we can guess something about the weather and seas because the ship
Dei Gratia (By Grace of God) sailed from New York for Gibraltar eight
days after *Mary Celeste* and followed a more northerly course, but would
have experienced broadly much the same general conditions.

Dei Gratia was a 295-ton British brigantine, a virtually new ship
having been built the previous year, 1871, near the small village of
Bear River nestled in a deep valley in south-western Nova Scotia, off the
Bay of Fundy near the mouth of a river called Bear River on Annapolis
Basin. Her principal owner was George F. Millar, a merchant of Bear
River. She was skippered by 34 year-old Captain David Reed Morehouse,
a master mariner of 13 years and widely regarded as an expert navigator.
The first mate was a big man and a knowledgeable seaman named
Oliver E. Deveau who hailed from St Mary's Bay, Nova Scotia, and had
commanded a brig himself. The son of Cyril Deveau and Madeleine
Comeau, he was born on 9 September 1837 at Plympton, Digby County,
Nova Scotia. He stayed at sea throughout his life, eventually becoming a
captain himself, and only retired in his early seventies when illness
forced him to leave his ship in Cuba and return home. He died on
10 September 1912, leaving a widow, a son (James Deveau) and two
daughters (Jessie and Addie).[1]

Dei Gratia had loaded a cargo of petroleum in New York and sailed on
15 November, for most of her voyage enduring what First Mate Oliver

Deveau described as 'very heavy weather'. This meant continuous gale force winds and tempestuous seas, for these were reported by numerous vessels arriving in ports along the eastern seaboard of Canada and the United States. *Mary Celeste* would also have experienced the same stormy conditions.

By about noon on Sunday, 24 November 1872, *Mary Celeste* was in latitude 36°56′ N, and longitude 27°20′ W. She had passed all but two of the nine islands of the Azores group. San Miguel, the largest of the islands was about 100 miles to the northeast and the smaller and beautiful island of Santa Maria almost 110 miles dead ahead.

According to the log slate *Mary Celeste* made reasonable headway doing about 8 knots throughout the afternoon and early evening, but about 7 p.m. the wind freshened and increased *Mary Celeste*'s speed to 9 knots.

The weather didn't look favourable, the wind coming in 'fresh' at 8 p.m., and at 9 p.m., with a storm probable, it was decided to take in her royal and topgallant sails. The ship's speed dropped back to 8 knots, which she would maintain throughout the night. At midnight the log records that *Mary Celeste* was sailing east by south and that it was raining. We know that there were stormy conditions over the Azores during the night; the author Charles Edey Fay, citing a letter from a representative of the Azores Meterological Unit, states that 'the records from Angra do Heroismo and Ponta Delgada – the only two stations existing in 1872 . . . – stormy conditions prevailed in the Azores on November 24 and 25, 1872. A cold front passed Angra do Heroismo between 3 and 9 p.m. on the 25th, the wind shifting then from S.W. to N.W. The minimum of pressure was 72 mm. and the wind velocity attained to 62 km. at Ponta Delgada at 9 p.m. on the 24th. Calm or light wind prevailed on the forenoon of the 25th but later became a gale force.'[2]

At 5 a.m. the log notes 'made the island of S. Mary's bearing E.S.E.'. *Mary Celeste* had covered some 90 miles during the night and was now approaching the western end of Santa Maria. Charles Edey Fay thought the course being pursued by *Mary Celeste* was slightly strange because it seemed opposite to the way it should have been heading, which was to the southeast, to pass through the Strait of Gibraltar to reach Genoa. It was also apparently dangerous, taking the ship between the north end of the island and the rocks of the Dollabarat Shoal to the northeast.

The log slate contained nothing but terse hourly entries that for the most part recorded nothing but the ship's speed and would not have contained any other information such as a death on board or sickness, but Mr Fay's concern raises the question of whether or not Captain Briggs or First Mate Richardson would have sailed such a course. Alternatively, Captain Briggs knew Gibraltar well enough to be known to Consul Sprague and to have joined a Masonic lodge there, so did his experience of the waters lead him to pursue an unconventional course? We will never know, but it certainly adds to the overall mystery.

At 8 a.m. the log slate noted, 'At 8, Eastern point bore S.S.W. 6 miles distant.' The log contained no further entries.

As mentioned above, the watches had noted the ship's speed on the log slate for every hour since midday the previous day and it seems fair to suppose that they would have continued to do so until midday when a new log slate would have been started (sea days begin at 12 noon). The log slate contains no such entries, from which it is probably safe to assume that whatever happened happened between 8 a.m. and 9 a.m. on 25 November 1872.

It was on Wednesday, 4 December 1872 land time or Thursday, 5 December 1872 sea time that *Dei Gratia* sighted *Mary Celeste*.

It isn't clear who first sighted the derelict. According to John Wright, second mate of *Dei Gratia*, seaman John Johnson was at the wheel and sighted *Mary Celeste* off the port bow at about 1.00 p.m. sea time and the state of the vessel's sails had caught his curiosity. Johnson had then called to Wright and pointed out the vessel. However, Captain Morehouse also claimed to have been the first to sight the vessel. He had just come on deck and had noticed the *Celeste*, which he judged to have been about six miles distant. Morehouse and Johnson probably saw her simultaneously.

Mary Celeste was bearing east-north-east, steering west-south-west on a starboard tack, whilst *Dei Gratia* was steering south-east-half-east on a port tack – in other words, *Mary Celeste* was sailing towards *Dei Gratia*.

Captain Morehouse studied the distant stranger through his glass and saw as Johnson had done that she carried little sail. Morehouse concluded that something was wrong and ordered *Dei Gratia* to sail toward her. Fifteen or twenty minutes later it was clear that *Mary Celeste* was yawing and Morehouse also thought he could see a flag of distress at her yard (it was in fact a flapping sail). He called Oliver Deveau, the mate, who was off duty below deck, who viewed the ship and immediately agreed with Morehouse that the vessel was in trouble.

Several hours passed as the two ships closed the distance between them, then at 3 p.m. they were within hailing distance. Captain Morehouse decided to 'speak' to the vessel and offer whatever assistance he could. They braced up the yards at once and hauled for the vessel. By this time they were four to five miles distant.

Mary Celeste was making about one and a half to two knots, heading westward – opposite to the direction of *Dei Gratia*, which according to the log was in latitude 38°20′ N, longitude 17°15′ W. *Mary Celeste*'s last position had been 37°01′ N, 25°01′ W, which means that *Mary Celeste* had sailed some 378 miles on her own.

The *Dei Gratia* came alongside – that is to say they passed her 300 or 400 yards off – and hailed her but got no answer and saw no one on the decks. Captain Morehouse ordered a boat lowered and Mate Deveau, Second Mate John Wright and seaman Johnson rowed over. Deveau and Wright clambered aboard, leaving Johnson in the small boat alongside.

The two men aboard the creaking and deserted stranger made a quick but remarkably detailed search of the ship and Mate Deveau later described her condition to the salvage hearing. According to Mate Deveau, the staysail had fallen down and was on the stove-pipe of the galley, the upper fore-topsail and foresail were gone, apparently blown from the yards, and the lower fore-topsail was hanging by four corners. The main staysail had been hauled down and was lying on the forward-house, and the jib and foretop staysail were set. All the rest of the sails, including the royal and topgallant, were furled.

Deveau said the 'rigging was in very bad order, some of the running rigging carried away, gone, the standing rigging was all right.' He elaborated, 'The rigging out of order was: fore-braces on port side broken; starboard lower-topsail brace broken; main peak halyards broken; the gear of the foresail all broken; clew-lines and buntings gone.' There were no spare spars (a spar is the general term for any wooden support used in the rigging of a ship) on the decks of the *Mary Celeste* whatever. The spar was lashed through the sheave-holes.

Mary Celeste had three hatches; the fore and main opened into the cargo hold and the lazaret opened to a small space below the main deck to the aft of the ship which was used to store provisions and spare gear. The fore-hatch and the lazaret hatch were both off. Through the fore-hatch Deveau was able to see the cargo was barrels marked 'alcohol'.

The wooden binnacle – the housing for the ship's compass and often containing other items – had been lashed on the top of the cabin above the deck but had been washed away from its place and 'was stove in', the glass broken. Deveau found a second compass in the Mate's room, fixed the binnacle and used it on the voyage to Gibraltar. He also found two nautical astronomical navigation instruments called quadrants, one in the Second Mate's room.

On boarding *Mary Celeste* the first things they did was to sound the pumps, otherwise to see how much water was in the bilges. Seawater could enter a ship in various ways, through small leaks, for example, or when it washed over the decks during a storm, and it would collect in the hold and bilges, spaces either side of the keel, where it could become noxious to an extent that in previous centuries it was capable of asphyxiating a man. To see how much water was collecting in the bilges and in the hold a sounding rod would be used – in much the same way as a dip-stick is used to find out how much oil there is in a car – and pumps employed to empty the water. Ships were regularly pumped, often every four hours. *Mary Celeste* did not leak very much and during the voyage to Gibraltar she took on very little water. Seaman Charles Lund testified: 'The *Celeste* made a little water afterwards, I cannot say how much, about 20 to 25 strokes. I cannot say how much water she made in the day. I pumped her out morning and evening and 25 strokes each time sucked the pipe. The *Dei Gratia* made more water than the *Celeste*.'

Oliver Deveau found $3^1/_2$ feet of water in the hold. This was quite a lot of water for such a small ship. Since *Mary Celeste* would have been pumped every few hours when manned the water can only have entered the vessel *after* she was abandoned, or it was a contributory factor in her abandonment. The testimony regarding the location of the sounding rod is therefore far more crucial than it might at first have appeared.

According to Second Mate John Wright, 'There was no sounding rod but a piece of iron with a piece of line attached to it, I found no proper sounding rod. I was able to sound with the piece of iron and line attached to it. It was found lying on the deck near the cabin . . .'. Charles Lund, who later helped Deveau bring *Mary Celeste* into Gibraltar, described this line as 'an iron bolt and a piece of line tied to it. The bolt was 6 inches to 1 foot long.' For some reason Deveau or Wright had left this line in the cabin, for that is where Lund found it. Although neither Wright nor Lund mentioned the sounding rod itself, both Deveau and Augustus Anderson did so. Anderson said, 'The Mate found a sounding rod on deck, but I did not see him find it. It was all wet and could not be used . . . He did not tell me what he did with it.' This is an important and perhaps crucial piece of testimony because in ordinary circumstances the sounding rod would have been put back in its proper place and kept dry, so finding it on the deck, where presumably it had been dropped, suggests that some-one had sounded the ship shortly before abandoning her. As Deveau explained to the Vice-Admiralty Court, it was required to make a log entry 'pumps carefully attended to', so the pumps would have been sounded every two or four hours, or at least every watch. The amount of water Deveau found showed, he thought, that she made little or no water, no more than about an inch every 24 hours, from which he concluded that all the water found in her had gone through the hatches or cabin.

In other words, Oliver Deveau knew from the experience of sailing *Mary Celeste* into Gibraltar that she took on very little water. He therefore concluded that the $3^{1}/_{2}$ feet found in the hold had to have entered over the decks and through the open hatches and cabin. We can further surmise that the sounding rod discarded on the deck indicates that the vessel had been sounded at the time of or immediately after whatever had caused the abandonment, and *if* the latter then it is reasonable to suppose that whatever had happened had given rise to concern that the ship was taking on water. The water, then, was a contributory factor in the aban-donment of *Mary Celeste* – the captain and crew thought she was sinking!

A few minutes after sounding the pumps Deveau went into the cabin, which contained the Captain's room, Mate's room, a w.c. and pantry. It was raised two feet above the upper deck and contained six windows, all battened up with canvas and boards. Deveau would remove the covering in the Mate's room but leave the rest as he found them. There was a great deal of water between decks. The forward-house on the upper deck was full of water up to the combing. In the cabin the skylight was open and raised and a great deal of water had got in, everything inside was wet, the clock was spoilt by the water, but the water had naturally run out. In the Mate's cabin he found the log book on his desk and the log slate on the cabin table. There were two charts in the Mate's cabin, one under the mate's bed and one hanging over it, one of them showing the track of the vessel up to the 24th. The ship's register or other papers concerning the ship were all missing, except some letters, account books and the mate's note book in which were entered receipts for cargo and other items.

In the Captain's cabin Deveau found Captain Briggs's charts and books, some in two bags under the bed, and two or three loose charts over the bed. There were no charts on the table. The bed was unmade, as if just vacated by its occupants, and bore the impression on the mattress of a child having been asleep in it – these unmade beds being further indications that disaster had struck *Mary Celeste* in early morning. The bedding was wet, Deveau thought probably by water that had come through the open skylight or somehow through the boarded-up windows near the bed. 'There had been rain and squalls the morning we found the *Mary Celeste*,' said Deveau, 'but I don't think it was that which wetted the bed.'

He said there was an old and dirty dress hanging near the bed which was not wet. There were also two boxes of clothing, one containing a mixture of male and female clothing, the other some remnants of material (presumably for Mrs Briggs's sewing). Neither box was locked, but at one point Deveau said the box containing clothing 'was shut' and a little later he said that 'both boxes were open'. The box of clothing was not wet, but in two drawers under the bed Deveau found more clothing, mostly men's, and that in the lower drawer was wet. The drawers also contained work-bags holding needles, threads, buttons, hooks and a case of instruments – a dressing case and other things in the drawers. Deveau also found in the Captain's cabin a valise-case which he could not or did not open, children's clothing and toys, and a pair of india-rubber over-shoes. There was also a writing desk and Mrs Briggs's melodeon in the cabin. Under the bed he found a sword in a sheath. He drew it, but noted nothing of interest about it and replaced it under the bed or somewhere nearby. The sword was a souvenir Briggs had bought during an earlier voyage to Italy.

In the forward-house there was a foot or so of water. Deveau didn't know how it had got there, although the door was open and the scuttle-hatch was off. In the fore-cabin there were a few old coats and a pair of sea-boots. A bag of dirty clothing, evidently belonging to Captain and Mrs Briggs, hung in the water-closet and was damp.

In the galley in the corner of the forward-house all the pots, kettles and other equipment were washed up, all the knives and forks were in the pantry, and no food was being prepared. There were no cooked provisions in the galley, only a barrel of flour one third gone and preserved meats in the pantry. There were plenty of provisions and plenty of water on board, Deveau estimated about six months' worth, and he and his men used some of the meat and potatoes.

There was no appearance of damage by fire nor any appearance of fire or smoke in any part of the ship, and Deveau said 'It did not occur to me that there had been any act of violence – there was nothing to induce one to believe or to show that there had been any violence.' In fact, everything appeared to be in its place, but the overall appearance was as if the ship had been left in a hurry. *Mary Celeste* had no davits at the side (davits hold a small boat such as a lifeboat to the side of the ship and assist with lowering and raising it like mini cranes) and carried her boat on stern davits, but a spar was lashed across these and for some reason the boat had been lashed across the main hatch. Deveau said 'there were no lashings visible, therefore I cannot swear that the *Mary Celeste* had any boat at all, but there were two fenders where the boat would be lashed. Assuming that there was a boat, there was nothing to show how the boat was launched, there were no signs of any tackles to launch her. We launched our boat that way from the rail of the vessel without tackle or hoisting her up with a tow rope only to secure her.'

Deveau appears here to be saying that there was no evidence that *Mary Celeste* had carried a boat and no indication of how a boat could have been launched. However, what he actually seems to have said is that there were no tackles to launch the boat. There was a way to launch the boat, however, because Deveau said he launched his boat 'that way' without specifying the way itself. In fact a section of rail appears to have been removed to facilitate launching the boat.[3]

It was clear what had happened to the captain, his family, and the crew of *Mary Celeste*: they had made a very hurried but ordered evacuation of the ship. Someone had sounded the vessel and presumably thought she was taking on a lot of water and sinking, and had not bothered to replace the sounding rod but had dropped it to the deck, suggesting haste. Men had released the railing and launched the small boat, someone had gathered the chronometer, sextant, navigation book, ship's register and other papers, but had not bothered with food or extra clothing, or even pipes and tobacco. They had then got into the small boat and at some point it had capsized and everyone had drowned. But what could possibly have happened on the ship to make those aboard believe they were in such imminent danger that they had no alternative but to hurriedly leave the ship?

When Deveau and Wright had completed their brief inspection and established that there was nobody on board, alive or dead, they rejoined Johnson in the boat and returned to the *Dei Gratia*.

Captain Morehouse noted in the *Dei Gratia*'s log:

> *December 5. Begins with a fresh breeze and clear, sea still running heavy but wind moderating. Saw a sail to the E. 2 p.m. Saw she was under very short canvas, steering very wild and evidently in distress. Hauled up to speak her and render assistance, if necessary. At 3 p.m. hailed her and getting no answer and seeing no one on deck . . . out boat and sent the mate and two men on board, sea running high at the time. He boarded her without accident and returned in about an hour and reported her to be the Mary Celeste, at and from New York, for Genoa, abandoned with $3^1/_2$ft. of water in hold.*

Oliver Deveau urged Captain Morehouse to let him take two men and bring *Mary Celeste* into Gibraltar, a voyage of some six hundred miles in a stormy December ocean. Morehouse was reluctant. He was responsibile for the safety of the men under his command and for safely delivering both his ship and her cargo of petroleum to their destination, and he knew that both ships would be endangered by a depleted crew. Deveau still felt inclined to attempt it, so Morehouse called all hands aft, explained the situation, pointed out the risk, and asked them whether they would be willing to share the extra risk and extra labour. They all agreed to do so.

At about 4 p.m. Deveau, with Charles Lund and Augustus Anderson, crossed to *Mary Celeste*, taking a barometer, compass and watch from *Dei Gratia*. Deveau took his own nautical instruments and Captain Morehouse gave them all the food the steward had cooked. Deveau boarded first, followed by Anderson. As soon as Deveau went on board he wore *Celeste* round, but made no sail. Deveau was able to follow *Dei Gratia* at the rate of $1^1/_2$ to 2 knots an hour during the night. The next few hours were spent sorting out the rigging and sails and pumping the vessel dry. Morehouse saw them at the pumps till dark, about 10 p.m. They also repaired the binnacle, according to Charles Lund, 'We put it into its place again – it may have taken 5 to 10 minutes to put it back again. The binnacle was not again carried away by bad weather whilst we were on board. If a sea had come over it might have again struck and carried away the binnacle.' It is an interesting observation, reflecting Lund's belief that the binnacle had been swept from its position by heavy seas.

Before midnight Morehouse wore *Dei Gratia* round and ran under the stern of *Mary Celeste*, asking whether Deveau felt safe and had got the ship pumped dry. Deveau said yes, but asked Morehouse not to leave him that night. They agreed that Deveau would make a flash if he felt in danger at any time during the night. Morehouse thought on one occasion that Deveau had done so, perhaps an indication that he was feeling tense about the whole enterprise, but Deveau hadn't made any light and at midnight he eventually made sail.

The wind fell very light and the two vessels kept together. The next morning about 9 a.m. Morehouse spoke to Deveau and asked him how he was getting on. Deveau said pretty well but that it was hard work, that he was still getting the sails in order and was shifting his fore-top gallant sail to a fore-topsail and planned later in the morning to set the two gib and all three staysails. When he had done as he intended the speed of the two vessels was nearly equal.

The weather remained moderate during the following days, just a few little squalls to contend with, and the vessels kept in sight of one another, only not being able to do so at night, and they spoke to each other two or three times on the way to Gibraltar. It was on the eve of arriving in Gibraltar that they encountered a major problem. The weather deteriorated and the seas became very rough, then a thick fog descended and at about 3.00 a.m. *Dei Gratia* lost sight of *Mary Celeste*.

Dei Gratia made it into Gibraltar at 4.00 p.m. and there were several hours of anxiety before *Mary Celeste* came into sight about 9.00 a.m., Friday, 13 December. Deveau quickly got pratique – meaning that he obtained permission to use the port – and headed for *Dei Gratia*. Morehouse, who was ashore and unaware of *Mary Celeste*'s arrival, was returning to his own ship when he saw and made his way towards her. Fortunately he caught sight of Deveau aboard *Dei Gratia* and immediately went to join him. Morehouse congratulated Deveau, who looked very fatigued and sleepy, who replied, 'Yes, but I don't know that I would attempt it again.' Morehouse then went aboard *Mary Celeste* with Deveau.

Deveau wrote to his wife:

My men were all done out when I got in here, and I think it will be a week before I can do anything, for I never was so tired in my life. I can hardly tell what I am made of, but I do not care as long as I got in safe. I shall be well paid, for the Mary Celeste . . .

Little did he know.

Notes and references

1   An obituary appeared in the *Digby Courier*, 20 September 1912.

2   A letter dated 27 May 1940 from Lieut. Col. J. Agostinho, Director of the Meteorological Service in the Azores, to the author Charles Edey Fay (*The Story of the 'Mary Celeste'*, Appendix X, p. 251).

3   A minute examination of *Mary Celeste* after her arrival in Gibraltar found what appeared to be be an axe cut on the rail of the vessel. Deveau was recalled on 4 March 1873 to give evidence at the salvage hearing, he was shown the piece of railing and agreed the cut looked as if it had been done with a sharp axe, but said he had not noticed it when aboard the ship and did not think it could have been done whilst his men were in possession of the vessel because they had found only an old axe on board. He then stated, 'I did not replace the rails of the ship found on the deck before I returned to the *Dei Gratia* the first time.' This appears to mean that a section of the rail had been removed by the crew of *Mary Celeste* and left on deck, that Deveau had found it there and had only replaced it when he took command of the vessel. It seems remarkable that Deveau had not previously mentioned the rail having been removed, clearly to facilitate launching the boat, and that he should only have mentioned it now in passing.

CHAPTER 6

Meet Mr Frederick Solly Flood

One of the first things Captain Morehouse did in Gibraltar was to cable news of the salvaging of *Mary Celeste* to a part-owner of *Dei Gratia*, John W. Parker, who was a partner in the brokerage business of Haney and Parker at 25 Coenties Slip, New York. Parker in turn notified the offices of J.H. Winchester & Co., who informed the various insurers, including the Atlantic Mutual Insurance Company, whose Disaster Clerk noted on page 192 of Disaster Book No. 93 the content of the cablegram:

> *FOUND FOURTH AND BROUGHT HERE 'MARY CELESTE'*
> *ABANDONED SEAWORTHY ADMIRALTY IMPOST NOTIFY ALL*
> *PARTIES TELEGRAPH OFFER OF SALVAGE. MOREHOUSE.*

On the same day the United States Consul in Gibraltar, Horatio Sprague, sent the following telegram:

> *GIBRALTAR, 13TH DECEMBER 1872*
> *BOARD OF UNDERWRITERS, NEW YORK*
> *BRIG 'MARY CELESTE' HERE DERELICT IMPORTANT SEND POWER*
> *ATTORNEY TO CLAIM HER FROM ADMIRALTY COURT.*
> > *[SIGNED] HORATIO J. SPRAGUE*

He also cabled his opposite number in Genoa, O.M. Spencer:

> *GIBRALTAR, 13TH DECEMBER 1872*
> *AMERICAN CONSUL, GENOA*

AMERICAN BRIG 'MARY CELESTE' HERE DERELICT IMPORTANT
SEND BILL LADING CARGO TO CLAIM FROM ADMIRALTY COURT.
[SIGNED] SPRAGUE, CONSUL

In reply to the first telegram, Alfred Ogden, who was Chairman of the Standing Committee on Salvages, Losses and Averages of the Board of Underwriters of New York (who was also Vice-President of the Orient Mutual Insurance Company, one of the main insurers of Mary Celeste), told Sprague:

PROTECT BRIG 'MARY CELESTE' WANT VOYAGE PERFORMED
OGDEN

The recovery of *Mary Celeste* was reported in *Lloyd's List*, a British newspaper reporting shipping movements and casualties, maritime news and other commercial information:[1]

> *Gibraltar, Dec. 13, 1872, 1.45 P.M. – The Mary Celeste (Aust. brigantine), from New York to Genoa, with alcohol, has been derelict at sea and brought here by three men of the Dei Gratia (British brigantine).*

> *Gibraltar, Dec. 14, 1872. – The Mary Celeste (British brigantine) is in possession of the Admiralty Court.*

The Times on 16 December also carried the news of the discovery under its heading 'Latest Shipping Intelligence' and by 19 December the story had reached the New York *Journal of Commerce*. The tale at this time was brief and to the point, but it did not take long for the peculiar circumstances of *Mary Celeste*'s discovery to attract the attention of the press and on 21 December the *Shipping and Commercial List* noted that:

> *The strange feature about the* Mary Celeste *is the fact that she was in seaworthy condition. There was no evidence that she had been run into, or that she had encountered unusually heavy weather. The inference is that there has been foul play somewhere, and that alcohol is at the bottom of it.*

The last sentence carried a slight implication that the shippers were guilty of fraud, and on 25 December the *Shipping and Commercial List* offered a correction in which they apologised for any imputation of the shipper's honesty but in doing so cast speculative aspersions on the *Mary Celeste*'s crew:

> *In our last issue we noted the fact, based on private despatches, that the brig Mary Celeste, hence for Genoa with a cargo of Alcohol, had been abandoned, and subsequently fallen in with and towed into Gibraltar; that as the vessel when found was in a seaworthy condition, apprehensions of foul play were entertained, and that Alcohol was probably at the bottom of it. It seems that the closing sentence of the paragraph was misconstrued into a reflection upon the honesty or good faith of the shippers, although it really bore no such interpretation. The shippers of the cargo of the Mary Celeste are known to us as being among the most honorable of firms, and not the slightest suspicion is entertained of fraud on their part, so far as we are aware. The impression we intended to convey was that the crew had possibly been making free with the Alcohol, and that foul play had resulted. This, of course, is mere conjecture, and until the affair has been fully investigated, the real cause of abandonment cannot be known – perhaps it never will be.*

This was just the start of the extraordinary speculations that would surround both the crew of *Mary Celeste* and *Dei Gratia* and which must have made Captain Morehouse, Oliver Deveau and the crew of *Dei Gratia* rue the day they set eyes upon the ocean wanderer. On 30 January 1873 the *Gibraltar Chronicle* would lay out the basic facts for suspicion and indicate the direction in which the suspicion was leading. During a long report, which was picked up and repeated in *The Times* in London on 14 February, it stated:

> *As regards the interior of the ship – a very minute survey showed most clearly that not only had the vessel not sustained any accident, but that she could not have encountered any seriously heavy weather. The whole of the hull, masts and yards were in good condition, and the pitch in the water–ways had not started, which must have been the case had any bad weather been experienced. The deck–house, made of thin planking and 6ft in height above the deck, was perfect, there not being a crack in the planking nor even in the paint. The seaman's chests and clothing found on board were perfectly dry, some razors even being quite free from rust. Moreover, a small phial containing oil for use with a sewing*

machine was found in a perpendicular position, which, together with a thimble and a reel of cotton discovered near it, had not been upset, as must have been the case if the ship had been subject to any stress of weather. Spare panes of glass were also found stowed away and unbroken. All the articles of furniture in the captain's cabin, including a harmonium, were in their proper places and uninjured by water, the music and other books also being dry. Finally, the conclusion arrived at by the surveyor, Mr Austin, is that there exists no apparent reason why the vessel should have been abandoned. But, in addition to the above facts, a sword was discovered which, on its being drawn out of its scabbard, exhibited signs of having been smeared with blood and afterwards wiped; further the top-gallant rail had marks on it apparently of blood, and both bows of the vessel had been cut, to all appearances intentionally, with some sharp instrument. No bills of lading nor manifest was found on board. The effects found in the captain's cabin were of considerable value and proved that a lady and child had been on board. The ship's log, which was found on board, showed that the last days work of the ship was on 24th of November, sea time, when the weather allowed an observation to be taken which placed the vessel at lat. 36.56 N., long. 27.20 W. The entries on the log slate were, however, carried on up to 8 a.m. on the 25th, at which time the vessel passed from west to east to the north of the island of Saint Mary's (Azores), the eastern point of which at 8 a.m. bore S.S.L six miles distant. The distance of the longitude of the places where the Mary Celeste was found from that of the island of Saint Mary's is 7.54. E., and the corrected distance of the latitude from the position last indicated in the log is 1.18 N., so that the vessel had apparently held on her due course for 10 days after the 25th of November, the wheel being loose all the time. But the log of the Dei Gratia shows that during this time, from the 25th of November to the day when she met with the Mary Celeste, the 5th of December, the wind was more or less from the north, and that she was on a port tack during the whole of that period. It appears, therefore, almost impossible that the derelict should have compassed the same time and distance of 7.54 L, at all events on the starboard tack, upon which she was met by the Dei Gratia, and the obvious inference is that she was not abandoned until some days after the last entry made in the log. Naturally, various theories are set up to account for this extraordinary series of facts, and *the finding of the sword and the blood stains are held to point to some deed of violence.*

The utter respectability of the crew of both vessels makes murder on the high seas highly improbable, but it cannot be denied that despite the abundant theories the circumstances of *Mary Celeste*'s abandonment seem to defy convincing explanation, and it is therefore hardly surprising that *Mary Celeste* should have been a talking point. What turned her into a *cause célèbre* in the annals of maritime mystery and remembered 130 years later was a pompous little man named Frederick Solly Flood who possessed the grand and imposing title of Her Majesty's Advocate-General and Proctor for the Queen in Her Office of Admiralty, and Attorney-General for Gibraltar.

He was born plain Frederick Solly in 1801 and was the son of Richard Solly, but on his father's death in 1820 he took by Royal Licence the additional surname of his maternal grandfather, the prominent Irish politician Sir Frederick Flood (1741–1824), whose property and fortune he hoped to inherit and which in 1824 he did indeed come into. He received a good education at Harrow and Trinity College, Cambridge, was admitted to Lincoln's Inn in 1824 and was called to the bar in 1828, joining the Midland Circuit and attending Warwick and Northampton Sessions. He had married Mary Williamson of Stoke Damerel, Devonport, and in due course he created a very successful legal practice, but his fortunes do not appear to have been as great as outward appearances suggest because at the advanced age of 71 years lack of funds effectively forced him to accept the position of Attorney General at Gibraltar. He was also a fairly prolific writer and towards the end of his life authored two papers for The Royal Historical Society, of which he was elected a Fellow in 1885, 'The Story of Prince Henry of Monmouth and Chief Justice Gascoign' (1886) and 'Prince Henry of Monmouth – his Letters and Despatches during the War in Wales, 1402–1405' (1889), and a book that was never published but had the daunting title *Abridged History of the Writ of Habeas Corpus Cum Causa as a Remedy against Unlawful Imprisonment*.

From the arrival of *Mary Celeste* in Gibraltar's harbour, Frederick Solly Flood was determined to establish that violence had been done aboard the vessel. As Consul Sprague wrote to the Department of State on 20 January 1873, 'The Queen's Proctor in the Vice Admiralty Court of this

City, who is also the Attorney General, seems to take the greatest interest in the case and rather entertains the apprehension of some foul play having occurred.'

What Consul Sprague thought of Solly Flood at this time is uncertain, but much later he suffered no misapprehensions and on 4 March 1885 he wrote with an admirable felicity of language to the Assistant Secretary of State in Washington,

> . . . Mr Flood is an Irish gentleman . . . he has always been considered an individual of very vivid imagination, and to have survived to some extent at least, the judicious application of his mental faculties; such is, I believe, the general opinion of the community at large, even among his most intimate and personal friends.[2]

'To have survived . . . the judicious application of his mental faculties' is a delicious turn of phrase, but the point is that Frederick Solly Flood seems to have been a man who was capable of seeing shapes in the shadows that simply weren't there and whose advanced years had impaired the process of strictly logical thinking. He was the sort of man who, once he had made up his mind about something, couldn't be shifted.

The salvage hearings opened at the Vice-Admiralty Court of Gibraltar on Tuesday, 17 December 1872 and were almost immediately adjourned until the following day, Wednesday, 18 December 1872.

The presiding judge, who for a time at least seems to have shared the opinions of Frederick Solly Flood, was Sir James Cochrane (1798–1883), who was born in Nova Scotia where *Mary Celeste* was built, the son of Thomas Cochrane, speaker of the House of Assembly of Nova Scotia. Sir James had formerly occupied Flood's position, having been Attorney General for Gibraltar from 1830 until 1841, in which year he had been appointed Chief Justice for Gibraltar, an office he held until he resigned in 1877. At the time of his resignation the Governor of Gibraltar, General Lord Napier of Magdala, said that 'During the long time that Sir James Cochrane has presided over the supreme court at Gibraltar he has eminently maintained the high character of the bench. The clearness of his judgment, the wisdom of his decisions, and his personal character have commanded the respect of all classes of the community. He has done much for the lower classes, and his firmness and perfect fairness have helped greatly to dispel from the city of Gibraltar the crime of using the knife, which was unfortunately once so prevalent.'

Appearing before Sir James were Frederick Solly Flood who represented the Queen in Her Office of Admiralty, Henry Peter Pisani who represented Captain Morehouse and the owners of *Dei Gratia*, George F. Cornwell acting for the owners of *Mary Celeste*, and Martin W. Stokes, acting for the owners of the cargo. The Registrar was Edward Jocelyn Baumgartner.

The whole of the first day's proceedings were taken up with the testimony of Oliver Deveu, who was recalled following a short adjournment on Friday, 20 December, corrected an earlier statement and gave further evidence. Testimony was then given by John Wright, the second mate, and seaman Charles Lund. On the following day, 21 December, seamen Augustus Anderson and John Johnson were heard. Johnson had little to say because he had remained in the small boat and not boarded *Mary Celeste* at all, and in any case he understood very little English and cross-examination would have been complicated by the need to use an interpreter. The hearings were then adjourned until 29 January 1873 when James H. Winchester gave his testimony. They were then adjourned yet again, this time until 31 January 1873.

On Monday, 23 December, Frederick Solly Flood ordered a special survey of *Mary Celeste*, and this was undertaken by John Austin, Surveyor of Shipping, and Ricardo Portunato, a diver. They visited the ship accompanied by Thomas J. Vecchio, Marshal of the Court, and Solly Flood, and undertook a thorough internal and external examination. Their reports, though long and somewhat tedious, make sometimes interesting but important reading:

Affidavit of John Austin, Surveyor of Shipping, Gibraltar,
I, John Austin of the City of Gibraltar, Surveyor of Shipping make oath and say.
1. That by desire of Thomas Joseph Vecchio Esqr Marshal of this Honble Court in company with him and Fredk. Solly Flood Esqr H. M's Advocate General for Gibraltar and Proctor for the Queen in her Office of Admiralty on Monday the 23rd day of Decbr last went on board a vessel rigged as a brigantine name unknown supposed to be the Mary Celeste *then moored in the port of Gibraltar and under an arrest in pursuance of a warrant out of this Honble Court as having been found derelict on the*

high seas and I then carefully and minutely surveyed and examined the state and condition of the said vessel and was occupied therein for a period of five hours.

2. On approaching the Vessel I found on the bow between two and three feet above the water line on the port side a long narrow strip of the edge of one of her outer planks under the cat-head cut away to the depth of about three eighths of an inch or about one inch and a quarter wide for a length of about 6 or 7 feet. This injury had been sustained very recently and could not have been effected by the weather and was apparently done by a sharp cutting instrument continuously applied thro' the whole length of the injury.

3. I found on the starboard bow but a little further from the stem of the Vessel a precisely similar injury but perhaps an eighth or a tenth of an inch wider wh. in my opinion had been effected at the same time and by the same means and not otherwise.

4. The whole of the Hull – Masts Yards and other Spars were in their proper places and in good condition and exhibited no appearances whatever that the vessel since she had undergone her last repairs or during her last voyage had encountered any seriously heavy weather. Some of her rigging was old but some of her ropes appeared to have been new at the commencement of her last voyage.

5. The peak halyards and throat halyards appeared to be the same with wh. she had been rigged during her last and more than once previous voyage. None of them had been recently spliced and they were all in good working condition. If the peak halyards had been carried away during her last voyage they must have been subsequently spliced wh. was not the case.

6. If the peak halyards had been carried away while the vessel was under sail and the vessel had been abandoned hurriedly and without letting go the throat halyards the gaff would have been carried backwards and forwards by the wind. The jaws of the gaff would thereby have been destroyed and the mainmast would have been cut into but the jaws of the gaff exhibited no signs of an [sic] recent injury and the mainmast was undamaged – in such a case also the Gaff would have ripped the mainsail to pieces.

7. Moreover the main boom would have swayed backward and forward and in the event of there being any strong wind either the sheets

would have been carried away or the bolts wld. have been torn out of their deck but they were all uninjured –

8. Upon examining the deck I found the butts and waterways in good condition the pitch in the waterways had nowhere started wh. it must have done extensively if the vessel had encountered seriously bad weather.

9. The Vessel had not bulwarks but was provided with a top gallant rail supported by wooden staunchions [sic] the whole of wh. were uninjured nor was there a single stanchion displaced. The water barrels on deck were in their proper places and secured in the ordinary manner but such that if the vessel had ever been thrown on her beam ends or encountered a very serious gale they wld. have gone adrift and carried away some of the stanchions of the top gallant rail.

10. Returning to the bow of the Vessel I removed the forehatch immediately under wh. was a new hawser wh. had never been used and was perfectly dry – Had any quantity of water found its way thro' this hatch the hawser would have exhibited signs of having been wetted. It exhibited none nor did any other of the articles wh. I observed there.

11. I found a forward deck house thirteen feet square and about six feet in height above the deck.

12. The deck house was made of thin planking painted white the seam between it and the deck being filled in with pitch a very violent sea would have swept the deck house away. A sea of less than very great violence would have cracked the pannelling [sic] and cracked or started the pitch throughout or at least in some parts of the deck.

13. It had not suffered the slightest injury whatever there was not a crack in the planking nor even in the paint nor in the pitch of the deck seams.

14. The port side of the deck house was divided into two cabins the forward one extended between nine feet six and ten feet across the deck and about six feet nine inches fore and aft the after cabin being on the same side was about six feet nine inches by six feet nine inches. The forward cabin entered by a sliding wooden door facing the bow of the ship.

15. Close in front of the door of the forward port cabin was a seaman's chest unlocked and at the sides of the door opposite to it was another also unlocked. Both were quite full of seamen's effects of a

superior description and mostly quite new. They were perfectly dry and not had the slightest contact with water.

16. Amongst the articles I observed in one of them was a new cigar case with metal clasp not in the slightest degree rusty. It contained nothing but 3 gold studs set with precious stones and a razor also equally unaffected by water. I also particularly noticed a pair of new instep boots and a pair of new high foul weather boots both perfectly clean a quadrant in its case together with a piece of chamois leather all perfectly dry and uninjured and unaffected by water.

17. I also carefully searched for marks of mildew on all the articles particularly on the boots and the rest of the clothing but could not discover any or any other mark of water wh. I believe I must have discovered if the Vessel had encountered any very bad weather.

18. I then examined the after Cabin on the port side wh. I believe to have been the second Mate's and it contained a seaman's chest similiar to those in the forward port Cabin and containing clothes wh. I carefully examined but none of which exhibited the slightest appearance of having been subjected to water.

19. The sills of the doors of these Cabins rise to the height of about a foot above the deck. If water had come into either of them to an extent to have flooded them an inch in depth a great part of the clothing wh. I observed would have shown signs of the water none of wh. were to be seen.

20. The Starboard Side of the Deck house to the extent of about six and a half feet in width aft and about 314 feet forward comprised the ships galley and was entered by a sliding door on the after side.

21. The stove and cooking utensils were in good order and exhibited no appearance of having suffered from exposure to water. Had any quantity of water found its way into the galley it would have immediately passed out thro' a scuttle hole on a level with the deck near the stove or thro' a hole wh. I found in the deck near the hearth into the hold.

22. The forward deck house was lighted by two windows on each side those on the port side were covered by a thin sliding shutter. The after window on the Starboard side was uncovered.

23. None of the shutters or of the windows were injured in the slightest degree. Some of them must have been greatly injured or wholly destroyed if the vessel had experienced very bad weather.

24. On the upper deck of the deck house I found the remains of two sails wh. apparently had been split some time or another in a gale and afterwards cut up as large lengths had been cut off with a knife or other sharp instrument and I subsequently found what I believe to be portions of those sails –

25. On going aft I examined a skylight wh. lights both the main cabin and the Captain's cabin. It consisted of six panes of glass on each side the whole of which had a small piece wanting. Had the ship experienced very bad weather the skylight unless it had been covered which it was not when I surveyed the vessel would have been greatly damaged.

26. The height of the Cabin is increased by means of a false deck raised about 15 inches above the deck of the vessel.

27. The entrance to the Cabin is by means of a companion through a door in the forward side and a sliding hatch.

28. On descending into the main Cabin I found at the foot of the companion an oblong piece of canvas wh. I believe to have formed part of one of the sails which had been split and which I had noticed on the forward house. It had been cut and fitted as a lining for a small recess to which it was carefully fastened with nails or screws and through a small brass hook apparently intended for the purpose of hanging a towel on had been carefully driven into one of the uprights.

29. This piece of canvas had evidently been fixed there before the vessel had sailed on her last voyage. On the port side of the main-cabin was the pantry entered by a door the sill of which was about an inch and a half above the level of the lower deck or floor of the cabin. On the floor of the cabin I found among other things an open box containing moist sugar a bag containing two or three pounds of tea an open barrel containing flour and open box containing dried herrings; also some rice a nutmeg some kidney beans together with several pots of preserved fruits and other provisions in tins covered with paper. The whole of these articles were perfectly dry and had not been in the slightest degree injured or affected by water.

30. On the plate rack was another piece of canvas apparently cut from off the sails which I had observed on the forward house. It was cut into the shape of a towel for which it was apparently used. On the Starboard side of the main cabin was the chief mate's cabin, on a little bracket in which I found a small phial of oil for a sewing machine in its proper perpendicular position a reel of cotton for such a machine and a thimble. If they had been there in bad weather then they wd. have been thrown down or carried away.

31. The chief Mate's bedding was perfectly dry and had not been wetted or affected by water. Underneath his bed place were the vessel's ensign and her private signal W T. The latter had been altered since it had been used. The letter W having been quite recently sown [sic] on.

I also found under the mate's bedplace a pair of heavy Seamen's boots for stormy weather greased cleaned and apparently unused and also two drawers containing various articles.

33. In the lower drawer were a quantity of loose pieces of iron and two unbroken panes of glass which wd. have been broken to pieces had the Vessel encountered any seriously bad weather.

34. In the lower drawer were among other things a pair of log sand glasses and a new log reel without any log line.

35. The whole of the furniture and effects in the cabin were perfectly dry and in good condition. None of the articles had been or were injured or affected by water.

36. In the cabin was a clock without hands and fastened upside down by two screws or nails fixed in the woodwork of the partition, apparently some considerable time previously.

37. On entering the Captain's cabin which is abaft the main cabin I observed and examined a large quantity of personal effects.

38. In the centre of the cabin against the partition was a harmonium in very good condition and near to it a quantity of books mostly of a religious kind and which with the exception of a few which I was informed by the Marshal had been removed by him out of the lowest drawer underneath the Captain's bedplace and which were damaged by water were in Excellently good condition.

39. I found also on the floor of the cabin a little child's high chair in perfectly good condition a medicine chest containing bottles and various medical preparations in good condition.

40. The whole of which articles were uninjured and unaffected by water.

41. The bedding and other effects were perfectly dry they had not been affected by water and were in good condition.

42. I am of opinion that some not large quantity of water had fallen on the floor of the cabin through the sky light and found its way into the bottom drawer under the captain's bedplace.

43. In the cabin I found one of the Vessel's compasses belonging to the binnacle. The card of it had been damaged by water.

44. I also observed in this cabin a Sword in its scabbard which the Marshall informed me he had noticed when he came on board for the purpose of arresting the vessel. It had not [word missing] affected by water but on drawing out the blade it appeared to me as if it had been smeared with blood and afterwards wiped. Both the cabins were provided with lamps to be lighted by means of petroleum. They and their glasses were uninjured.

45. On the port side of the Captain's cabin was a water-closet near the door of which opposite to a window imperfectly covered on the outside was hanging a bag which was damp and had evidently been much wetted by rain or spray or both coming in at the window.

46. I was informed by the Marshal that upon his going on board the Vessel for the purpose of arresting her he had found the bag full of clothes mostly belonging to a lady and extremely wet.

47. On the Starboard side of the cabins were three windows two of which intended to light the Captain's cabin were covered with canvas similar to that of which the torn sails were made and apparently cut from it the canvas being secured by pieces of plank nailed into the frame work of the cabin the third window intended to light the chief Mate's Cabin no appearance of having ever been covered and the glass was injured on the side of the Cabin facing the bow of the vessel was another window secured in the same manner and with the same materials as those intended to light the Captain's cabin.

48. On the port side there was a window which lighted the water closet. It was partially covered in the same manner as that last mentioned. There was a port for another window to light the pantry but it had been effectually closed up by a wood made to fit into it.

49. Returning to the deck I found one of the pumps in good order the valve of the other had been removed for the purpose of passing a sounding apparatus into the well.

50. The sounding apparatus wh. consisted of a metal bolt attached to a line was lying near & was in good order.

51. I then carefully examined the binnacle which I found secured to the deck of the cabin between two battens the original batten on the Starboard Side had been replaced by another roughly made. It was farther secured by cleats on each side.

52. The binnacle was constructed to hold two compasses and a lamp between them with a pane of glass separating the lamp from each compass. Both these panes of glass were cracked perpendicularly and apparently from the heat of the lamp only.

53. One of the compasses was in good working condition and did not appear to have been otherwise during the voyage. The other was missing being the one which I found in the Captain's cabin.

54. The binnacle itself did not appear to have sustained any damage.

55. In my opinion it never could have been carried away by a sea which wd. not have destroyed it & washed it overboard.

56. Such a sea wd. also have swept the decks and carried away the skylight off the cabin the top gallant sail' & stanchions and besides doing other damage probably have thrown the Vessel on her beam ends.

57. The whole appearance of the Vessel shows that the Vessel never encountered any such violence.

58. I next examined the after or lazaret hatch which is secured by an iron bar and went into the after hold.

59. I found here barrels of stores and other provisions in good order & condition & in their proper places. The whole of these wd. have been capsized if the Vessel had been thrown on her beam ends or encountered any very violent weather.

60. I also saw there a barrel of Stockholm tar standing in its proper position with the head of the barrel off, none of it appeared to have been used. Had the Vessel encountered any very heavy weather this barrel wd. have been capsized or at all events some of the tar wd. have been spilt, but not a drop of it had escaped.

61. I found no wine or beer or spirits on board. I made the most careful & minute examination through every part of the Vessel to which I had access to discover whether there had been any explosion on board & whether there had been any fire or any accident calculated to create an alarm of an explosion or of fire & did not discover the slightest trace of there having been any explosion or any fire or of anything calculated to create an alarm of an explosion or of fire.

62. The Vessel was thoroughly sound staunch and strong & not making water to any appreciable extent.

63. I gave directions to Ricardo Portunato an experienced Diver minutely & carefully to examine the whole of the hull and bottom of the said Vessel her stem, keel, Sternpost & rudder while I was engaged on board in surveying her, and he remained under water for that purpose for a time amply sufficient for that purpose.

64. I have now perused and considered the paper writing marked A produced & shown to me at the time of the swearing this my affidavit & which purports to be an affidavit by said Ricardo Portunato in this cause on the 7th day of Jany. now instant.

65. Having carefully weighed & considered the contents thereof & all & singular the matters aforesaid I am wholly unable to discover any reason whatever why the said Vessel should have been abandoned.

Affidavit of Ricardo Portunato, Diver

In the Vice-Admiralty Court of Gibraltar. The Queen in Her Office of Admiralty Ag't. – The Ship or Vessel name unknown supposed to be called the Mary Celeste and her Cargo found derelict.

I, Ricardo Portunato of the City of Gibraltar, Diver make oath and say as follows:

1. I did on Monday the 23rd day of Decbr. last by direction of Thomas Joseph Vecchio Esqr. Marshal of their Honble. Court and of Mr. John Austin Surveyor of Shipping for the port of Gibraltar proceed to a ship or vessel rigged as a Brigantine and supposed to be the Mary Celeste then moored in the port of Gibraltar and under arrest in pursuance of a warrant out of their Honble. Court as having been found derelict on the high Seas for the purpose of examining the State and condition of the hull of the said vessel below her water line and of ascertaining if possible whether she had sustained any damage or injury from a collision or from having struck upon any rock or shoal or otherwise howsoever.

2. I accordingly minutely and carefully examined the whole of the hull of the said Vessel and the stern keel, stern post and rudder thereof.

3. They did not nor did any or either of them exhibit any trace of damage or injury or any other appearances whatsoever indicating that the said Vessel had had any collision or had struck upon any rock or

shoal or had met with any accident or casualty. The hull Stern, [sic]
keel Sternpost and rudder of the said Vessel were thoroughly in good
order and condition.

4. The said Vessel was coppered the copper was in good condition
and order and I am of opinion that if she had met with any such
accident or casualty I shld. have been able to discover and shld. have
discovered some marks or traces thereof but I was not able to discover
and did not discover any.[3]

On 22 January 1873 Frederick Solly Flood summarised the results of
these reports – as he saw them – in a letter to the Marine Department
of the Board of Trade in London. He explained that *Mary Celeste* was
perfectly seaworthy, well found and provisioned, had encountered no
seriously heavy weather, and bore no sign of fire or an explosion, and
nothing aboard suggested a cause for abandonment. However, the survey
showed that both bows had been recently cut by a sharp instrument and
that a sword was found which appeared to be bloodstained and to have
been wiped before being returned into the scabbard. There were what
appeared to be bloodstains on the starboard top-gallant rail and a cut
apparently made by a sharp axe. In the hold a barrel of alcohol appeared
to have been tampered with. 'My own theory or guess,' wrote Flood, 'is
that the crew got at the alcohol and in the fury of drunkenness murdered
the Master whose name was Briggs and wife and child and the Chief
Mate, that they then damaged the bows of the vessel with the view of
giving it the appearance of having struck on rocks or suffered from a
collision so as to induce the Master of any vessel which might pick them
up if they saw her at some distance to think her not worth attempting to
save, and that they did sometime between the 25th Novbr. and the 5th
Decbr. escape on board some vessel bound for some North or South
American port or the West Indies.'[4]

Flood added a supplement to the letter the following day in which
he expressed doubt that *Mary Celeste* would have reached the position where she was found if she had been abandoned at 8.00 a.m. on
25 November, and expressed the view that she had 'in fact not been
abandoned till several days afterwards, and probably also that she was
abandoned much further to the Eastward than the spot where she was
found'.

On 7 January Frederick Solly Flood made a further examination of *Mary Celeste*, paying particular attention this time to what he described in his letter to the Board of Trade as 'marks of violence', and was this time accompanied by the Marshal of the Vice Admiralty Court, Captain Fitzroy of HMS *Minotaur*, Captain Adeane of HMS *Agincourt*, Captain Dowell of HMS *Hercules*; Captain Vansittart of HMS *Sultan*, and by Colonel Laffan, R.E. All of them, said Flood, 'agreed with me in opinion that the injury to the bows had been effected intentionally by a sharp instrument'.

The evidence of murder on the high seas was growing. Or at least the tenacious Mr Flood thought it was and towards the end of the month he sought scientific evidence from a Dr J. Patron, who was instructed to undertake a careful and minute examination of the ship, particularly the deck, top-gallant rail, cabin floor and a few other places, along with the sword.

Analysis by Dr. J. Patron of Supposed Blood-stains

Gibraltar,

30th January *1873*

At the request of Her Majesty's Attorney General I proceeded on board of the American brig Mary Celeste *anchored in this Bay for the purpose of ascertaining whether any marks or stains of blood could be discovered on or in her hulk.*

After a careful and minute inspection of the deck of the said vessel some red brown spots about a millimetre thick and half an inch in diameter with a dull aspect were found on deck in the forepart of the vessel these spots were separated with a chissel [sic] *and carefully wrapped in paper No. 1.*

Some other similar spots were equally gathered in different parts of the deck and wrapped in papers numbered, 2, 3, and 4. Paper No. 5 contained a powder grated from a suspicious mark seen on the top-gallant rail part of which was obtained on board and part from a piece of timber belonging to the said vessel in Her Majesty's Attorney General chambers.

I carefully examined the cabin both with natural and artificial light; the floor, the sides of the berths, mattrasses [sic] *etc. were minutely searched and nothing worth calling attention was seen that could have any relation with the object of my enquiries.*

On the 31st January at 2 o'clock I received from the hands of Mr. Vecchio Marshal of the Supreme Court the five papers above mentioned and numbered 1, 2, 3, 4, and 5 and a sword with its sheath found on board the said vessel.

The spots which were in paper No. 1, 2, and 3 were cut in small pieces of about a quarter of an inch long and broad passed through a white thread and suspended half an inch from the bottom of tubes containing a small quantity of distilled water.

The contents of paper No. 4 were put in a small filtering bag as their minuteness would not allow any other process of maceration and the same was done with the contents of paper No. 5.

The maceration went on in the five tubes for two hours and a quarter; the distilled water remaining after this period as clear and bright as in the very beginning of the experiment.

Notwithstanding I left the things as they were till the next day and 23 hours' maceration did not produce any alteration in the transparency of the liquid. The water being then heated with the spirit lamp as no precipitate or cloudy aspect appeared, I consider the experiment over and of a negative character. The stains on the pieces of timber remained unaltered in their aspect and the finger which was passed over them was not tinged or stained in any degree their aspect remaining as it was before maceration. The contents of paper No. 5 macerated in the bag were then examined with a microscope and nothing particular was seen but a few particles of rust (carbonate of iron) and some fragments of vegetable substance (fibres of wood).

The sword presented on its blade about the middle and final part, some stains of a more suspicious character; although few very small, and superficial, their aspect was reddish and in some parts brilliant like albuminous coloured substance, my first impression was that they were really blood stains, examined with an eight or ten diameter magnifying glass these stains presented an irregular and granulated surface; the granules becoming smaller in proportion of their distance from the central and thickest part. After an hour and three quarters maceration the transparency of the liquid remained unchanged; heat produced no cloudy alteration in it and the result was as negative as in those of the stains found on the deck.

The largest of these reddish spots was carefully grated from the blade and put under a microscope of Doctor Hartnack objective No. 7 and ocular No. 3 corresponding to a magnifying power of 330 diameter. A yellow and imperfectly crystallised substance resembling Citrate of Iron presenting here and there some red granules was seen with some fragments of vegetable ramified fibres; but no blood globules could be detected. Three other stains were tested with Hydrochloric Acid and after a perceptible effervescence a yellow stain was produced of chloride of Iron; the insufficiency of the liquid could not permit of any other experiment.

The blade heated under the flame of the spirit lamp recovered a natural brilliancy after the removal by heat of the superficial crust the sheath of the sword was clean inside and with no mark of any kind.

From the preceding negative experiments I feel myself authorized to conclude that according to our present scientifical knowledge there is no blood either in the stains observed on the deck of the Mary Celeste *or on those found on the blade of the sword that I have examined.*
(Sig'd) J. PATRON[5]

Dr Patron's conclusion must have disappointed Flood, especially his conclusion that the stains on the deck of *Mary Celeste* and on the blade of the sword were not blood, and it may be testimony to just how serious a blow they were to Flood that whilst Dr Patron's conclusions were widely known, his report remained unopened for fourteen years.[6]

On 31 January George F. Cornwell appeared before the court and laid out his petition that James H. Winchester, upon payment of salvage and salvage expenses, be allowed to take charge of *Mary Celeste*, but Judge Cochrane, perhaps persuaded by Frederick Solly Flood's arguments, declared that further investigation should take place before the release of the vessel was sanctioned.

On 5 February 1873 the USS *Plymouth* arrived at Gibraltar homeward bound from Villefranche, via Lisbon, and the Coast of Africa, and the US Consul, Horatio Sprague, formally asked Captain R.W. Shufeldt to undertake an examination of *Mary Celeste*. Shufeldt did so the following day, and submitted a brief report to Sprague before leaving Gibraltar on 7 February. Shufeldt acknowledged that his examination was cursory and his knowledge of the story imperfect, but he rejected the idea of mutiny. He had found no evidence of violence aboard the vessel, the damage to the bows, which featured heavily in Flood's visions as deliberate damage to give the impression of the ship having run upon some rocks, he thought to be no more than 'splinters made in the bending of the planks which were afterwards forced off by the action of the sea'. He gave it as his opinion that Mary Celeste had been abandoned in a moment of panic, possibly following a rough gale and in the belief that she was taking on more water than was the case. He thought it possible that there was a passing vessel and the Captain had made a snap decision to seek safety aboard her and that all aboard would in due course turn up in some far-flung port. 'But if we should never hear of them again, I shall nevertheless think they were lost in the boat in which both Master & crew abandoned the Mary Celeste & shall remember with interest this sad and silent mystery of the sea.'[7]

The proceedings lumbered along, but on 25 February some significant headway was made when Consul Sprague prevailed upon Frederick Solly Flood to allow Mary Celeste to be restored to her owners and be allowed to proceed to Genoa with her cargo of alcohol.

But the suspicions of Mr Frederick Solly Flood were not abandoned. If anything they were gaining adherents, the Nautical Gazette of New York, on 29 March 1873, having reported Captain Shufeldt's conclusions almost verbatim, expressed 'grave misgivings as to the fate of the crew' and stated that 'the Secretary of the Treasury [William A. Richardson] is evidently impressed with the same doubts'. This indeed he was, having issued only a few days earlier, on 24 March, instructions to customs officers that he be immediately informed of any clues to the fate of Mary Celeste's crew, and mentioning in the course of his memo the supposedly bloodstained sword and railings and the damage to the ship's bows.

Before proceeding it might be useful to see for future reference what those who actually examined Mary Celeste in Gibraltar had to say, especially as there is some slight reason to think that the reports may not have been free from bias. It is noticeable that John Austin, the Surveyor of Shipping, made several statements that may have been made in an effort to support Frederick Solly Flood's conviction that foul play had taken place aboard Mary Celeste. In particular he contested the testimony of

Mate Oliver Deveau and Seaman Charles Lund that the peak halyard was broken and gone; one theory advanced at the time and which has gained widespread acceptance since is that those abandoning *Mary Celeste* had used the peak halyard to secure the yawl to the *Celeste*, that the rope had broken and the yawl had drifted away from the ship. If the peak halyard was broken and gone as the *Dei Gratia* crew members claimed, and if those aboard *Celeste* had indeed used it to secure the small yawl to the *Celeste*, then it would have been self-evident that the crew expected something to happen but anticipated returning to *Celeste* if it did not. In other words, the broken halyard would suggest that the crew planned to come back and had not been done away with by the *Dei Gratia*'s crew. Austin also denied much evidence of *Mary Celeste* having encountered bad weather, saying that the bedding was not wet and referring in particular to a phial of oil near to Mrs Briggs' sewing machine which was upright, a position he maintained it would not have retained if the vessel had encountered heavy seas. It is to be supposed that the beds could have dried out by the time Mr Austin came to examine them, but the oil raises other problems. Would it have stayed upright during the days of *Mary Celeste*'s lone wanderings or during the voyage under Deveau's command into Gibraltar? Austin's conclusion *prima facie* seems a piece of reasoning contrived to support the view that the ship had encountered no natural hazard of the sea.

As the drama of the Vice Admiralty Court unfolded, a drama of a different kind took place in the Bay of Biscay. When in New York and preparing to sail, Captain Benjamin Briggs had daily awaited the arrival of his brother, Captain Oliver Briggs, in *Julia A. Hallock*, but *Mary Celeste* had had to sail before the *Hallock* reached port. She in fact arrived a few days later, took on a fresh cargo and in due course sailed for Gijón, Spain, discharged her cargo and took on 50 tons of coal as ballast, then sailed for Barcelona. Disaster struck in the Bay of Biscay, a vast inlet of the Atlantic Ocean bounded on the north and east by France and by Spain on the south, where the vessel ran into a gale and began taking on water. Men manned the pumps, but apparently they were blocked with coal dust and on 8 January 1873 *Julia A. Hallock* foundered and, with the exception of Second Mate Perry, all hands were lost, including Captain Oliver Briggs. Perry clung to some wreckage for four days before having the extraordinary good fortune of being rescued.

Notes and references

1   Edward Lloyd who ran a coffee house in Tower Street and later in Lombard Street which became a meeting place for merchants, particularly those with an interest in shipping, in January 1692 began publishing a weekly newsletter called *Ships Arrived at and Departed from several Ports of England, as I have Account of them in London . . . [and] An Account of what English Shipping and Foreign Ships for England, I hear of in Foreign Ports.* This became known as *Lloyd's List* and after Lloyd's death publication was taken over by the association of underwriters, incorporated in 1871 as the Corporation of Lloyd's – better known as Lloyd's of London. It is the second-oldest continuously published newspaper in the world.

2   Quoted in Charles Edey Fay, *The Story of the 'Mary Celeste'*, p. 144.

3   Ibid., pp. 236–38.

4   Ibid., pp. 78–80.

5   Ibid., pp. 236–38.

6   In July 1887, Worthington C. Ford, head of the Bureau of Statistics in the Department of State, requested Consul Sprague for additional information about the analysis and Sprague in turn turned to Edward J. Baumgartner, still Registrar of the Vice-Admiralty Court, who found Dr Patron's report in the files, still sealed. As Baumgartner wrote, '. . . it being rather remarkable, however, that the analysis or report so brought in was brought in under seal on the 14 March, 1873 and the seal remained unbroken until I opened it for the purpose of giving you the copy.'

7   Quoted in Charles Edey Fay, op. cit., pp. 85–7.

. . . .

CHAPTER 7

Meanwhile

On 23 December *Dei Gratia* sailed with her cargo of petroleum for Genoa, where she arrived on 16 January 1873. Captain Morehouse had remained in Gibraltar, entrusting *Dei Gratia* to the capable hands of Oliver Deveau, but neither the ship nor Deveau had received permission to leave and their action not only resulted in some stinging criticism from Judge Cochrane, but also, and perhaps more seriously for the men involved, in a salvage award that was considerably lower than it might otherwise have been.

Judge Cochrane observed that

The conduct of the Salvors in going away, as they have done, has, in my opinion, been most reprehensible and may probably influence the decision as to their claim for remuneration for their services, and it appears very strange why the Captain of the Dei Gratia *who knows little or nothing to help the investigation, should have remained here, whilst the First Mate and the crew who boarded the Celeste and brought her here should have been allowed to go away as they have done.*

Captain Morehouse's behaviour *is* explicable and probably more understandable than Judge Cochrane's rebuke credited: *Dei Gratia* had been held in Gibraltar for eleven days and during that time the crew had had to be paid and port charges had been incurred. On top of that the shippers wanted their cargo delivered and delays could have incurred penalty payments, so it was imperative that the owners cut further losses by continuing the voyage, and whilst Morehouse had nothing germane to offer the investigation of the court or to satisfy the suspicions of Flood, as the representative of *Dei Gratia*'s owners in Gibraltar he was the only person there empowered to speak for them. His decision to stay in Gibraltar and send Deveau off with *Dei Gratia* is therefore understandable, as indeed it must in reality have been to Judge Cochrane, but in retrospect it was obviously wrong to send away the principal witnesses.

As for the interests of *Mary Celeste* and her owners, as well as the New York underwriters, Captain Winchester had given up Christmas festivities with his family and friends and on 25 December had boarded the Cunarder RMS *Abyssinia*, bound for Liverpool via Gibraltar, where she arrived on 15 January. Here he kicked his heels for a week or two, his appeals that he be allowed to put a new captain aboard *Mary Celeste* and hire a crew to get the ship's cargo delivered to its owners falling on unresponsive ears. Solly Flood demanded that Winchester post sureties amounting to $15,000 dollars before he would order the release of the vessel, but Winchester was unable to meet this because before leaving New York he had not made any arrangements to transfer funds and he was not known in Gibraltar where the authorities refused to accept his note. So *Mary Celeste* remained in the harbour, running up expenses to add to the salvage costs and with the chances that the shipper of the freight *Mary Celeste* was supposed to pick up following the delivery of her cargo in Genoa would ship with someone else.

Eventually desperation drove Winchester in the first week of February to leave Gibraltar and go to Cadiz where he hoped he could raise the necessary funds from an old friend, a ship-broker named Bensusan. In Cadiz he learned that his friend had died. However, Winchester was fortunate that on 28 January 22-year-old Captain Henry O. Appleby[1] had arrived in Cadiz in command of the brigantine *Daisy Boynton*. Appleby had been at school with Captain Winchester's daughter and knew Captain Winchester well enough to help him out. *Daisy Boynton* had discharged her cargo and received her freight money, which Appleby lent to Winchester.

Curiously, Winchester did not return immediately to Gibraltar but instead went to Lisbon and on 6 February telegraphed Consul Sprague informing him of his intention to return to New York aboard the Anchor Line steamer *Caledonia*, then about to leave that port.

In a letter to Consul Sprague dated 10 March 1873 Winchester gave a more detailed explanation of his actions, saying that he had left his wife in ill-health and whilst in Gibraltar had been anxious about her, that he also believed that his business in New York was suffering because of his absence and that his time kicking his heels in Gibraltar had run up expenses he could not afford. On top of all this, he said, he had been informed by a reliable source that Judge Cochrane and Attorney General Flood were employing delaying tactics to hold onto *Mary Celeste* while they sought evidence to support their conviction of foul play. Winchester said he was told that the two men even planned to arrest him on a charge of hiring crew members to kill Captain Briggs and the officers. Winchester added, revealing how far things in Gibraltar had gone, that whilst he knew the idea was ridiculous he felt 'from what you and everybody else in Gibraltar had told me about the attorney general, I did not know but he might do it . . .'.

Winchester arrived in New York on 25 February 1873 where he found his wife's illness had worsened.

The idea that Captain Winchester would have hired others to murder the captain and crew of *Mary Celeste* sounds ludicrous, but if the annals of crime teach us anything it is that ludicrous things often happen. Captain Winchester was a well-known and highly respected businessman, but other well-known and highly respected businessmen have also resorted to murder. However, it is extremely unlikely that Winchester could have been guilty of such a crime. He was a close friend of the Briggs family, Benjamin's father, Captain Nathan Briggs having commanded the *J.H. Winchester*, which was owned by Winchester and at one time had been the carrier of the largest cotton cargo ever loaded in New Orleans. Mate Richardson was also married to Frances Spates, the niece of Captain Winchester's wife.

Mary Celeste was finally released by the court at the end of February. A new skipper had been sent out from New York, Captain George W. Blatchford from Wrentham, Massachusetts, who took possession of *Mary Celeste* and, on 6 March, signed a receipt for the possessions of Captain and Mrs Briggs, baby Sophia and the crew, which would in due course be shipped back to the United States. He was cleared to sail on 7 March and after a couple of days getting the ship readied to sail, *Mary Celeste* left Gibraltar on 10 March and reached Genoa without mishap 11 days later. It is interesting to note that two months earlier *Dei Gratia* had taken 24 days to complete the same journey. *Mary Celeste's* cargo of 1,700 barrels of alcohol, of which nine had leaked and were empty, was in excellent condition.

Mary Celeste was cleared to sail from Genoa on 17 May, but according to the *Maritime Register* she remained in port for a few days over three months and it is not clear why she remained in port for so long. She eventually sailed for Boston on 26 June, arriving on 1 September and sailing again on 13 September.

On 14 March 1873, four days after *Mary Celeste* sailed from Gibraltar, Chief Justice Cochrane delivered judgment in the salvage case. *Mary Celeste* was valued at $5,700.00 and her cargo at $36,943.00, making a total of $42,673.00. The salvers were awarded £1,700, less the costs of the analysis of the bloodstains which was deducted from that amount. It was considerably less than what they no doubt expected and rightfully should have received, and the crew of *Dei Gratia* and her owners were apparently and understandably very angry and disappointed. It was no doubt with a heavy heart that Oliver Deveau took command of *Dei Gratia* on 17 March and sailed from Genoa to Messina. She arrived there on 21 March and on her arrival a painting of the ship was made. The ship sailed soon after and after a brief stop at Gibraltar she sailed for New York, reaching her home port on 19 June.

On 19 November Consul Sprague notified the Department of State that he had dispatched the effects of Captain and Mrs Briggs to the United States and on 11 December the Collector of Customs in New York made a report that they had been received safe and sound. We don't know what happened to them all, including the crew's five chests and a canvas bag, but we know that Mrs Briggs's sewing machine and beloved melodeon reached the home of Benjamin's mother, as did the Italian sword, the stain on which had caused so much trouble.

Note and reference

1   The story about Captain Appleby is told by Charles Edey Fay in *The Story of 'Mary Celeste'*, and was related to him by Captain Appleby in 1930 and in subsequent letters from his daughter, Mrs Thomas J. Port. Mr Fay recorded that Captain Appleby died in 1931 at the age of 80.

CHAPTER 8

. . . .

Wild and fanciful tales

Such was the celebrity of the mystery of *Mary Celeste* that she inspired several weird and wonderful tales. The fiction falls into three categories: fiction that was presented as nothing more than fiction; fiction which was guesswork and speculation but advanced a plausible theory (or which the author thought was plausible) and could be fact; and fiction that offered a theory, plausible or otherwise, that was intended to be taken for fact. These tales embrace everything from an early offering from one of the giants of storytelling, through a shameless and intentional hoax to an episode of the classic radio series *The Goon Show*, and on the way it grabs Bela Lugosi, the troubled star best known for his portrayal of Dracula and also these days for his appearance in the Ed Wood classic *Plan Nine From Outer Space*.

Few people or incidents pass into the English language as a common form of description and it is testimony to the impact of the story of the disappearance of her crew that *Mary Celeste* has achieved that distinction, and it is surprising how often one hears the vessel's name invoked to describe somewhere strangely deserted. What one actually hears said, however, is not that the room or building seemed like the *Mary Celeste*, but that it was strangely deserted like the '*Marie Celeste*'. Furthermore, in the popular mind the ship was unaccountably deserted, not abandoned, and the galley table was littered with unfinished meals and mugs of lukewarm coffee, and that the aroma of fresh tobacco smoke still lingered in the Captain's cabin. The name 'Marie Celeste' and these trapping of fictional but spine-chilling detail owe themselves to a short story called 'J. Habakuk Jephson's Statement'.

The story was published in the January 1884 issue of the prestigious *Cornhill Magazine*, founded in 1860 by George Smith. It became the most important magazine in the latter half of the nineteenth century, its first editor being William Makepeace Thackeray and its contributors drawn from among the most popular writers of the day: Wilkie Collins, George Eliot, Mrs Gaskell, Thomas Hardy, Henry James, James Payn, Charles Reade, Robert Louis Stevenson, and Anthony Trollope among them. It is evident then that the publication within its pages of 'J. Habakuk Jephson's Statement' was quite an achievement for its young author who, as a practising doctor, had to publish it anonymously, something which no doubt caused many of its readers, including Frederick Solly Flood and Horatio Sprague, to imagine that it was supposed to be a genuine, auto-biographical narrative.

The narrator of the tale is Joseph Habakuk Jephson, a Harvard doctor and a consulting physician and specialist on consumption at the Samaritan Hospital of Brooklyn, who is described as 'a distinguished advocate for Abolition in the early days of the movement, and whose pamphlet, entitled 'Where is thy Brother?' exercised a strong influence on public opinion before the war.' According to the story, Jephson is one of the passengers aboard *Marie Celeste*, a fellow passenger being a half-caste named Septimius Goring. Goring, who had long hated white people and had murdered countless numbers of them as he travelled across the United States, had conceived a plan to rule a black nation which in its early stages involved hijacking *Marie Celeste* with some co-conspirators and sailing her to Africa. Those aboard the ship were duly killed but Jephson had escaped, because at some time earlier an old black woman living on the plantation he owned had given him a strange stone with a hole in the middle, which by luck turned out to be part of an idol revered by the black tribe Goring had gone to rule. Jephson was given his freedom and cast out to sea with water and food, his survival in the hands of God, and was fortunately rescued within days. He made it to Liverpool and from there back to the United States.

The story was vividly told but factually inaccurate, the errors about *Mary Celeste* many and varied: the vessel's name was given as *Marie Celeste,* her owners were given as a firm of Boston-based importers, her port of departure is given as Boston, her destination Lisbon, her sailing date was wrong, her skipper is called J.W. Tibbs, the captain's child is a boy called 'Doddy', her cargo is wrong, the skipper of *Dei Gratia* is called Dalton, and so on. Moreover, the details of J. Habakuk Jephson's career are wrong in ways that would never have been made by a man who had actually lived them. For example, the battle of Antietam (Sharpsburg), fought between 16–18 September 1862, is incorrectly placed *after* Gettysburg, the turning point of the Civil War, fought between 1–3 July 1863. Anyone who had actually served in the Civil War or who knew much about it would not have made such a mistake. Nevertheless the tale was taken seriously by some people and hotly denounced. Frederick Solly Flood loudly declared that 'J. Habakuk Jephson's Statement' was 'a fabrication from beginning to end', which of course it was, and rather melodramatically claimed that it might damage England's relations with foreign countries. US Consul Horatio J. Sprague asked *Cornhill Magazine* to investigate the origins of the fraudulent article.

'J. Habakuk Jephson's Statement' was in fact one of the first literary efforts by Arthur Conan Doyle, later to achieve enduring fame as the creator of the consulting detective Sherlock Holmes. Born on 22 May 1859, in Edinburgh to Charles and Mary Doyle, after several very unhappy years at a Jesuit boarding school in England, Doyle had entered the University of Edinburgh Medical School and met Dr Joseph Bell, the prototype for Sherlock Holmes, and had begun writing, *The Mystery of the Sasassa Valley* being his first published work. In 1880 he had signed as a ship's surgeon aboard the Greenland whaler *Hope of Peterhead*, and between February and September sailed the coasts of Labrador and Greenland. Doyle was appalled by the brutality of the seal-hunting but was fascinated by a whale hunt and enjoyed the camaraderie. The Arctic adventure affected him greatly and he would even christen his detective hero after the vessel, initially calling him Sherringford Hope. The Artic also provided the inspiration for the short story 'Captain of the Pole-Star' that in due course would be the title of a collection of short stories featuring 'J. Habakuk Jephson's Statement', which found its inspiration in Doyle's next voyage.

Returning to Liverpool, he almost immediately signed aboard the African Steam Navigation Company's 20-year-old 1,500-ton steamer *Mayumba*, a passenger ship showing wear and tear, regularly plying between Liverpool, Portugal and West Africa. It was an unhappy voyage for Doyle, who nearly died from typhoid, but a fellow passenger was the incredible Henry Highland Garnet (1815–82), US Consul to Liberia, who was probably the inspiration for both J. Habakuk Jephson and, if not for Septimius Goring, at least for Goring's ambition to found a black nation. Garnet was a thoroughly remarkable man. Born a slave, he escaped with his parents in 1824 to New Hope, Pennsylvania. In 1840 he graduated from the abolitionist Oneida Institute near Utica, New York, and as a theologian began a career in churches in New York City, Washington DC, and eventually as president of Avery College in Allegheny, Pennsylvania. He was a strident abolitionist, remembered today chiefly for his celebrated 'Address to the Slaves of the United States' during the National Convention of Coloured Citizens in Buffalo, New York, in 1843, and as the first black man to address the US House of Representatives. He was appointed minister to Liberia, where he died in Monrovia on 13 February 1882.

Garnet had something of a profound impact on Doyle, who had hitherto shared the widespread general feeling that black people were evolutionarily inferior and less civilised, at one point having written, 'My own experience is that you abhor them on first meeting them, and gradually learn to dislike them a very great deal more as you become better acquainted with them.'[1] Garnet, an intellectual who had also direct experience of the iniquities heaped upon his people, changed Doyle's views and Doyle incorporated Garnet's abolitionist views in the character of J. Habakuk Jephson. Garnet also wished to found a black nation, and Doyle invested this wish into the otherwise repulsive Goring.

Doyle was paid £30 for the story, almost the equivalent of a year's rent, was pleased that his story had been so convincing that it could stir up that level of controversy, and pleased, too, that readers who recognised that the story was a fiction thought it was written by Robert Louis Stevenson. In his *Memories and Adventures* Doyle wrote, 'What gave me great pleasure and for the first time made me realize that I was ceasing to be a hack writer and was getting into good company was when James Payn accepted my short story "Habakuk Jephson's Statement" for *Cornhill.* I had a reverence for this splendid magazine with its traditions from Thackeray and Stevenson and the thought that I had won my way into it pleased me even more than the cheque for £30, which came duly to hand.' The gloss was nevertheless taken off his success by the story being published anonymously. 'I won my way into the best journals, *Cornhill, Temple Bar*, and so on; but what is the use of that when the contributions to those journals must be anonymous? It is a system which tells very hardly against young authors.' It was nevertheless a system which had its advantages, 'How well I can see a dear old friend running after me in the street, waving a London evening 'paper in his hand. "Have you seen what they say about your *Cornhill* story?" he shouted. "No, no. What is it?" "Here it is! Here it is!" Eagerly he turned over the column, while I, trembling with excitement, but determined to bear my honours meekly, peeped over his shoulder. "The *Cornhill* this month," said the critic, "has a story in it which would have made Thackeray turn in his grave." '[2]

Consul Sprague was not pleased with the story, a copy of which he sent to the Department of State in Washington, with an accompanying letter:

UNITED STATES CONSULATE
HONORABLE JOHN DAVIS,   *Gibraltar, January 12, 1884*
Assistant Secretary of State, Washington.
SIR:
My attention has been called to an article which appears in the Cornhill *Magazine for this month, entitled 'J. Habakuk Jephson's Statement' in which is referred the American brigantine* Mary Celeste *of New York, which was met at sea on the 4th December 1872 in latitude 38°20' longitude 17°15' W. by the British brigantine* Dei Gratia, *and brought into this port as a derelict, the full particulars of which were at the time duly transmitted to the Department.*

It having ever since remained a mystery, regarding the fate of the master and crew of the Mary Celeste, *or even the cause that induced or forced them to abandon their vessel which, with her cargo, were found when met by the* Dei Gratia *to be in perfect order, I ask to myself, what motives can have prompted the writer of the article in question to refer to this mysterious affair, after the lapse of eleven years; especially as the statement given, is not only replete with inaccuracies as regards the date, voyage and destination of the vessel, names of the parties constituting her crew, and the fact of her having no passengers on board beyond the master's wife and child, but seems to me to be replete with romance of a very unlikely or exaggerated nature.*

As the Department cannot fail to feel a certain interest to ascertain whether there be the least suspicion of truth in any portion of what is stated in the article referred to in the Cornhill *Magazine, I have taken the liberty to call its attention to it, especially as it may have the opportunity of examining the author of this extraordinary composition.*

With reference to the crew of the Mary Celeste, *I beg to enclose herewith a list of their names, according to her clearance for Genoa at the New York Custom house; also copy of a communication I received in 1873 from Prussia, referring to two of the crew, represented as being brothers, and evidently of German extraction.*

I am, Sir,   Your obedient Servant,

[Signed] Horatio J. Sprague, U. S. Consul.

Enclosures:

1.   *List of crew of the Mary Celeste.*

2.   *Copy of a letter from T. A. Nickelsen.*

Consul Sprague received a brief reply from the Department of State:

DEPARTMENT OF STATE

Washington, April 2, 1884

HORATIO J. SPRAGUE ESQ.

Consul of the United States, Gibraltar

SIR:

I have to acknowledge the receipt of your despatch numbered 451 of the 12th of January last, relating to the statement of J. Habakuk Jephon [sic] which appears in the Cornhill Magazine *for January 1884 in regard to the brigantine* Mary Celeste *of New York, which vessel was met at sea by the British brigantine* Dei Gratia *and brought into the port of Gibraltar on the 4th. of December 1872, as a derelict.*

The article to which you refer has been read with attention and much interest. The mystery which surrounds the fate of the master and crew and the passengers, or even the cause that induced or forced them to abandon their vessel, is in no wise satisfactorily explained in that statement, and it is conceived that, from the information we now possess, no solution of the mystery has yet been presented.

Under the circumstances, the Department has not deemed it essential to pursue any particular enquiries into the antecedents of the writer of the article in question, leaving the matter to a further development of the facts which time alone may or will develop.

Agreeing with the interest you have expressed in the matter, the Department will be gratified to receive any further information upon the

subject that may reach you in the future.
I am, Sir, Your obedient servant,
[Signed] John Davis, Assistant Secretary.

'J. Habakuk Jephson's Statement' was a tale that turned the mystery of *Mary Celeste* into a *cause célèbre* and ensured that it would be forever remembered in the pages of maritime history. Doyle did not intend it to be taken seriously, however, but others were not so noble and writing solutions to the *Mary Celeste*, particularly true histories by survivors, became something of a cottage industry, popular when the full facts of the case were not as easily obtainable as they are today.

The story of Abel Fosdyk

In 1913 the hugely successful *Strand Magazine*, today largely remembered for its publication of Conan Doyle's Sherlock Holmes stories, invited its contributors and readers alike to suggest solutions to the mystery of *Mary Celeste*. Among the reader responses was an account that purported to be true, came from a seemingly impeccable source and gave a first-hand solution to the enigma. The story came from Mr A. Howard Linford, MA, of Magdalen, Oxford, headmaster of Peterborough Lodge, Hampstead's largest preparatory school. According to a letter to the editor of the *Strand*:

> *Sir – A friend has brought to my notice your article on the Marie*
> *Celeste. When I read it the name struck a familiar chord, but it was some*
> *days before I could remember under what circumstances I had heard it.*
> *At last, however, I recalled an old servant, Abel Fosdyk, committing to*
> *my charge, on his deathbed, a quantity of papers contained in three*
> *boxes; amongst these he told me would be found the account of (the)*
> *Mary Celeste. I suppose he said 'the', but I had at the time no notion of*
> *what Mary Celeste meant, and imagined it was a woman. I paid but little*
> *heed, and merely sent the boxes away to a safe keeping, not anticipating*
> *that they would ever be opened again. Before commenting on the matter*
> *I would like to emphasize the fact that I do not vouch for the truth of*
> *anything narrated. No word on the subject was ever mentioned by the*
> *writer to me. But the fact that for thirty years he kept not only a diary but*
> *also a set of shrewd observations on all that passed, and wrote much and*

well without our knowing anything of what he was doing, shows him to
have been a man of exceptional reticence and self-control.

As for the document, I would rather let it speak for itself; but at the
same time I must confess that I have been greatly impressed by the
following facts: A brig called Marie Celeste, sailing under a Captain
Griggs. By your courtesy I have now seen the official report, and find in
every instance the papers in my possession are correct. Further, the
official papers mention a peculiar damage to the bows and two square
cuts on the outside. This, I think, has never till now been made public,
yet there again the papers I send you enter most minutely into this
alteration of the bows. Finally I find, on enquiry, that the autumn of 1872
was famous for its extraordinary storms in the Atlantic, so much so that
a leading article in the Times likens it to the period of storms so well
known to have prevailed at Cromwell's death. One can easily imagine
a captain, working day and night in such conditions, going gradually out
of his mind.

Of course, minute errors will always creep in when relating facts a
long time after their occurrence. It is evident to me these facts were
written down nearly twenty years after they happened, and no one knows
better than myself how easily dates may be forgotten or the sequence of
events confused.

I now leave the M.S. in your hands.[3]

The story, then, purported to be a true account disclosed in a
manuscript left among the effects of Abel Fosdyk. As support there
was a a photograph of a little girl, and some drawings made by Linford's
son, a schoolboy at Harrow. Linford even supplied Abel Fosdyk's manuscript, a portion of which was reprinted in the *Strand*, and it looked like
the magazine had a scoop!

Abel Fosdyk said that he had to leave America – his reasons were
undisclosed – and had managed to get secret passage aboard the *Celeste*
because he was an old and close friend of her skipper, Captain Griggs. For
about a month the ship encountered ferocious and terrifying storms,
and the daily strain began to tell on the captain, who became increasingly
irritable and eccentric in his behaviour.

During the voyage Captain Griggs had come upon his daughter, who
was seven or eight years old but called 'Baby', playing precariously on

the bowsprit. He chastised her, but knowing that children will do what they are told not to do, he ordered the ship's carpenter to make a safe platform from an old table for her to play there. The carpenter did so, cutting deep grooves either side of the bow – thus explaining the marks that had so intrigued Frederick Solly Flood.

As the days passed the captain's behaviour became increasing erratic and he began to challenge the first mate about an incident that had happened some time earlier when a man had fallen overboard and the mate had failed to jump into the water after him. The captain stated that the mate was a coward, the mate in turn replied that he was so weighed down with clothing that had he gone into the water he would surely have drowned. At this the Captain became insanely irate, changed his clothing and dived into the water with two of his men to prove that it was possible to swim when dressed. Everyone aboard crowded onto the platform to watch the spectacle, but under their combined weight the platform collapsed and everyone plummeted into the sea – and to the sharks! Fosdyk escaped this dietary end because he actually fell onto the platform and managed to cling on, drifting away from *Celeste* and eventually washing up on the African coast, from where he managed to get passage to Marseilles, and from there to England, where he arrived in the summer of 1874.

The story captured the imagination of readers around the world, and it neatly answered a lot of the points that had so disturbed Solly Flood and others, but alas it was a fabrication and once again the factual mistakes should have been a dead giveaway. Captain Briggs was called Griggs, Morehouse was named as Boyce, Albert Richardson was called Harry. Fosdyk himself replaced the real steward Edward W. Head, and the crew had expanded to thirteen and included someone called Williamson and a black youth with the now totally non-pc nickname 'Darky'. The account was also shot through with anachronisms instantly recognised by mariners, such as 'we heaved to' instead of the more likely nautical 'hove to'. A correspondent to the New York *Nautical Gazette* remarked that 'the fellow who wrote that doesn't know a poopdeck from a jib downhaul.'

What has never been answered is why Mr A. Howard Linford MA, headmaster of Peterborough Lodge, Hampstead, and a man apparently widely respected, should have peddled a spurious account of the *Mary Celeste* as if it was factual.

The story of Captain Lucy

*GREAT SEA MYSTERY **CLEARED UP**.*
What happened to the Mary Celeste.
Derelict Gold: Crew's Escape with Stolen £3,500

So proclaimed the *Daily Express* on 24 September 1924, headlining its scoop 'discovery' of 70-year-old Captain R. Lucy, RNR, whose name the newspaper claimed was well known all over the Mediterranean – for what we're not told, but presumably for his experience and utter probity – and who had been distinguished for his service in the Dardanelles during the First World War and had been the recipient of the Croix de Guerre and the Italian Cross of Merit.

According to Captain Lucy, 42 years earlier when serving as mate aboard the *Island Princess* plying business in the South Seas, he had met a man named Triggs in the Bay View Hotel, Melbourne, who was in need of a job. Lucy managed to get him aboard his own ship as bos'n and during the subsequent voyage Triggs, a name which Lucy came to believe was assumed, told him in strict secrecy that he had been bos'n of *Mary Celeste*. As the *Island Princess* island-hopped in those romantic and dangerous waters, the story of the disappearance of the crew was revealed.

When *Mary Celeste* was a day or so away from her destination of Genoa she came across a derelict steamer, the name of which was not discernible on her stern or bows because of rust. She was boarded and in the purser's cabin they found a large iron safe which they forced open and found inside the veritable fortune of £3,500 in silver and gold. Captain Briggs decided to keep the money, taking £1,200 for himself and giving £600 to the mate and £400 to Bos'n Triggs, and dividing the rest between the men. They then scuttled the steamer.

Back aboard *Mary Celeste* the men began to worry about what they had done and decided to scuttle their own ship, but the sea was calm and the weather was good and the vessel had recently been seen by men aboard a passing ship. In the absence of any reason why *Mary Celeste* should founder and sink, the crew decided that their best bet was simply to abandon *Mary Celeste*, get to land and split up, each man taking his ill-gotten gains to a personal destination. Taking the treasure and some provisions, the men piled into a boat, reached land and went their separate ways.

Despite the sheer improbability of the story and literary devices designed to deter investigation and verification – such as Triggs not being the man's real name, the name of the steamer being unidentifiable because of rust, and the men abandoning ship because they had stolen money that nobody knew or would have suspected they had – Captain Lucy's story was widely accepted as the true solution to the mystery, accepted hook, line and sinker even by the *Evening Standard* newspaper.

The story of John Pemberton

The most outrageous theory about the fate of the crew of *Mary Celeste* was the now almost forgotten but at one time scandalous fiction weaved and presented as fact by Laurence J. Keating. Whereas Arthur Conan Doyle had written a fiction, Mr A. Howard Linford perhaps had never meant to do more than give verisimilitude to his fiction that would get it noticed and win the 'competition', and Captain Lucy may have innocently recited some shipboard yarn in the genuine belief that it was true, the story of John Pemberton was an elaborate hoax that culminated in one of the longest and most detailed books ever written about *Mary Celeste*, replete with full-colour fold-out charts and maps. The story of John Pemberton is today an almost forgotten literary hoax that has never been fully documented, little being known about Keating or his intentions. In its day it was almost unbelievably successful and the outrage many people felt, particularly the relatives of those who had been aboard *Mary Celeste*, has influenced almost every account, authors highlighting the many errors in what has long been unnecessary detail.

The hoax began in the July 1926 issue of *Chambers Journal* which contained an article entitled 'The Truth about the *Marie Celeste*. A Survivor Story'. It was written by someone calling himself Lee Kaye – this was not the author's real name, but his real initials, L.K. – and it purported to be an account of what happened aboard *Mary Celeste* given to the author by a survivor named John Pemberton, who had been the cook aboard the vessel. Furthermore, unlike previous survivors who were dead and could not be questioned, John Pemberton was still very much alive, living in Liverpool and ready to receive visitors (at least in theory). Lee Kaye also claimed to have spoken to another survivor, the bos'n and ship's carpenter aboard *Mary Celeste*, a man named Jack Dossell, also known as 'Chippy' Russell.

The narrative was distinguished by a wealth of detail and colour that made the story enticingly believable. For example, it was claimed that 'Chippy' Russell, who had died near Shrewsbury in 1917, had peddled an ointment around the Shropshire towns for several years and would have been widely remembered because handling his concoction had turned his hands green.

There were no doubt many people in Shropshire who did indeed remember the green-handed 'Chippy' peddling his wares, even though he was the complete figment of an inventive writer's imagination.

According to the article in *Chambers Journal*, John Pemberton had served aboard the *Marie Celeste* since 1870 and in September 1872 had been with the vessel in New York where she was being loaded with a cargo of railway timber and a very large shipment of barrelled whale oil that was so big it was being split between *Marie Celeste* and *Dei Gratia*. This brought Captain Briggs and Captain Morehouse into regular contact with one another, and using a plot idea that would be adapted by the author of the Hammer movie *The Mystery of Mary Celeste*, Captain Morehouse came to the assistance of Captain Briggs by lending him three of his crew when Captain Briggs encountered trouble putting a crew together. According to Lee Kay, *Dei Gratia* left port on 2 October and sailed to deliver a consignment of wines to Queenstown, the plan being that she would sail from there and meet up with *Marie Celeste* at Santa Maria in the Azores, where Briggs planned to pick up some crew and return the men he had borrowed to *Dei Gratia*.

Trouble began almost as soon as Mrs Briggs came aboard and, as is so often the case in reality, it began with small seeds. Mrs Briggs wanted her piano put where Mate Hullock wanted to place his sea chest, and from this minor but niggling acorn of dispute an oak tree of hatred would grow.

Marie Celeste – as Pemberton called the ship, perhaps understandably given the way that Conan Doyle's fictional invention dominated the popular memory of the mystery – sailed on 7 October and by the end of the month she had encountered rough weather. According to Pemberton (and contrary to the evidence of John Austin's survey in Gibraltar) on 24 November a sudden gust of wind took the vessel over on her starboard beam. The piano had been lashed in place, but broke free in the violence of the storm and crushed Mrs Briggs against the bulkhead, causing injuries so severe that she died very soon afterwards. Captain Briggs became almost insane with grief and blamed Mate Hullock, who was a thoroughly unpleasant bully and had aroused very little liking among the men on board. Hullock in turn blamed the man at the wheel and ordered him thrown overboard. The crew refused to do it, and threw the piano overboard instead, but that night Captain Briggs disappeared and Hullock suggested that he had 'gone after the piano'.

The days passed and discipline virtually collapsed as the men took to drinking and brawling. Mate Hullock had a fight with a crewman who had been shanghaied in New York and who tumbled over the side. Neither Hullock nor any other crew member tried to save him and he drowned.

A short time later *Marie Celeste* reached Santa Maria and the natives sailed out from the shore in bumboats laden with fresh fruit, assorted trinkets and other items for sale. The arrival of the bumboats gave those aboard *Marie Celeste* an opportunity to quit the ship and it was a chance Mate Hullock and two others quickly grasped, going ashore and disappearing. The only men left aboard were the three men put aboard *Marie Celeste* from *Dei Gratia* and the narrator of the tale John Pemberton.

The four men continued the journey to Gibraltar and in due course they were overhauled by *Dei Gratia*. Morehouse's men described what had gone on aboard the ship since leaving New York and Morehouse realised that he could claim *Marie Celeste* as salvage, knowing that he could trust his own men, who were never listed as having been aboard, and that Hullock and the others were unlikely to ever reveal themselves. Pemberton had little choice but to go along with the plan and keep silent. In due course the two ships reached Gibraltar and a couple of weeks later were awarded a handsome salvage reward. Pemberton had kept himself well away from anyone's gaze and was assumed to have vanished along with the rest of the crew.

Lee Kaye was an excellent storyteller and he spiced his tale with assorted claims that seemed to give his fantasy an air of persuasive and disarming honesty. He claimed, for example, that *Marie Celeste* was sold to a British business concern named Bellamy & Company and for many years carried china-clay from Plymouth to Philadelphia. Said Kaye, many old Plymouth longshoremen would remember *Marie Celeste* at her customary berth in Millbay Dock. And no doubt some did.

The story was full of errors, of course. The ship was called *Mary Celeste* not *Marie Celeste* and the real crew bore no resemblance to Mate Hullock and company. The *Mary Celeste*'s cargo was alcohol, not whale oil or railway timbers, there is no real indication that Captains Briggs and Morehouse knew each other, the sailing dates were wrong, as were other dates given in the narrative, and the piano was in reality a melodeon. Sophia Matilda Briggs isn't mentioned, the story depicts the salvage claim going through without a hitch in Gibraltar and a substantial reward given, neither – to the regret of the *Dei Gratia*'s crew – being the case, while the sale to Bellamy & Company was a complete invention.

Other parts of the story have struck commentators as absurd, but it's easy to pick out improbabilities when one knows the story is a fiction, but not always so easy for those at the time reading what purported to be a true story. For example, some commentators have pointed out that Mrs Briggs would hardly have been playing the piano during a severe storm, but readers could always have supposed that she was singing hymns and praying for safe passage through the tempest. It is easy to see why the *New York Herald Tribune* of 26 July 1926 observed of John Pemberton's story that 'there are none to dispute the truth of his story'.

Two years later, in 1929, there appeared a highly detailed book written by Laurence J. Keating and called with successfully disarming honesty *The Great Mary Celeste Hoax*.[4] It corrected some of the errors in the magazine version, among them, as the title shows, the ship's name – albeit claiming that her intended name was *Mary Sellars* – but it was still error-filled and it even robbed Joshua Dewis of the distinction of having built the vessel, Keating bestowing this distinction on someone named Henry M. Colfax. It was nevertheless an impressive book, chunky, with a full-colour frontispiece of what was supposed to be *Mary Celeste*, plans of the deck and interior and replete with full-colour fold-out charts and maps.

John Pemberton was the man of the hour and many newspapers were very keen to meet and interview him, but he proved elusive until he was tracked down by a 'Special Correspondent' of the *Evening Standard*. On 6 May 1929 the newspaper carried an interview under the headline:

A TALE THAT JOSEPH CONRAD MIGHT HAVE WRITTEN.

There was even a photograph of the old man, but the whole story was a fabrication and the photograph was of Laurence J. Keating's own father.

The Great Mary Celeste Hoax outraged a lot of people, not the least of them being Benjamin Briggs's son, Arthur Briggs, and his cousin, Dr Oliver Cobb, both of whom wrote to the newspapers, notably the *Boston Post* (8 August 1926), and Mrs Priscilla Richardson Shelton, the sister of Mate Albert Richardson, who gave an interview to the *New York Herald Tribune* (29 July 1929). It is not known whether the hoax was innocent in intent, just a bit of fun, or whether it was a serious attempt to deceive, to foist a fiction on a gullible public as if it was fact, but it highlights a problem that has hit the headlines quite a few times over the years, namely the use – or rather the misuse – of real people in fiction and the distress this causes the descendants.

'Faction', as the mixture of fact and fiction is known, frequently causes problems, especially as far as Hollywood is concerned, where historical fact has rarely been allowed to interfere with a good story. The responses of Arthur Briggs and the other relatives of *Mary Celeste*'s crew would have been understood by the descendants of First Officer William McMaster Murdoch, Lieutenant RNR, who was portrayed in the movie *Titanic* as being responsible for the collision, taking a bribe to let a man into a lifeboat, and shooting a passenger. In the movie he finally shoots himself. The reality appears to be that Murdoch acted honourably and bravely and was trying to release a collapsible boat when swept away to his death by the sea. His heroism was witnessed by several people, among them Charles Lightoller and Harold Bride, fellow seamen, and a passenger, Archibald Gracie.

In 1957 the writer Macdonald Hastings, then planning a book about *Mary Celeste* which eventually was published in 1972, wrote an open letter to the *Liverpool Daily Post* for information about Laurence J. Keating. He received only one reply, from a Captain T.E. Elwell in the Isle of Man. In that letter, dated 4 October 1957, Captain Elwell described Keating as 'the worst type of Liverpool Irishman'. Elwell wrote:

> *I knew Laurence Keating well. He was, or is, – I have no knowledge of his death – a liar, a confirmed plagiarist, and quarrelsome withal. Early in 1923, a friend of mine, named Robert Flaherty, who knew him brought*

him to see me. At that time I was writing an article on the Mary Celeste *which appeared in* Chambers' Journal *on July 2, 1923. Keating had never heard of the mystery, and said the whole thing was a fairy tale. When my article appeared, he was eaten up with jealousy, and asked if I was going any further with it. I said 'No', I have written all I mean to write on the subject.*

I saw no more of Keating – didn't want to – but my friend, who lived near Keating, told me that he was engaged on some spoof about the mystery, and that my friend had been asked by Keating for ideas as to how to treat the thing. My friend told him that if he was determined on spoof, something could be done about a salvage wrangle between the skippers of the Mary Celeste *and the* Dei Gratia.

Laurence J. Keating died on 16 March 1944 after a lengthy illness, having lived with his sister, Margaret McDonald, for forty years or so.

Macdonald Hastings had the luck to read a number of letters written by Laurence J. Keating to an acquaintance named F.J. Lambert, 'A psychiatrist might be interested in the inventions, which the fellow seems to have believed out of his own imagination,' Hastings wrote. Keating 'was one of those strange men who believed what he wanted to believe. The Irishry in him may have guided him as it guided Mr Solly Flood.'

Many other individuals have come forward claiming to be survivors or to have met survivors or to otherwise possess private information, and assorted imaginative tales emerged from the waterfront bars to gain acceptance and belief. Captain A.E. Dingle, who wrote many popular sea stories during the 1930s and 40s, said a compatriot aboard the barque *Lady Elsie* at the turn of the century claimed to be a cousin of a man who had been aboard *Mary Celeste* on that fateful voyage in 1872. The man's name was Bundy, which, of course, was not the name of anyone aboard that vessel at that time.

In 1937 Arthur Cocker, the skipper of a barge sailing between Sheffield and Hull, claimed that as a cabin boy aboard a grain trader *Kentishman* his ship had come across the deserted *Mary Celeste* and boarded her. An axe was deeply embedded in the mainmast, he said, and he claimed that he possessed documents and notebooks taken from the captain's cabin that cast the mystery in a new light, the nature of which he did not state.

Theorists were plentiful too. The writer Arthur Morrison (1863–1945), best known for his tale of East End poverty *Child of the Jago* and the early detective stories featuring Martin Hewitt, suggested that those aboard *Mary Celeste* had been the victims of a religious fanatic. This theme was picked up by J.G. Lockhart in his book *Mysteries of the Sea* in 1925, who was also influenced by the story of the brig *Mary Russell*, whose skipper, William Stewart, went berserk and killed seven people during a voyage from Barbados for Cork in 1828 after a dream in which God appeared to him. The presence of the handsome rosewood melodeon and books of largely religious music aboard *Mary Celeste* suggested a religious disposition and Lockhart supposed that Captain Briggs had been overcome by madness, slaughtered all those on board and later killed himself in a moment of lucidity when the full horror of what he had done was borne in on him. But, as Mr Lockhart explained in a subsequent volume:

> *In* Mysteries of the Sea *I put forward a solution which a number of people were kind enough to approve, and which others, perfectly reasonably, regarded as too farfetched to be permissible. My solution was suggested to me by the horrible and authentic story of the* Mary Russell, *a brig sailing from Barbados to Cork in 1828, whose Captain suddenly went off his head and, with the assistance of two apprentices, first bound and then butchered the greater part of his crew, only two men, both badly injured, managing to escape from him and to hide in the hold. I suggested that the presence of the harmonium and of religious books and music in the cabin of the* Mary Celeste *might possibly be the clue to a similar tragedy; that the Captain, a man of excellent character, might have developed religious mania, and, with the strength and cunning of the homicidal lunatic, have attacked, overpowered, and murdered his wife and child and crew, taking them one by one and unawares; and that finally, the mad Captain of an empty ship, he may have recovered his senses, as homicidal maniacs generally do, and, horrified by his crimes, have thrown himself overboard.*
>
> *All this was merely conjecture, of which little more could be said than that, although there was not a jot of positive evidence in its support, it roughly accounted for most of the facts as I have given them.*
>
> *Since the appearance of* Mysteries of the Sea, *however, I have accumulated much fresh material, and have had access to sources of*

information of the existence of which I was ignorant at the time of writing. In particular, I am indebted to Dr Oliver Cobb; to Mr Sprague, the American Vice-Consul at Gibraltar; and to one or two other gentlemen, mostly resident in the United States, for particulars the study of which compels me to admit that my 'solution' in Mysteries of the Sea *is as valueless as these other 'solutions' I have criticized.*[5]

If the mystery of *Mary Celeste* was not to be explained by a mad and fanatical skipper, then it could be explained by a mutinous crew, a suggestion Lowell Thomas attributes in his book *The Sea Devil's Fo'c's'le* to Felix, Graf von Luckner, who appears as ill-informed about the facts as most early theorists, yet as uncritically certain of the rightness of their solution.

If not the captain and crew of *Mary Celeste*, how about the crew of *Dei Gratia*? Harold T. Wilkins, in the July 1932 issue of *Quarterly Review*, also embraced the foul play theory, but did so on the faulty premise that *Dei Gratia* had sailed ten days before *Mary Celeste* and must have waited in mid-ocean for *Celeste* to turn up. Wilkins then proposed that all or most of *Celeste*'s crew had been lured aboard *Dei Gratia* and slaughtered (nobody having examined *Dei Gratia*). The theory collapses, of course, when it is appreciated that *Dei Gratia* sailed eight days *after Mary Celeste* and was the heavier and slower of the two vessels, and that had *Mary Celeste* not been abandoned she would have reached Gibraltar long before *Dei Gratia*. Wilkins was critical of the Vice Admiralty Court proceedings and of the 'scientific' evidence such as the analysis of the sword, and he thought that Captain Morehouse and Oliver Deveau would have had a tough time had they faced a murder trial. The only bolster to his theory was a letter he said he'd received from Mrs Priscilla Shelton, the sister of *Celeste*'s mate, Albert Richardson, but it isn't clear how it supported him.

If not murder by the captain or the crew of either ship, how about death coming to those aboard *Mary Celeste* by something else? J.L. Hornibrook in *Chambers Journal* in 1904 suggested that all aboard *Mary Celeste* were snatched from the vessel by a giant octopus or squid! He imagined that the helmsman was snatched by a tentacle and that his screams brought everyone else on deck, each being snatched in their turn and dragged below the waves. Absurd as the theory sounds, it is surprisingly within the realms of possibility.

For years sailors have told tales of monsters of the deep including the huge, many-tentacled giant squid, dubbed the kraken by the Greeks, which is said to have eyes the size of footballs, a beak which can tear through bone and wood, and tentacles that could reach as high as a ship's mainmast and sink the biggest ships. Erik Ludvigsen Pontoppidan, the Bishop of Bergen, in his *The Natural History of Norway* (1752) wrote of Norwegian sailors' tales of a squid the size of an island and said that such tales had circulated since the twelfth century. He described the kraken as one and a half miles across and that this included '. . . the creature's arms, and, it is said, if they were to lay hold of the largest man-of-war, they would pull it down to the bottom.'

There is a well-known picture by Pierre Denys de Montfort published in his 1802 *Historie Naturalle Générale et Particulière des Mollusques* of a giant cephalopod embracing a ship and Herman Melville immortalised the mysterious creature when he wrote about a duel-to-the-death between a squid and a sperm whale in his 1851 classic *Moby Dick*. A giant squid also famously appears in Jules Verne's *20,000 Leagues Under the Sea*.

In 1875 members of the crew of the barque *Pauline* reported seeing a sperm whale with a sea-serpent wrapped around its mid-section dragging the whale beneath the surface of the sea. The sea-serpent or snake, as it appears to have been described, was probably the tentacle of a giant squid, scientifically known as *Architeutis dux*, an elusive creature of the deep that prefers the depths of the sea and is rarely seen alive near the surface. In fact sightings of the creature, the largest invertebrate on the planet, either dead or alive, are rare and probably don't number above two hundred and fifty. The only specimens are dead animals either washed ashore or found inside whales. One of the largest washed ashore was a 50 ft, 550 lb (250 kg) specimen found on a beach in Hobart, Tasmania, in July 2003, and the largest on record measured about 60 ft (18 metres), including the length of its tentacles. To put this into perspective, it would be just over half the length of *Mary Celeste*. This is considerably smaller than the no doubt exaggerated mile and a half reported by Pontoppidan, but there could be bigger ones!

Giant squid are known to have mistaken ships for sperm whales and to have attacked them. In the 1930s a Norwegian tanker *Brunswick* was attacked several times by a giant squid which failed to grip the steel surface of the hull and was quickly torn to pieces by the ship's propellers. In 2003 news services reported the claim by veteran French yachtsman Olivier De Kersauson who was taking part in the round-the-world Jules Verne Trophy that a giant squid had clamped on to the hull of his boat when he was in waters off the Portuguese island of Madeira. It was comparatively small, only 26ft long or thereabouts.

Old mariners' tales claim that the tentacles of a giant squid have swept a crewmember or two from the deck of a ship, and it is perfectly possible that tentacles with their plate-sized suction cups could have done so. It isn't very likely that this could account for the loss of everyone aboard *Mary Celeste* – and it certainly wouldn't account for the loss of the ship's papers and navigation instruments, the lifted rail and the missing yawl.

One thing about a good mystery is that one can always return to it. Having advanced the giant octopus theory in 1904, Mr Hornibrook returned to the theme of the disappearance of the crew from *Mary Celeste* in March 1933 with an article in *Chambers Journal* in which he suggested that *Mary Celeste* had been attacked and boarded by Riff pirates who operated off the Moroccan coast and according to Mr Hornibrook's source, Captain J.L. Vivian Millet, were still active in the early 1870s. Again the theory could be true; pirates were no doubt active then as they are still active today – on 5 January 2004 heavily armed pirates seized the tanker *Cherry 201* and her cargo of 1,000 tonnes of palm oil in the Malacca Strait and held the crew to ransom, shooting dead four crew members when the ship's owner failed to pay the demanded 400 million Rupiah (about US$50,000) for their release. A short time later ten pirates armed with machine guns opened fire from a wooden fishing boat on a tugboat towing a barge in the northern Malacca Straits. Whether or not Riff pirates were active in the 1870s remains to be seen. Riff pirates were Moroccan fishermen in rowing boats operating out of tiny coves on the western side of the harsh Guelaya peninsula, which juts out into the Mediterranean at the far western end of Morocco, who in the mid-nineteenth century attacked European shipping passing through the Strait of Gibraltar and ransomed the cargos and crew. The British merchant ship *Violet* was captured by Guelayi pirates in December 1851, four of the six men aboard being ransomed. The pirates were a major political and diplomatic issue for about 25 years until they were crushed by Muhammad bin Abu, the governor of the region, backed by the Moroccan government and European powers.

The award for the most contrived theory probably goes to the ingenious solution advanced by the Canadian author of maritime matters, Frederick W. Wallace, in his influential account of the Atlantic Canadian sailing ships *In the Wake of the Wind-Ships* (London: Hodder & Stoughton, 1927). He suggested that *Mary Celeste* had become becalmed near a collier or with a vessel loaded with explosives, a fire or some other cause having led the crew of the other vessel to abandon ship. The vessel then drifted ever closer to *Mary Celeste*, forcing her crew to abandon ship too.

Notes and references

1 Quoted in Martin Booth, *The Doctor, the Detective and Author Conan Doyle*, London: Hodder & Stoughton, 1997, p. 75.

2 Author Conan Doyle, *Memories and Adventures*, London: John Murray, 1924.

3 Mr Macdonald Hastings, who later edited the *Strand*, thought that probably this was not Mr Linford's original letter to the editor, but one contrived when it had been decided to publish the story.

4 Laurence J. Keating, *The Great Mary Celeste Hoax, a Famous Sea Mystery Exposed*, London: Heath Cranton, 1929.

5 John Gilbert Lockhart, *The 'Mary Celeste' and Other Strange Tales of the Sea*, London: Rupert Hart-Davis, 1952.

CHAPTER 9

From Hammer to Goon to postage stamp

Mary Celeste has proved an inspiration for very few plays and films, although the few there have been have featured in some of the most historic programmes in their respective media, particularly radio, where the mystery has featured in one of the earliest radio dramas, one of the most famous radio series in the United States, and as an episode of the famous Goon Show. All this, as well as being the subject of the second movie to come from the cult Hammer Studios, later synonymous with horror movies, particularly its coupling of Peter Cushing and Christopher Lee.

Lawrence du Garde Peach (1890–1972), who was awarded an OBE in 1972, seems to be largely forgotten today, but this sometime university lecturer was a distinguished playwright in his day and wrote over four hundred plays, many broadcast by the BBC, and several movie scenarios, the most famous of which is probably *The Tunnel* (1936), a science fiction drama about building a tunnel under the Atlantic to link Britain and the United States. One of his earliest radio plays was about *Mary Celeste*.

As with the first of almost anything, there is doubt and dispute about the first radio dramatic presentation in Britain. According to an article in *Modern Wireless* ('Putting Over Radio Drama', March 1931) by the writer and broadcaster Val Gielgud, the first radio drama was an excerpt from a Shakespeare play in 1923. Writing of this event, Gielgud said: 'How many of us thought when the old British Broadcasting Company broadcast the quarrel scene from "Julius Caesar" some eight years ago that from that small beginning would evolve an entirely new art – radio drama?' This single scene from Shakespeare's *Julius Caesar* was broadcast on 16 February 1923 and starred Shayle Gardner and Hubert Carter.

There seems little doubt about the first true radio drama, a play not just specifically written for the radio but a play which understood and utilised the medium. It was *Ingredient X* by L. du Garde Peach and broadcast on 1 August 1929. The techniques of radio drama, wholly unremarkable today, were highly original back in the 1920s and required thought processes and dramatic skills that many traditional playwrights used to the stage were unable to grasp or master. *Ingredient X* is therefore testimony to L. Du Garde Peach's skill and ability, and it made full use of the new medium's ability to employ short scenes, quick changes of location, terse dialogue, and the sort of dramatic realism largely impossible in a stage play. The action in *Ingredient X* switched between a ship sinking in a storm, explorers in a jungle and a shareholders meeting in a London Board Room.

Among these very early plays was L. Du Garde Peach's *The Mystery of the Mary Celeste*. Many of the real people aboard the ship were featured in the drama, among them Benjamin and Sarah Briggs, Mate Andrew Gilling, Steward William Head, and crew members Harbens, Lorensen, Gottlieb and Volkirk. Captain Morehouse and Oliver Deveau from the *Dei Gratia* also appear. However, the story very quickly parts company with reality when Captain Briggs is portrayed as what L. Du Garde Peach described as 'a religious fanatic of the New England type'. It is certainly remarkable how frequently Briggs's religion, neither uncommon at the time nor overstated in such memories of the man as we possess, is perverted into fanaticism!

A lot of the play concerns interaction between the rough and uncouth Mate Gilling and the haughty and indignant Mrs Briggs, and there is a nice touch of humour when Captain Briggs's religious fanaticism turns to insanity and Mate Gilling locks him in his cabin. Mrs Briggs is outraged by this act of mutinous behaviour and accuses Gilling of misjudging her husband, claiming that no doubt all religious people seemed mad to him. 'No, ma'am,' replied Gilling, 'Not all of 'em. Some I grant you. But when it comes to a man threatening to smash the steering gear, throw the sails over the side, and trust in the Lord to bring the ship seven hundred miles to port – I reckon that's a symptom.'

Madness also featured in the 1936 movie *The Mystery of the Mary Celeste*, the second movie from the newly-founded Hammer Films and a film distinguished as being Hammer's first brush with the horror genre for which the studio would in future years become synonymous.

Hammer was created by William Hinds and Enrique Carreras. Hinds was a London-based entrepreneur who established a chain of bicycle shops, hairdressers and jewellers, and also managed a theatrical booking agency. He had briefly 'trod the boards' using the name Will Hammer in a variety comedy duo called Hammer and Smith. The act had gone nowhere very quickly but Hinds was able to invest in theatres and by the 1930s owned four, all in seaside locations. Deciding to move into the movie business, in November 1934 he formed a film company called Hammer Productions and took three offices in Imperial House on Regent Street in London. The following year he went into partnership with Enrique Carreras.

Carreras was born in Spain in 1880 and came to England at the turn of the century. In 1912, he bought with his brother Alphonse a theatre in Hammersmith, London, that would eventually become the first of the Blue Hall chain of variety halls. In 1923 they bought their first cinema, the Harrow Coliseum, and as his chain of movie houses began to grow, Enrique Carreras formed his own distribution company, Exclusive Films. Hinds went into partnership with Carreras at Exclusive and while Hinds gave himself over to film distribution, the business at Hammer was conducted by Henry Fraser Passmore, who produced five films for Hammer between 1935 and 1937, the first being *The Public Life of Henry the Ninth* and the second, in 1936, *The Mystery of the Mary Celeste* (aka *The Phantom Ship*).

The story calls the ship *Mary Celeste* rather than the by then general *Marie Celeste* and the names of those aboard and aboard *Dei Gratia* generally follow those of the real people. Captain Benjamin Briggs, Sarah Briggs, Anton Lorenzen, Tom Goodschard, Andy Gilling, Arian Harbens and Volkerk Grot all follow or are approximate to real people aboard *Celeste*. Captain Morehouse becomes Captain Jim Morehead, Oliver Deveau becomes Olly Deveau, and the story also features Horatio Sprague and James Winchester. Solly Flood features but not by name and is actually uncredited, as is the judge.

Captain Briggs (Arthur Margetson) asks his love Sarah (Shirley Grey) to marry him and join the ship for a honeymoon voyage to Italy. She agrees, but has another suitor, Briggs's friend Captain Morehead (Clifford McLaglen), who, bitterly let down, becomes Captain Briggs's enemy.

Meanwhile, *Mary Celeste* is preparing to set sail and First Mate Toby Bilson (Edmund Willard), given the task of hiring crew, is having trouble signing men aboard and is happy to sign up Volkert Grot (Herbert Cameron), unaware that he had been paid by Morehead to arrange for Briggs to have an 'accident'. The 'accident' happens soon after the ship leaves port, several members of the crew either dying or vanishing mysteriously as those remaining realise that a murderer is among them. The film is distinguished by a very effective use of reaction shots to convey the horror and brutality of some of the crimes, and the tension is well handled.

The British version opened and closed with the court of inquiry at Gibraltar, but these scenes were cut from the American version and the footage seems to have been lost, but otherwise the film seems intact, albeit not in very good quality. This applies to the widely available DVD version taken from the original 35mm nitrate export negative, but the film is a period piece well worth watching. It isn't a memorable film and probably wouldn't be remembered at all today if the cast hadn't included Bela Lugosi, the movie star best known for his portrayal of Dracula and, today, unfortunately for dying halfway through the monumentally awful but now cult movie *Plan Nine from Outer Space*, being replaced by an 'actor' who didn't in the slightest resemble him. Although *The Mystery of Mary Celeste* is run-of-the-mill 1930s B-feature fare, Lugosi, who was trying to escape being typecast as a horror actor, is very good in the movie as a religious zealot and alcoholic, psychologically scarred from a brutal shanghaiing aboard *Mary Celeste* in the past.

Apart from Lugosi, none of the cast members were particularly notable and none went on to achieve long-lasting fame. Dennis Hoey, who plays Tom Goodschard, a villainous would-be rapist, went on to play Inspector Lestrade in the Sherlock Holmes series starring Basil Rathbone and Nigel Bruce (Arthur Margetson, who played Captain Briggs, joined him in one of those films).

The Goon Show

At 2 Strutton Ground, Westminster, not far from Scotland Yard, there is a pub called Finnegan's Wake, one of several Irish theme pubs of that name belonging to a chain. It is a shrine, although there is nothing outside and little inside to show it. This pub was once called The Grafton Arms and was owned by a scriptwriter, Jimmy Grafton, who in the 1950s and 1960s wrote several popular television series for Dickie Henderson, Harry Secombe, Arthur Askey and Dick Emery. In the immediate post-war years the pub was a popular meeting place for actors, producers and comics, and it was here that the young Peter Sellers, Harry Secombe and Michael Bentine got together with a young comic who rented a room upstairs, Spike Milligan. Spike had already met Harry Secombe during the war and they had found that they shared a common humour. During the war Peter Sellers and Michael Bentine had worked together on an RAF Gangshow, and they met Secombe, who in turn introduced the pair to Milligan. The quartet sometimes performed what was then wholly original madcap comic pieces in the smoke-filled bar and a showbiz writer named Bill Boorne coined the expression 'The Goon Club' to describe them.

Grafton urged the group to go to the BBC, but as is so often the case in the history of the BBC, and has increasingly become so in television and radio generally over the years, the Corporation was deaf to the innovative humour. Eventually a young producer named Pat Dixon took a tentative interest and on 28 May 1951 the BBC broadcast the first episode of a series called *The Crazy People*, scripted by Spike Milligan and Larry Stephens, edited by Jimmy Grafton and produced by Dennis Main Wilson, who would become one of the greatest and most revered names in radio comedy. It was a humour without a middle ground, you either liked it or hated it, and that still applies over fifty years later. At the time it seems that detestation was the reaction of the majority of people, but as the series progressed the listening figures increased. For the second series, which began on 22 January 1952, the title was changed to *The Goon Show* and it gradually underwent a variety of changes: Michael Bentine left to start his own highly successful individual career, Dennis Main Wilson was replaced by Peter Eaton, the format of the show dropped sketches and adopted a single-plot storyline. By series four the show had taken on the form and shape by which it is so widely remembered today.

At the end of series four the team did a one-off special which Spike Milligan wrote with Erik Sykes and the two comic geniuses collaborated on all but the first six scripts of series five, which was broadcast through the BBC Transcription Service in New Zealand, South Africa and elsewhere. Series five included some of the most memorable episodes of the early Goon Shows – *The Dreaded Batter Pudding Hurler of Bexhill-on-Sea* and *Nighteen Eighty-Five* (a take-off of George Orwell's *Nineteen Eighty-Four*, then recently and famously televised). The eighth episode of the fifth series, scripted by Milligan and Sykes, and produced by Peter Eaton was 'The Mystery of the Marie Celeste (Solved)'. It was broadcast on 16 November 1954.

In the story, such as it is, the heroic idiot Neddie Seagoon (Secombe) reads a newspaper advertisement placed by the arch public school cad Grytpype-Thynne, in this tale of the high seas being cast as the famous author of sea stories and described as 'a tall, vile man, dressed in the naval uniform of a seagoing sailor. Under his left arm he held a neatly rolled anchor, while with his right he scanned the horizon with a pair of powerful kippers.' The Captain is offering a reward of £5,000 to anyone furnishing conclusive proof of the fate of the captain and crew of the *Marie Celeste*. Seagoon offers to solve the mystery and his search for the solution takes him first to Denis Bloodnok (Sellers), normally a major but for this episode an admiral:

> Seagoon: *Admiral, I was told you had associations with the ill-fated* Marie Celeste?
>
> Bloodnok: *All lies. Do you hear me, lies! I was in Bangalore at the time. I deny every word. She's lying I tell you. Lying! And so is Alice and Mary, and all the other women I molested. They're after my piggy bank, do you hear me!*
>
> Seagoon: *Admiral, please . . .* Marie Celeste *was found abandoned at sea.*
>
> Bloodnok: *Oh, poor girl, how she must have suffered . . .*

Seagoon explains about the reward which he promises to share with all those who help him and Bloodnok sends him to the shipyards of Henry Crunn (Milligan) where *Marie Celeste* was built. Seagoon gets Crunn to build a replica of the ship and in due course he finds a crew and sets sail, planning to follow the exact route of the first ship and to rendezvous with Grytpype-Thynne aboard the British sloop HMS *Gladys*. As the *Gladys* comes into view, Seagoon learns that his crew is the original crew of *Marie Celeste* and that they had deliberately vanished because they planned to share in the reward they knew that one day somebody would offer to anyone who could find out what had happened to them. With the solution to the *Marie Celeste* in his grasp, Seagoon brings *Marie Celeste II* within hailing distance of HMS *Gladys* – but there is nobody aboard and she is eerily deserted. Neddie offers a reward of £5,000 for the solution to the mystery of the disappearance of the captain and crew of HMS *Gladys* and receives a visit from Grytpype-Thynne – who offers to tell the story . . .

Suspense

One of the longest running shows on American radio was *Suspense*. It was launched on CBS in 1942 and lasted until 30 September 1962. Along with many programmes from the Golden Age of Radio, *Suspense* graduated to television, where it was broadcast live from New York on Tuesday evenings from March 1949 until August 1954, reappearing briefly in 1964 when it was hosted by Sebastian Cabot. Billed as 'Radio's Outstanding Theatre of Thrills', it was particularly distinguished for starring some of the biggest names in Hollywood, among them Judy Garland, Cary Grant, Frank Sinatra, Peter Lorre, Agnes Moorhead and Orson Welles. It was also notable for giving actors the opportunity to play parts they did not normally get, such as dramatic parts being given to comedians like Bob Hope, Lucille Ball and Jack Benny. The most famous episode of the series was *Sorry, Wrong Number*, written by the premier radio scribe Lucille Fletcher. In this story a panicked, bedridden woman, played brilliantly by Agnes Moorhead, perhaps best remembered for her role as Endora, the mother of witch Samantha Stevens in the television series *Bewitched*, tries to convince a telephone operator she has overheard a murder plot on a crossed line. First broadcast on 25 May 1943, it was repeated seven times and was filmed in 1948 with Barbara Stanwyck in the lead role.

There were approximately 945 episodes of *Suspense* of which over 900 still exist, including two dramatisations of a story by Gil Dowd about

Mary Celeste, the first broadcast on 8 June 1953, the second on 27 December 1955. The story begins with great promise: a man named Sam Newcombe is heard breathlessly fleeing the police after murdering three people (his sweetheart Grace, a man he'd found her with, and Grace's mother, who had always tried to turn Grace against him because he hadn't managed to become a master mariner) and seeking refuge on the docks, where he manages to stow away aboard *Mary Celeste*. The story goes downhill from this point. Newcombe initially intends to confess, but is dissuaded when he discovers that the captain's wife is called Grace. Thereafter he falls out with several crew members and especially earns the enmity of one called Hubbard whose hatred and innate brutality causes him to try to kill Newcombe with a marlin spike dropped from a height. After a while Newcombe confesses his crime to the skipper's wife, who becomes scared and Newcombe flees to the hold and attempts to hide from the captain and crew, but they find him and lock him up. A short time later he hears some sort of disturbance, then an unbroken and eerie silence as if all activity aboard ship had stopped. When his daily meal doesn't arrive he breaks free of the room. Going on deck he finds the ship deserted, everyone on board having vanished. Newcombe manages to make his own escape from the ship, but first writes his story and seals it in a bottle.

The story has very little to do with the real *Mary Celeste*, the ship being hardly more than a device to tell a not very realistic story about a murderer's escape, and the theory accounting for the disappearance of the crew is that undersea currents had swept up a sand island on which the 'Marie Celeste' ran aground. It is supposed that all aboard had walked ashore and that the island had then sunk.

The story may not have stood up to the test of time, unlike many of the tales in *Suspense*, which were actually excellent given that they fitted into a half-hour slot, about five minutes or more of which was taken up with opening and closing credits and sponsorship messages, but it won audience appreciation sufficiently for the tale to be broadcast twice. In one version Sam Newcombe was played by Van Heflin (1910–71), a very popular actor in his day who is perhaps best remembered today for his particularly powerful and understated portrayal of homesteader Joe Starrett in *Shane*, a movie whose literate script and excellent cast, notably Alan Ladd as the mysterious eponymous gunslinger, made it one of the finest westerns of all time. He was ideally cast as Sam Newcombe, having a genuine love of the sea, and would probably have been a sailor had he not found fame as an actor. In 1971 he had a heart attack while swimming, but somehow managed to reach the pool's ladder. When found later in the day he was rushed to the hospital, but never recovered consciousness and died on 23 July. His cremated remains were scattered on the ocean. The second version of the story starred John Dehner (1915–92), a movie actor who guest-starred in numerous TV series in the 1950s and 1960s.

Postage stamps

Mary Celeste has featured on several postage stamps, including one from the Maldives in a series called 'Mysteries of the Universe', in which she is called 'Marie Celeste', further testimony, as if any were needed, of the influence of Conan Doyle's story.

Mary Celeste has in fact appeared twice on stamps for the Maldives, a collection of beautiful white-beached atolls in the Indian Ocean, once correctly named on a RF5 stamp, as well as incorrectly named in the 'Mysteries . . .' series.

Gibraltar has likewise issued stamps featuring *Mary Celeste*. In 1967 a set of 15 definitive stamps with values from a halfpenny to £1 featured a variety of ships, *Mary Celeste* appearing on the £1 denomination. In February 1997 Gibraltar released a set of four stamps, two with a 28p value and two with a 30p value. The 28p stamps portrayed *Mary Celeste* passing Gibraltar, and the men of *Dei Gratia* boarding the ship. The 30p stamps had a picture of the crew leaving *Mary Celeste*, and one of *Mary Celeste* being found by *Dei Gratia*. This set of four seems to be the most difficult to get hold of these days.

CHAPTER 10

Other maritime mysteries

June 11th, 1881, – At 4 a.m. the 'Flying Dutchman' crossed our bows. A strange red light, as of a phantom ship all aglow in the midst of which light the masts, spars, and sails of a brig 200-yards distant stood out in strong relief as she came up on our port bow. The lookout man on the forecastle reported her as close on the port bow, where also the officer on the watch from the bridge clearly saw her, as did also the quarterdeck and the midshipman, who was sent forward to the forecastle, but on arrival there no vestige or sign whatever of material ship was seen either near or right away on the horizon, the night being clear, the sea calm. Thirteen persons altogether saw her, but whether it was van Demien of the 'Flying Dutchman' or what else must remain unknown.

The Tourmaline *and* Cleopatra, *who were sailing on our starboard bow, flashed to ask whether we had seen the strange red light.*

At 10.45 a.m. the ordinary seaman who had this morning reported the 'Flying Dutchman' fell from the topgallant foretopmast crosstrees and was smashed to atoms. At 4.15 p.m. after quarters we hove to with the headyards back, and he was buried at sea. He was a smart royal yardman and one of the most promising young hands in the ship, and everyone feels quite sad at his loss. At the next port we came to the Admiral was also smitten down.

This account of a sighting of the most famous phantom ship of the sea is taken from *The Cruise of Her Majesties Ship Baccante* by John H. Dalton,[1] published in 1886 and compiled from the notebooks, letters and private journals of Prince Albert Victor and his younger brother George,

Prince of Wales. It is doubtful that one could wish for a more reputable source, and in addition to the princes the spectre was seen by about thirteen people aboard the *Inconstant* and an unspecified number of people aboard the *Tourmaline* and *Cleopatra*. What they saw is another matter, of course, but it probably need not be doubted that they saw *something*.

The spectral ship is often referred to as the Flying Dutchman, but the name properly belongs to its captain, a maniacal Dutchman who challenged the wrath of God and was condemned to sail the oceans for eternity, bringing death and destruction to all who sighted him (as, indeed, it did to those aboard the *Inconstant*), and the tale is unquestionably the most famous and probably the oldest legend of the sea, being at least five hundred years old and perhaps with origins in stories dating from before the birth of Christ.

It is a confused story and there are numerous elaborated versions in which the details change; even the captain is variously called Vanderdecken, Van Diemien, Van Straaten, or Van-something-else. In the best-known version it is Captain Vanderdecken whose ship is gripped by a violent storm as he was voyaging around the Cape of Good Hope. The terrified passengers pleaded with the demented skipper to find a safe port or at least shorten sail and try to ride out the storm, but Vanderdecken only laughed and began singing blasphemous songs. His crew were greatly alarmed by his behaviour and attempted to take control of the ship, but Vanderdecken hurled the ringleader overboard and the would-be mutineers fell back with the passengers in horror and terror, placing their lives in the mercy of God, to whom they offered fervent prayers. Then the clouds parted and a glorious light bathed the forecastle revealing a wonderful figure who some said was the Holy Ghost and others claimed was God. The figure told Vanderdecken that as he took pleasure in tormenting his passengers and crew, henceforth he would sail the ocean for eternity, always in the grip of a howling storm and bringing doom to all who sighted him. He was condemned to eat only red-hot iron and drink only gall, and his only company was a cabin-boy who would grow horns from his head and have the muzzle of a tiger and the skin of a dogfish – all of which seems very unfair to the poor cabin-boy who had hitherto played no independent part in the story and presumably had been as afraid of Vanderecken as everyone else. With that the figure disappeared along with the passengers and crew.

One variant has it that the Dutchman was in fact a German named von Falkenberg and instead of cursing and challenging God, he is supposed to have wagered his soul in a game of dice played with the Devil and lost. In a similar story he is a murderer doomed to sail for eternity aboard a ship deserted of all life except for two shadowy figures playing dice for his soul, and the same theme is applied to the story of a Dutch skipper named van Straaten.

It's possible that the story touches base with reality in the shape of a seaman named Bernard Fokke who skippered a ship called *Libra Nos* and who some claim was a real person. Fokke was a brilliant seaman and excellent navigator whose skill enabled him to make remarkably fast voyages, so fast in fact that envious, jealous and superstitious captains claimed that he was in league with the Devil. The fact that he was an extremely ugly and violent man only leant support to the story and one day when he did not return from a voyage it was claimed that the Devil had finally collected his due.

The story of the Flying Dutchman has inspired many works of fiction. A poem by Thomas Moore (1779–1852) alludes to a superstition among sailors about a ghost ship called the 'Flying Dutchman'. The German writer H. Schmidt wrote of it in 1812 in *Der ewige Segler* (*The Eternal Seafarer*) and according to Sir Walter Scott his pirate poem 'Rokeby', published the following year, is based on 'a well-known nautical superstition concerning a fantastic vessel, called by sailors the "Flying Dutchman", and supposed to be seen about the latitude of the Cape of Good Hope. She is distinguished from earthly vessels by bearing a press of sail when all others are unable, from stress of weather, to show an inch of canvas.'

In the May 1821 issue of *Blackwood's Edinburgh Magazine* there was an anonymous tale entitled 'Vanderdecken's Message Home, or The Tenacity of Natural Affection', which doesn't refer to the supernatural as such, or to the curse, but is a scary tale about a vessel that hails passing ships to give them letters to deliver, but all the addressees turn out to have died long before. The story appears to have been known to Richard Wagner who adapted the letters theme.

The story was particularly popular in Germany when *Bruchstücken aus Karl Berthold's Tagebuch* (*Fragments from the Diary of Karl Berthold*) by 'Oswald' (pseudonym of Martin Hieronymus Hudtwalcker) appeared in 1826, in which year a melodrama called *The Flying Dutchman: or The Phantom Ship* was staged at the Adelphi Theatre in London. Written by the dramatist Edward Fitzball (1792–1873), who in his autobiography placed his tale in the tradition of Mary Shelley's *Frankenstein* and Weber's opera *Der Freischütz*, it had a farcical stage villain who was allowed ashore once every century to seek a bride to share his destiny. While on earth he must remain silent so it becomes a miming part. Again it may have influenced Wagner because it contains elements he used.

Joseph Christian Freiherr von Zedlitz's *Das Geisterschiff* (*The Ghost Ship*) appeared in 1832, and the Frenchman August Jal produced the most widely known version of the tale in his *Scenes de la vie maritime.* The undoubted inspiration for Wagner, however, was the German lyric poet Heinrich Heine (1797–1856) who wrote of the phantom ship first and briefly in 1827 in the second volume of *Reisebilder* (*Travel Pictures*), and later at greater length in 1834 in the pseudo-autobiographical *Aus den Memoiren des Herren von Schnabelewopski* (*From the Memoirs of Lord von Schnabelewopski*). Wagner may also have known of Frederick Marryat's *The Phantom Ship*, published in 1839. Richard Wagner, of course, produced a magnificent and powerful opera, *Der fliegende Holländer* (*The Flying Dutchman*), which used many of the themes of the earlier stories, including Vanderdecken being allowed ashore to find a woman whose love can redeem him.

The Flying Dutchman isn't the only spectral ship. In 1949 it was estimated that there were more than 100 'well-established' cases of vessels haunting just the north-east coast of the United States and the most famous is the 'Spectre of New Haven' first mentioned by a New Englander named John Winthrop who kept a journal and in 1648 noted that

> *There appeared over the harbor at New Haven in the evening, the form of the keel of a ship with three masts, to which were suddenly added all the tackling and sails, and presently after, upon the top of the poop, a man standing with one hand akimbo under his left side, and in his right hand a sword stretched out toward the sea. Then from the side of the ship which was toward the town arose a great smoke, which covered all the ship, and in that smoke she vanished away; but some saw her keel sink*

into the water. This was seen by many, men and women, and it
continued about a quarter of an hour.

Cotton Mather spoke with people who witnessed this apparition and
wrote of it in his *Magnalia Christi Americana* published in 1702, observing: 'Reader, There being yet living so many Credible Gentlemen, that
were Eye-Witnesses of this *Wonderful* thing, I venture to Publish it for a
thing as *undoubted*, as 'tis *wonderful*.'

Unfortunately Mather had not in fact spoken with witnesses as he
claimed but had received the tale third-hand in a letter from James
Pierpont, pastor of the First Congregational Church of New Haven. Since
Pierpont was only pastor there from 1685 (until 1714), he could not have
seen the ship event himself and he didn't say who the reliable witnesses
were. He even got the date wrong, giving it as 1648:

In the Year 1647, besides much other Lading, a far more Rich Treasure of
Passengers, (Five or Six of which were Persons of chief Note and Worth
in New-Haven) put themselves on Board a New Ship, built at Rhode-
Island, of about 150 Tuns; but so walty, that the Master, (Lamberton)
often said she would prove their Grave. In the Month of January, cutting
their way thro' much Ice, . . . they set Sail. Mr. Davenport in Prayer with
an observable Emphasis used these Words, Lord, if it be thy pleasure to
bury these our Friends in the bottom of the Sea, they are thine; save
them! The Spring following no Tidings of these Friends arrived with the
Ships from England: New-Haven's Heart began to fail her: This put the
Godly People on much Prayer, both Publick and Private, That the Lord
would (if it was his Pleasure) let them hear what he had done with their
dear Friends, and prepare them with a suitable Submission to his Holy
Will. In June next ensuing, a great Thunderstorm arose out of the
North-West: after which, (the Hemisphere being serene) about an Hour
before Sunset a SHIP of like dimensions with the aforesaid, with her
Canvas and Colours abroad (tho' the Wind Northernly) appeared in the
Air coming up from our Harbour's Mouth, which lyes Southward from
the Town, seemingly with her Sails filled under a fresh Gale, holding her
Course North, and continuing under Observation, Sailing against the
Wind for the space of half an Hour. Many were drawn to behold this
great Work of God; yea, the very Children cry'd out, There's a Brave
Ship! At length, crouding up as far as there is usually Water sufficient for

such a Vessel, and so near some of the Spectators, as that they imagined
a Man might hurl a Stone on Board her, her Maintop seem'd to be blown
off, but left hanging in the Shrouds; then her Missen-top then all her
Masting seemed blown away by the Board: Quickly after the Hull brought
unto a Careen, she overset, and so vanished into a smoaky Cloud, which
in some time dissipated, leaving, as everywhere else, a clear Air.[2]

Perhaps the greatest claim Mather's story has to notoriety, however, is that it was inspiration for Henry Wadsworth Longfellow's 'The Phantom Ship'.

The most famous ghost ship off the coast of America is probably the *Palatine*, the subject of a famous poem by John Greenleaf Whittier. Legend has it that in 1752 the *Palatine* was swept aground by a storm on the rocks of Block Island, Rhode Island, and the wreck was set alight by fishermen, but a woman was trapped aboard and burned alive, since which time the spectre of the flaming ship has been seen countless times offshore.

Interestingly, while detailed research has shown that no ship called *Palatine* was wrecked off Block Island in 1752, in 1738 a ship called the *Princess Augusta* did run aground there in a storm and sank. She was carrying 350 refugees from the Lower and Upper Palatinate in Germany. The homeland of the passengers aboard *Princess Augusta* was clearly transferred to the name of the spectral ship, and the sinking was changed to being set alight in order to fit a natural phenomenon witnessed there.

This tale shows how stories can have a foundation in real events even though all the names and details are changed and some authorities have argued that the origins of the Flying Dutchman story could stretch back to Greek myths and even more plausibly to the Norse saga of Stote in which a Viking steals a ring from the gods and is later found as a skeleton in a robe of fire seated on the mainmast of a black spectral ship. Other authorities have suggested that the story dates from the adventures of the Portuguese navigator Bartholomes Diaz (*c.*1450–1500) whose prowess as a skipper assumed a superhuman quality in his biography by Luis de Camois and who in 1488 discovered the Cape of Good Hope, around which the Flying Dutchman was supposed to be travelling when he incurred God's displeasure. There is some suggestion that there really was a Captain Vanderdecken; others point to a somewhat nebulous tale about two Dutch merchantmen whose crews sighted the wraith of a vessel they knew to have been lost in the Pacific.

The relevance of the Flying Dutchman legend is that it could have been born out of a real event such as an encounter with a strangely abandoned vessel such as *Mary Celeste* drifting aimlessly at sea. Books about maritime mysteries tell of several of these vessels, albeit almost always so briefly as to cause one to doubt their veracity. Some of the tales are so fascinating that were they true then they would be worth telling in detail, such as the story of the *Fannie J. Wolsten*. A schooner, she was abandoned in 1891 and apparently drifted an estimated 9,000 miles before running aground and breaking up off the coast of New Jersey four years later!

Three vessels are said to have been found abandoned in 1888. One, the schooner *William L. White*, was abandoned off Delaware Bay during the great blizzard of March 1888 and sailed alone for some ten months covering about 5,000 miles. Two schooners, *Ethel M. Davis* and *David W. Hunt*, abandoned off the east coast of the United States in November 1888, are each supposed to have drifted some 5,000 miles on their own, while the schooner *Twenty-one Friends*, abandoned off Chesapeake Bay in March 1885, apparently turned up off Cape Finisterre nine months later having travelled more than 3,500 miles.

Perhaps one of the most remarkable of such stories concerns the wool clipper *Marlborough*, which vanished in 1890 on a voyage between Australia and England and is said to have sailed alone for 23 years, eventually being found off the coast of Chile. It is highly doubtful that a vessel could have sailed the oceans unmanned for so long, but it takes little imagination to appreciate the effect on the mind of such a derelict apparition suddenly looming out of the night, or eerier still, out of the fog.

One version of the story has *Marlborough* carrying a cargo of $2,000,000 worth of gold bullion. She left port for England in 1890 and was never seen again. One story claims that she is ice-bound near the south pole, another comes from the crew of the British ship *Johnson* who sighted the vessel off the coast of Chile in 1913. The derelict's sails were hanging in shreds and covered with some kind of green mould, her timbers were dangerously rotten and a small boarding party found six skeletons on the bridge, ten more in the crew's quarters and several others were scattered about the ship. The source of the story seems to be a sober enough article in the *Evening Post* (Wellington, New Zealand) of 13 November 1913.

However, abandoned ships are comparatively rare, especially ones where the fate of the crew remains unknown and inexplicable. There is no shortage of stories, for garrulous old-time mariners apparently loved to swap such stories in waterfront bars and there has always been a market for sea stories among incredulous landlubbers, be they about abandoned ships or sea monsters. Several examples are given by Lt-Commander Rupert T. Gould in a slim volume called *The Stargazer Talks*:

> In August 1840, the deserted French ship Rosalie *was picked up off Nassau, in the Bahamas, with sail set, in perfect order, and with a valuable cargo on board. Apparently, she'd been abandoned only a few hours before – yet nothing was ever heard of her crew.*
>
> *Then again, on 21 April 1849, the Dutch schooner* Hermania *was found drifting, about ten miles S.E. of the Eddystone, by the fishing-vessel* Fame *of Rye. She was dismasted, and had obviously been in collision, but was still quite sound. Valuables were found on board, and clothing indicating that – as in the case of the* Mary Celeste *– the captain's wife and child had been on board with him. Her only boat was lying in its chocks, uninjured. Nothing was ever heard of the crew.*
>
> *On 28 February 1855, the* Marathon *of Newcastle fell in with the* James B. Chester, *a good-sized sailing-ship, in about 300 N., 400 W. – some 600 miles S.W. of the Azorea. She, too, was in perfect order, but abandoned. Her papers were missing, and it's uncertain whether all her boats were on board.*
>
> *Last, and queerest of all, comes the case of the abandoned derelict, in seaworthy condition, which the British ship* Ellen Austin *encountered, in mid-Atlantic, in the year 1881. She put a small prize-crew on board the stranger, with instructions to make for St. John's, Newfoundland, where she was bound herself. The two ships parted company in foggy weather – but a few days later they met again. And the strange derelict was once more deserted. Like their predecessors, the prize-crew had vanished – for ever.*[3]

It is not always easy to verify such stories as these, partly because the facts and details get changed as the story passes through numerous tellings and retellings, as with the story of the Palatine lights, where the date changed and the place of origin of the ship's passengers became the name of the ship itself. This proved to be the case with the first of the abandoned vessels mentioned by Gould, *Rosalie*.

Page 6 of *The Times* for Friday, 6 November 1840 carried the following news story:

> **SHIP DESERTED** – *A letter from Nassau in the Bahamas, bearing the date 27th of August, has the following narrative:*
> *A singular fact has taken place within the last few days. A large French vessel, bound from Hamburgh to Havanah, was met by one of our coasters, and was discovered to be completely abandoned. The greater part of her sails were set, and she did not seem to have sustained any damage. The cargo, composed of wines, fruits, silks, etc., was in the most perfect condition. The captain's papers were all secure in their proper places. The soundings gave three feet of water in the hold, but there was no leak whatsoever. The only living things on board were a cat, some fowles, and several canaries half-dead with hunger. The cabins of the officers and passengers were very elegantly furnished, and everything indicated that they had only recently been deserted. In one of them were found several articles belonging to a ladies toilet together with a quantity of ladies wearing apparel thrown hastily aside, but not a human being was to be found on board. The vessel, which must have been left within a very few hours, contained several bales of goods addressed to different merchants in Havanah. She is very large, recently built, and called Rosalie. Of her crew and passengers no intelligence has been received.*

The Times carried no further information about *Rosalie* and no additional information could be provided by Lloyd's of London and the Musée de la Marine in Paris, but Lloyd's did turn up a record of a ship called *Rossini* that ran aground on the Muares (the Bahama Channel) on 3 August 1840 *en route* to Havana from Hamburg. It appears that her passengers and crew were rescued and taken to safety, and that two weeks later, on 17 August, the British wrecking ships *Resolute* and *Seaflower*, under the command of Benjamin Curry and John Baptiste, salvaged *Rossini* and took her to Nassau, where they filed a claim for salvage. There can be little doubt that *Rosalie* and *Rossini* are the same vessel – they have similar names, both were bound from Hamburg to Havana;

they were found in the same general area and in the same month of the same year. The Vice Admiralty Court minutes mention an affidavit presented by Curry and Baptiste which refers to the 'curious circumstances' under which the vessel was found, but we have no idea what those 'curious circumstances' were. It may mean no more than that neither the salvers nor the authorities in Nassau were aware that *Rossini* had run aground two weeks earlier and that her passengers and crew had been taken to safety. Whatever the 'curious circumstances' were, there is little or no mystery about Rossini and the story demonstrates how these tales can quickly lose touch with what actually happened.

The *Hermania* and the *James B. Chester* have proved elusive and their very existence as yet remains to be demonstrated, despite the latter allegedly being brought into Albert Docks, Liverpool, where a large crowd supposedly gathered to see her arrival.

The story of *Ellen Austin* is indeed a strange one, though not for the reasons Lt-Commander Rupert T. Gould thought, and although Gould was an able, intelligent and objective researcher, his story of *Ellen Austin* demonstrates yet again how these maritime mysteries grow and change in telling.

Ellen Austin was real enough. She was an American schooner, 1,812 tons, 210 feet in length, and built in 1854 at Damariscotta, Maine, becoming one of the Swallowtail Line vessels operated by Grinnell, Minturn & Co., a prominent transatlantic packet company founded about 1822 and plying the New York and Liverpool route, where it did a thriving business taking Irish immigrants to a new life in the New World.

The details of her fate change from telling to telling: one afternoon – some accounts tell us it was the afternoon of 14 July – in 1881, when the British (or American) schooner (or brig) *Ellen Austin* was becalmed in mid-Atlantic, the lookout sighted a twin-masted schooner off the starboard bow. *Ellen Austin*'s skipper, a man named Baker, surveyed the schooner through his glass and noted that the stranger was not flying a flag and that no name seemed to be painted on the tailboards. The vessel also looked deserted, with no sign of life. Over the next few days the vessels drifted closer together and by mid-afternoon of 20 July they had drawn close enough together to make it feasible to lower a boat and cross to the stranger to take a closer look. With a crew of two (or four) Baker rowed across to the stranger and pulled himself over the side. He found the vessel seaworthy, her cargo intact and secure, and her lifeboats all secure in the davits – yet there was not a soul aboard. Baker decided to claim the ship and its cargo as salvage and put a skeleton crew aboard, telling them to follow *Ellen Austin* to St John's, Newfoundland (Gould says St John's, but other accounts variously state that *Ellen Austin* had been bound for Boston but had been forced to divert to St John's by bad weather; another account says that the vessel was bound for New York). In due course the winds picked up and the two vessels were able to make headway, but after two days they found themselves in the grip of a violent storm. They were on the perimeter of a hurricane, which to the southeast was blasting the eastern Bahamas and would move on to Georgia, Alabama and Mississippi, where it would leave 700 people dead in its wake. The storm separated the two vessels and although Captain Baker searched for his prize, no sign was seen of her and eventually dwindling supplies forced him to abandon the hunt.

Some tellers of the tale end the story here, others, like Commander Gould, give an unlikely elaboration. When the storm cleared *Ellen Austin* and the mystery schooner were still in sight of one another. Captain Baker anxiously hailed his men aboard the mystery ship but received no word in reply and lowered the boat. Gripped by a feeling that a terrible history was repeating itself, he rowed across to the schooner, and found his men gone, the ship deserted, the supplies his men had taken with them untouched, and no evidence to suggest that they had even been aboard.

Gould leaves the tale here, of course, but some tellers, presumably unable to resist over-egging the pudding, claim that the promise of a handsome payment induced some of his remaining crew to go aboard the stranger and try to bring her into port. Armed with guns, told to stay within hailing distance and to ring the mystery schooner's bell every quarter-hour, the skeleton crew sailed on. All went well, but after a few days a thick mist enveloped the two ships. The schooner's bell was rung every fifteen minutes from within the impenetrable blanket of grey fog, but the faint, reassuring sound was suddenly silent and was heard no more. The mist lifted and the schooner and the men on board had vanished, never to be seen again.

This second vanishing is an eerie elaboration and even the first vanishing lacks independent confirmation and could be a fiction. There are also complications to the story. The story is set in 1881, but in that year the ship changed her name to *Meta* and as far as is known she sailed only once in that year as *Ellen Austin*. This was a voyage from London to New York lasting from 5 December 1880 until 11 February 1881 and as far as we know it was uneventful. It was, however, a curiously long voyage, which could suggest that she encountered bad weather and we know that there was a severe blizzard and great loss of life at sea between 17–21 January 1881.

Some versions set the story later in the year, in August, and tell of a violent hurricane. The hurricane in August 1881 was real and 700 people were indeed killed in Georgia and South Carolina, and Savannah and Augusta in Georgia suffered extensive damage. If the incident took place in August 1881 then *Ellen Austin* would have been called *Meta*. Of course, if the story was told by someone who had served aboard *Ellen Austin* then the recent name change might not have been familiar enough to the teller to spring to mind as he related the tale to a journalist or to fellows in some waterfront bar.

From the foregoing it will be seen that whilst there are many mysteries of the sea – and the myths surrounding the so-called Bermuda Triangle have added considerably to the elaborated and exaggerated stories of maritime disappearance – few such stories have traceable foundation in fact and when they do, as in the case of the 'Rosalie', the factual foundation isn't as mysterious as it may at first seem. *Mary Celeste* is distinguished from such stories, she has a well-attested history, albeit disputed in some of the details, and we genuinely have no idea why the captain and crew abandoned a perfectly seaworthy ship.

Notes and references

1   John H. Dalton, *The Cruise of Her Majesties Ship* Baccante. *Compiled from the Private Journals, Letters, and Note-Books of Prince Albert Victor and Prince George of Wales*, London: MacMillan, 1886. Two volumes.

2   Cotton Mather, *Magnalia Christi Americana: Books I and II*, edited by K.B. Murdock, Cambridge: Belknap Press, 1977, pp. 169–70.

3   Rupert Gould, *The Stargazer Talks*, London: Geoffrey Bles, 1946.

. . . .

CHAPTER 11

Theories of abandonment

Contrary to the popular imagination, the mystery of *Mary Celeste* is not what happened to her skipper, his family and the crew, since we know that they abandoned ship in the yawl and that the heavily overloaded little boat probably capsized and all aboard were drowned. The mystery is *why* the crew abandoned a perfectly seaworthy ship.

Whatever that something was, it would appear to have happened some time after 8.00 a.m. on Monday, 25 November 1872, and probably quite soon after: up to that time there had been hourly notes on the log slate; there was no cooked food in the galley, no sign of any cooking in preparation or of an interrupted or finished meal; the beds were unmade and the Captain's bed bore the imprint of a child having been asleep there. The weather must have been reasonable because the boat seems to have been launched without the crew attending to the sails, which suggests that there was little more than a light breeze, and this is confirmed by the meteorological records which show that a calm or light wind prevailed that morning. The cabin skylight was also open, which suggests the weather was fair, which is again indicated by the hatch covers being lifted, presumably to air the hold – unless they were lifted after the something that happened. From the evidence provided by the ship herself it is therefore reasonable to deduce that whatever happened was without warning, dramatic and serious enough to greatly alarm an experienced master-mariner and to cause the ship to be abandoned in considerable haste.

An opinion to which some credence must be given is that of Dr Oliver W. Cobb because he knew the people involved and during a life-long interest in the case amassed a great deal of information – although some of it was wrong; he believed, for example, that the beds were made and that the hatch covers were upside down on the deck, as if blown off rather than lifted. Neither detail is true, or at least neither detail is supported by the testimony given at the Vice Admiralty Court hearings. Such details might appear minor, but they play a part in consequent theories, including Dr Cobb's, which is one of the most influential and was expressed several times over the years, including in his interesting account of the Briggs's family, *Rose Cottage*.

As the entry in the log book made at noon, November 24th, indicates light southerly wind, the Mary Celeste was then probably under full sail. This enables us to reconstruct what probably happened. At some time after noon of November 24th, Captain Briggs determined to take in sail. He may have interrupted Mr. Richardson's letter writing. The royal and topgallant sail, the flying jib, main topmast staysail, middle staysail, gaff topsail and the mainsail were furled.

The vessel was still on the starboard tack as is shown by the jibs being set on the port side. That the yards were braced around so as to back the squaresails is evident from the position of the yards when the salvors went on board. The movable section of the rail abreast the main hatch had been taken out and laid on deck where Mr. Deveau said that he left it until he went on board the second time. All the above movements indicate good seamanship and preparation to leave the vessel. We do not know why, but I think that, the cargo of alcohol having been loaded in cold weather at New York early in November and the vessel having crossed the Gulf Stream and being now in comparatively warm weather, there may have been some leakage and gas may have accumulated in the hold. The captain, having care for his wife and daughter, was probably unjustifiably alarmed and, fearing a fire or an explosion, determined to take his people in the boat from the vessel until the immediate danger should pass.

Knowing what the duty of each man should be, it is comparatively easy to reconstruct the scene with the evidence which we have. The boat was launched on the port side. The captain got his wife and daughter into the boat and left them in charge of Mr. Richardson with one sailor in the boat while the captain went for his chronometer, sextant, Nautical Almanac *and the ship's papers.*

Mr. Gilling with one sailor would be getting the peak halyard ready to use as a tow rope. Another sailor would tend the painter of the boat and a fourth sailor would be at the wheel. The cook gathered up what cooked food he had on hand and some canned goods.

There is some evidence of haste in the act of leaving the vessel. The sailors left their pipes. The main staysail was not furled. The wheel was left loose. The binnacle was displaced and the compass broken, probably in a clumsy attempt to get the compass quickly.

It may well have been that just at that time came an explosion which might have accounted for the fore hatch being upside down on deck, as found.[1] It was currently reported at the time that the captain left his watch and money in his desk and that money was found in the sailors' chests by the salvors – probably small sums of money if any, and the captain's watch probably became a keepsake for somebody. These articles do not appear in the court record and are not mentioned in the memorandum of personal effects which Mr. Sprague, the American Consul, submitted.

*Whatever happened, it is evident that the boat with ten people in her left the vessel and that the peak halyard was taken as a tow line and as a means of bringing the boat back **to** the* Mary Celeste *in case no explosion or fire had destroyed the vessel. Probably a fresh northerly wind sprang up, filled the squaresails and the vessel gathered way quickly. The peak halyard, made fast at the usual place on the gaff, would be brought at an acute angle across the bulwarks at the gangway. With the heavy boat standing still at the end, I do not wonder that the halyard parted. This would tally exactly with the evidence given in court that 'the peak halyard was broken and gone'. This fact was impressed upon the sailors as they had to get a coil of rope from the lazaret and reeve off a new peak halyard before they could set the mainsail.*

When the tow rope parted, these people were left in an open boat on the ocean as the brig sailed away from them. The wind that took the vessel away may have caused sea enough to wreck them. They perished – let us hope quickly. Nothing has appeared in all these sixty-seven years to tell us of their end. What we know and can surmise from the facts has been told here.[2]

The theory is attractive and has been given considerable credence. It suggests that normal activity had gone on aboard *Mary Celeste* until something happened with the cargo, ominous rumblings threatening an explosion or maybe there was an actual small explosion of gaseous fumes. There followed an ordered but hurried evacuation of the ship, the peak halyard being used to tie the yawl to *Mary Celeste* to keep the two together and enable those in the yawl to return to the ship in the event of the supposed danger not happening. The halyard in due course separated and the little yawl was cast adrift, soon to be capsized and drowning those aboard.

However, whilst it is true that *Mary Celeste* was carrying 1,700 barrels of alcohol and that any thought of an explosion in the vicinity of such a flammable cargo would certainly have been sufficient to panic even the most experienced of those on board, there is no evidence of an explosion aboard *Mary Celeste*. Oliver Deveau and his men did not see any sign of one, although it must be observed that the close packing of the cargo in the hold may have prevented signs of a minor explosion being visible, but John Austin, the Surveyor of Shipping at Gibraltar, saw no signs of an explosion either, and whilst he too may have missed them, there were no reports of any signs of an explosion when the cargo was unloaded in Genoa, where the cargo itself was in excellent condition. The possibility of fumes is an altogether different matter. *Dei Gratia* had sailed eight days after *Mary Celeste* and between 15 and 24 November the weather was too stormy for the hatches to be lifted, except for the main hatch which was lifted once for an hour only. If stormy weather had also prevented *Mary Celeste's* crew from lifting her hatches then explosive gases could have gradually accumulated in the hold during the voyage. Had there been any explosion in the hold then *Mary Celeste* would almost certainly have been destroyed and today would be a forgotten name in the tragic catalogue of vessels mysteriously lost at sea, but panic could have been caused if vapours were seen escaping from the hold and there has been a lot of discussion about the possibility that vapours could have been created by temperature changes between New York and the Azores. However, the temperature changes needn't worry us as they were small, 56°F in New York harbour and roughly 66°F off the Azores, insufficient to have materially affected the cargo. Overall, however, whether or not there were any fumes, they would have quickly dissipated when the hatch cover was lifted and it would have been seen that any anticipated danger had passed.

The idea advanced by Dr Cobb and others that the crew of *Mary Celeste* secured the yawl to the ship by the peak halyard – a rope used to hoist the sails – brings up a conflict in the testimony. Oliver Deveau said that the halyards were 'broke' and another crew member said they were 'broke and gone' – the meaning of 'gone' being the same then as it is now, as in 'ceased to function' (as we might say 'the lightbulb's gone') – but the Surveyor, John Austin, described the halyards as old, used for some time, and having not been spliced. Whether or not the yawl was secured to *Mary Celeste* by the main peak halyard, which duly snapped, is something we cannot know, but seems unlikely. To begin with, if, as Dr Cobb suggested, they feared that *Mary Celeste* was in danger of imminently being blown to smithereens, it's unlikely that anyone would have thought to unreeve what was probably over two hundred feet of rope or, indeed, see much point in securing the yawl to the vessel they thought about to explode. In fact, it is difficult to think of any reason why those aboard *Mary Celeste* would have wanted to secure the yawl to the ship – if they thought *Mary Celeste* was sinking, as was suggested by the ship having been sounded and the sounding rod being dropped to the deck, they would not have secured the yawl to the vessel by a rope, but one man, maybe Captain Briggs, who had a significant financial investment in *Mary Celeste*, or First Mate Albert Richardson would have stayed on board until certain she was sinking, then abandoned ship. Abandoning ship was not a decision to be lightly taken. It was an extreme action taken in a desperate situation, the last action of people who believed it to be the only way of saving their lives.

Another solution to the mystery is that *Mary Celeste* had become becalmed. The weather records add apparent support to such a possibility, it being recorded that there were calms and light airs around the islands of the Azores that morning. The theory suggests that the strong currents were carrying *Mary Celeste* towards the dangerous Dollabarat Rocks, some twenty miles from Santa Maria, and that the crew took to the yawl in an effort to reach the safety of land before the vessel ran aground but were swamped, and the winds picked up and carried *Mary Celeste* to safety and immortality in the realms of mystery. However, the set of the sails suggest that this was not the case because if the ship was becalmed the crew would have set every available sail to catch whatever wind there was. This had not been done. Furthermore, the idea of the ship being becalmed doesn't explain the ship having been sounded and the sounding rod being dropped to the deck, or the orderly but hurried evacuation. Nor would *Mary Celeste* have been abandoned by everyone on board or, indeed, by anyone on board, until running aground was inevitable.

A theory advanced on an internet site by Captain Dave Williams[3] takes a completely opposite point of view, arguing that far from the seas being calm, they were severely turbulent because of a 'seaquake' – an earthquake at sea – that caused the sea to rise and fall violently and erratically and for *Mary Celeste* to be shaken with such severity that nine barrels of alcohol were released from whatever secured them so that they broke open and emptied their contents into the hold, from where the alcohol quickly entered the bilges. He also suggests that the cooking stove had recently been used to cook a meal and that it emptied its still hot contents into the galley – open 'fire' and heavy alcohol fumes making a dangerous combination that caused the crew to fear an explosion.

Citing information from the Acoustics Division of the US Naval Research Laboratory, Captain Williams says that every year a major seaquake has happened within 60 miles of Santa Maria in the Azores and says that the area is one of the most seismically active areas in the world, home of the East Azores Fracture Zone and Gloria Fracture Zone. He also cites a source at the National Geophysical Data Center in Boulder, Colorado, as saying that although an 8.5 magnitude seaquake occurred in the area late in December 1872 and which might have been heralded by large foreshocks for up to a month before the event, the absence of seismic instruments and historical records makes it impossible to say whether a seaquake happened in November.

Captain Williams speculates that the crew were sounding the ship when the quake struck, which would explain the sounding rod being dropped to the deck. The violent shaking caused other damage, such as knocking the compass from its stand, and released nine barrels of alcohol so that the contents flowed out and into the bilges, permeating the whole ship with alcohol fumes. The crew lifted the hatches and opened the sky lights to release the fumes and try to air the lower decks. It is speculated that the stove, released from its chocks, was lit in preparation for cooking a meal, and spewed forth sparks and embers, threatening an explosion.

Captain Williams makes an interesting and valid observation that we don't have any description of the yawl carried aboard *Mary Celeste*, and he convincingly argues that it may have been large enough to accommodate everyone aboard, which would explain why it was lashed to the main hatch, being too big to be carried on the stern davits. He extrapolates that the yawl may therefore have been equipped with one or two sets of oars, a sail and maybe emergency provisions. Such a vessel could well have survived the seas for quite some time, as that was its purpose.

The theory is very appealing and Captain Williams proposes an explanation for most of the curious features aboard *Mary Celeste* – such as the hatches being lifted and skylights opened, and the theory deserves to be explored in greater detail and with full source citations, particularly for the claim by Captain Williams that five months after *Mary Celeste* was found abandoned two rafts were found off the coast of Spain with five badly decomposed bodies tied to them, one with an American flag. One would also like to see more accounts of seaquake encounters, particularly the reaction of those aboard ships that encountered them to see how they behaved, but the problem with the theory is that when *Mary Celeste*'s cargo was taken off the vessel there were nine empty barrels, their contents having apparently leaked during the voyage and a loss that the shippers seem to have accepted as within expectations. There seems to have been no suggestion that the barrels had broken free or been broken open by accident or design. If they had emptied as a consequence of natural seepage during the voyage or when the ship was in Gibraltar, then there would have been no alarming alcohol fumes.

Secondly, Oliver Deveau said that the galley did not show signs of having recently been used to prepare a meal or that a meal had been cleared away. It is possible that a meal had been cooked, eaten and everything washed up and tidied away, but that the stove remained lit, but there is no evidence for it and much depends on what meals would have been eaten aboard *Mary Celeste* and when, particularly whether a midday meal would have been prepared and what it would have been. We know that the crew were still aboard *Mary Celeste* at 8.00 a.m. because someone noted in the log that at that time the eastern point of Santa Maria was six miles distant. We know, too, that if normal practice had been maintained aboard ship there would have been further log entries at least at midday if not earlier had there been anybody aboard to make them. Their absence suggests that the ship was abandoned between 8.00 a.m. and midday. The unmade beds and the impression of a child's body in one of them would seem to suggest that either the child was unwell, or that the morning had not progressed very far when whatever happened happened. The state of the galley suggests that either breakfast hadn't been begun or that it had been eaten and cleared away, but nothing indicated that the steward had begun to prepare any lunch, assuming that a midday meal was eaten. There is therefore real doubt that the galley stove would have been lit.

Finally, if *Mary Celeste* had encountered a seaquake sufficiently violent to release and break open nine barrels of alcohol and possibly release the galley stove from its securings and empty its contents on the galley deck, other signs of the turbulence would surely have been visible. There was a phial of sewing machine oil in a perpendicular position, for example, and although one questions whether it could possibly have remained like that throughout the period between abandonment and the ship being examined in Gibraltar, the fact that the authorities seized upon it and argued that the ship otherwise showed no signs of having encountered violent or heavy seas, suggests that the vessel had not in fact encountered anything as violent as the seaquake suggests.

Finally and perhaps less importantly, the evidence seems to indicate that *Mary Celeste* was abandoned in an orderly but hurried fashion, those aboard doing little more than grabbing a few navigation instruments, but ignoring extra clothing, supplies and personal possessions, and abandonment suggests that whatever was feared likely to happen was thought to be so dangerous that it wasn't safe for anybody, not even Captain Briggs, to stay aboard. The seaquake theory does not allow for this. We have to allow for alcohol fumes to permeate the ship, with the crew taking the time to lift the hatches and open the skylights to allow fresh air into the ship. Presumably there would have been time, too, to get water to extinguish the cinders from the galley stove. The cargo *was* volatile and the possibility of an explosion must have been a constant anxiety, but lifting the hatch covers shows that steps would have been taken to lessen the danger. Would abandonment have seemed the safest and best option – particularly if the sea was still rough with aftershocks? – and even if it was, it must be doubted that it would have been the only option for everyone aboard.

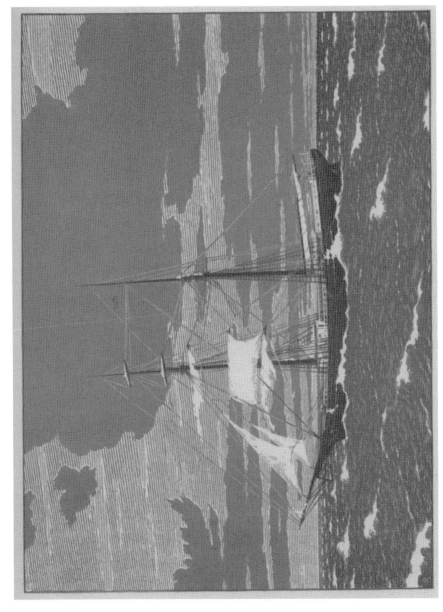

PLATE 1 ◆ *A wood engraving by Rudolph Ruzicka of Mary Celeste as she appeared when sighted by Dei Gratia.*
Peabody Essex Museum.

PLATE 2 ◆ *The Amazon, as Mary Celeste was known before being renamed. This unsigned painting, possibly by Honoré Pellegrin, was made at Marseille in November 1861.*

PLATE 3 ◆ *Captain Nathan Briggs, Benjamin's father, struck by lightning as he stood in the doorway of his home.*

From Oliver W. Cobb, *Rose Cottage*, Reynolds DeWalt, 1965.

PLATE 4 ◆ *Captain Benjamin Spooner Briggs shortly before he took command of* Mary Celeste.

New Bedford Whaling Museum.

PLATE 5 ◆ *Benjamin Spooner Briggs as a young man.*

Peabody Essex Museum.

PLATE 6 ◆ *Benjamin Spooner Briggs as a young man.*

Peabody Essex Museum.

PLATE 7 ◆ *Oliver Briggs, Benjamin's brother, lost at sea shortly before the disappearance from* Mary Celeste.

From George S. Bryan, *Mystery Ship: The Mary Celeste in Fancy and in Fact,* published by J.B. Lippincott, 1942, © HarperCollins.

PLATE 8 ◆ *Rose Cottage where Benjamin Spooner Briggs grew up in Marion, Massachusetts.*
From Oliver W. Cobb, *Rose Cottage*, Reynolds DeWalt, 1965.

PLATE 9 ◆ *Mrs Briggs and their son Arthur Stanley Briggs.*

Peabody Essex Museum.

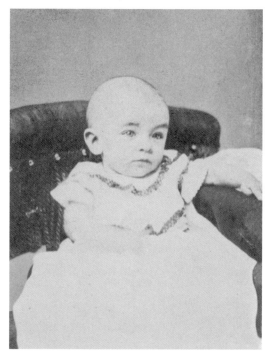

PLATE 10 ◆ *Sophia Matilda Briggs.*

PLATE 11 ◆ Mary Celeste *crew member Arian Martens and his wife.*

PLATE 12 ◆ *Albert G Richardson, first mate of* Mary Celeste.

Peabody Essex Museum.

PLATE 13 ◆ *Dei Gratia from a painting made at Messina, Sicily by Giuseppe Coli in April 1873.*

Peabody Essex Museum.

PLATE 14 ◆ *David Reed Morehouse, captain of* Dei Gratia.

Peabody Essex Museum.

PLATE 15 ◆ *Oliver Deveau, first mate of* Dei Gratia.

Peabody Essex Museum.

PLATE 16 ◆ *Mrs Briggs' melodeon.*

Peabody Essex Museum.

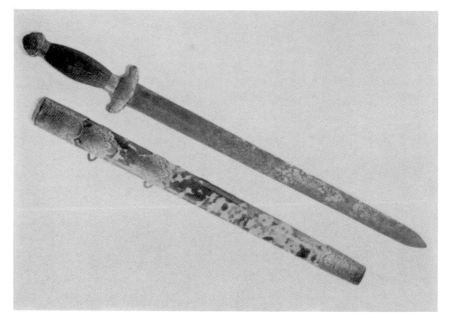

PLATE 17 ◆ *The sword believed to be the one found on board* Mary Celeste.

Peabody Essex Museum.

As with so many theories, the seaquake, though a very appealing and well-argued one, has the captain and crew abandoning ship in the aftermath of something having already happened and when to some degree they had already taken measures to combat its effects. Abandoning a ship for a small boat is a desperate measure and not one likely to be taken without extraordinarily good reason. It isn't something one would do because of something that *might* happen, it's something one does because one is absolutely certain that something *will* happen.

Gershom Bradford gives a highly plausible theory in his short but useful account of the *Mary Celeste* mystery[4] that was based initially on the blown-away sails and the quantity of water found below. When other theorists address these points it is usually assumed that both were caused by a squall that happened *after* the ship had been abandoned, but Mr Bradford points out that this would have meant that *Mary Celeste* had all five sails set when the yawl was launched, which would have been possible but extremely difficult to the point where Mr Bradford suggested that seamen with a knowledge of sail would probably conclude that the ship was abandoned *before* the sails were lost. I'm not so sure that this line of reasoning is accurate as many of those who studied the case in its early days, like Dr Cobb, had experience and/or knowledge of being under sail and if they didn't comment on the improbability of *Mary Celeste* being abandoned whilst under full sail, we should perhaps conclude that it was not quite as improbable as it seems. Nevertheless, Mr Bradford's observation is a valid one.

Mr Bradford also drew attention to the small hatches being uncovered when Deveau and his men first boarded *Mary Celeste*. The hatch covers were either lifted by members of the crew or they were blown off, the latter being deemed unlikely given the absence of any evidence of an explosion. The hatches could have been lifted to investigate noises in the hold or to release any gases and fumes that could have built up during the voyage, but this would have allowed the gases to escape and the potential for an explosion would have been less than the risks inherent in abandoning a ship under full sail and the dubious safety of the small and overloaded yawl.

The third key factor in Mr Bradford's deliberations was the amount of water in the 'tween decks, the galley and cabin. *Mary Celeste* was examined at the time and it was concluded that she had not been boarded by a heavy sea or been on her beam-ends, nor was she leaking. The water had entered the ship through the hatches, companionways and the skylight over the cabin. Whilst those aboard might have lifted the hatches during a storm if they feared an explosion in the hold, they would hardly have opened the cabin skylight. The open skylight therefore suggests that the ship was enjoying fair weather when she was abandoned and that the water *must* have entered the vessel *after* she had been abandoned and when there was nobody on board to shut the skylight and cover the hatchways. But, of course, this would mean that *Mary Celeste* had been under full sail when abandoned, which was possibly too hazardous to have been considered and means that the sails must have been torn away in a storm *before* abandonment. The contradictions make one's head spin, but Mr Bradford resolved this conundrum by postulating a waterspout.

The characteristics of a waterspout, he wrote, 'are: a vicious wind: a radical difference in barometric pressure between, that within the spout and that outside, and an accompanying deluge of water.' A waterspout would have hit the ship, the winds would have torn the sails away, the barometric pressure would have popped off the hatch covers, and water would have poured below.

A waterspout is a tornado at sea, a whirling column of wind and water, and within the waterspout the barometric pressure is dramatically low. They form when high layers of cool air blow across a body of water while warm moist air sweeps up from below; they can vary dramatically in size from a few feet to a mile or more in height and, importantly in their application to the Mary Celeste theory, they can measure from hundreds to just a few feet wide. They also move at different speeds, some moving as fast as 80 miles an hour, others 2 miles an hour, and the wind within the spout can vary from 60 to 120 miles an hour. It has been suggested by Dr Joseph Golden, a distinguished waterspout authority with the National Oceanic and Atmospheric Administration (NOAA), who conducted a lot of significant early research during the 1960s and 1970s and is the authority most commentators have followed, that a significant fraction of the so-called Bermuda Triangle incidents, a large proportion of which are losses of small boats, are caused by waterspouts, waterspouts being more common in the area of the Florida Keys than anywhere else in the world.[5] Waterspouts most often form in the regions of high water temperature, such as the typical area designated the Bermuda Triangle – the Gulf of Mexico, Florida Straits to the Bahamas and northward along the route of the Gulf Stream along the East Coast of the United States. At first glance the waterspout theory would therefore seem an implausible solution to the *Mary Celeste* mystery because she was a long way from the tropics when abandoned, but waterspouts are not restricted to warm water areas. They have been observed in cold weather and cold water; in December 1920, for example, witnesses aboard the steamer *British Marquis* reported that within two hours they had seen no fewer than 20 waterspouts in the English Channel. She avoided all of them, but one that suddenly formed directly ahead caused a screaming wind to sweep across her decks.

Waterspouts may also explain the Fortean phenomena or rains of strange objects from the sky: lizards that poured down over Montreal, tadpoles on New York, live fish on Providence, Rhode Island, and so on.

It is uncommon for a vessel to be struck by a waterspout, which is usually visible enough to be seen and for a vessel to take action to avoid. Nevertheless, there are several known examples. The *Lilian Morris*, a sailing ship, struck a 500-foot-wide waterspout that tore its masts, sails, and swept a man overboard. A story told in a copy of the *Nautical Magazine* cited by Gershom Bradford, who unfortunately doesn't give a date and which I have not been able to locate, records the experience of a Captain Steele of the ship *Mersey*, sailing from Liverpool to Oporto, Portugal, in 1842. He was some 36 miles off the coast when a waterspout passed his vessel and engulfed a schooner some distance ahead. Thunder boomed and lightning cracked overhead in a fearful storm, and when the waterspout passed after fifteen minutes the schooner was lost. Waterspouts also reportedly sank five ships at Tunis on the North African coast in 1885 and a tornadic waterspout that hit Port Royal Sound in South Carolina on 2 July 1814 sank the US schooner *Alligator* with a loss of 25 of its 40-man crew.

Willis E. Hurd, associate meteorologist in the Climate and Crop Weather Division of the Central Office of the Weather Bureau until his retirement in 1944, produced ocean-weather reports for publication in the *Monthly Weather Review* and for use of the Hydrographic Office of the Navy and the latter published many of his special articles on ocean weather on pilot charts, one of which referred to the barque *Ceylon*, struck by spout on 10 April 1885, her canvas stripped away, along with the main and mizzenmast, and the mate killed and other crewmembers injured.

The White Star liner *Pittsburgh* was struck head on by a waterspout in mid-Atlantic on 30 March 1923. Apparently the bridge and chart room were damaged and the officers' quarters were flooded. Sadly the *Pittsburgh*, having been renamed *Pennland*, was bombed and sunk on 25 April 1941 by German aircraft in the Gulf of Athens.

On 15 January 1956 a waterspout of considerable size engulfed a tug towing eight barges some seven miles off the coast of Japan, killing four men and sinking three of the barges. In 1980, a waterspout on San Antonio Bay in Texas struck a shrimp boat, flipping it over before it sank.

Could a waterspout have struck *Mary Celeste*? We know that on 24 November the vessel was experiencing westerly winds in the southern semi-circle of a depression that was passing to the north of *Mary Celeste*, and we know, too, that this was suitable to the creation of a waterspout. A relatively small and harmless spout, narrow and travelling at an angle, could have struck the ship without doing a great deal of damage; indeed, it would have left the vessel no worse than had she encountered a storm, but the barometric pressure within the spout would have been extremely low and as the spout passed over the ship the marked difference in pressure between the inside and outside of the ship could have caused the hatch covers to blow off – in the same way that the walls of a building explode outward when struck by a tornado.

We can't be any more certain about when *Mary Celeste* was abandoned than that it was before midday, but there was no evidence of food being prepared or cooked in the galley, the beds were unmade and there was an impression of a child in the bed. All this seems consistent with early morning, probably not long after the 8.00 a.m. log entry had been made. The waterspout probably appeared out of nowhere, as happened with the *British Marquis*, and hit *Mary Celeste* with a deluge of swirling water that blew off the hatches and tore away the sails. The captain and many of the crew, perhaps still asleep, would have been awakened suddenly and engulfed by this tumultuous hell of wind and water pouring into the cabins through the skylight.

As quickly as the hell had arrived, it went away. There would have been an eerie silence almost as terrifying as the sudden screech of winds in the spout, and the crew would have been shaken and disorientated. Uncertain of what had happened and how much water the ship had taken on, Captain Briggs would have ordered that the ship be sounded.

Here we have to allow for a piece of hypothesising. Mr Bradford suggests that the excessively low barometric pressure pushed bilge water up the pump well, where for a while it would have been prevented from returning to the hold by a valve in the lower box of the pump. If the ship was sounded, it would have appeared that she had taken on far more water than was the case, from which it would have been concluded that she was holed below the waterline. This was the opinion of Mate Deveau, it seems, for when asked in court to venture an opinion of the cause of the abandonment, he had said, 'My idea is that the crew got alarmed and by the sounding rod being found alongside the pump, that they had sounded the well and found a quantity of water in the pumps, at the moment, and thinking she would go down, abandoned her.'

Disorientated, scared, and now alarmed by the prospect of being aboard a rapidly sinking ship, the order is given for the yawl to be launched.

The theory doesn't answer all the questions. Although waterspouts can be strange things, as can tornados on land, one would nevertheless expect the sails and rigging overall to have displayed greater damage than they did. This doesn't completely negate the possibility of a waterspout striking *Mary Celeste*, but it is something to think about. Also, when launching the yawl it should have been apparent that *Mary Celeste* was not any lower in the water than usual, but it's equally possible that if gripped by panic and with the evidence of the sounding, this was ignored.

Whatever caused *Mary Celeste* to be abandoned, Mate Oliver Deveau's observation about the sounding rod is very likely the key to the solution. Someone had sounded the ship and they had dropped the sounding rod on the deck instead of replacing it where it was kept. This suggests that *Mary Celeste* was sounded shortly before being abandoned and that something about the sounding had caused considerable alarm and the sounding rod had simply been dropped on the deck. We can only assume that the sounding gave the impression that the ship was taking on water, but we know that she was not. Whatever those aboard *thought* had happened, be it an explosion in the hold or not, has to have given the impression that the vessel was taking on water. If it wasn't a waterspout, what could it have been?

Notes and references

1   That the hatch was found on the deck upside down appears to be one of the myths that found its way into even the most sober accounts of the mystery. The hatches appear to have been lifted in the normal fashion.

2   Oliver W. Cobb, *Rose Cottage*, New Bedford, MA: Reynolds-DeWalt Publishers, 1968.

3   'Was the Mary Celeste Abandoned During a Seaquake', http://www.deafwhale.com/maryceleste/

4   Gershom Bradford, *The Secret of Mary Celeste and Other Sea Fare*, London: Foulsham, 1967.

5   Quoted by Bruce B. Smith, 'Waterspouts', http://www.crh.noaa.gov/apx/science/spouts/waterspouts.htm

CHAPTER 12

Afterwards

The subsequent life of *Mary Celeste* is uncertainly known. One of her most recent biographers suggested that she 'rotted on the wharves where nobody wanted her,' but this certainly wasn't the case. From the surviving records it seems clear that Sylvester Goodwin, Daniel T. Sampson, and Sampson Hart, who apparently had lent Captain Briggs monies with which he'd bought *Mary Celeste*, all sold their shares to James H. Winchester, who was briefly the sole owner. On 10 October 1873 he sold a quarter share to J.Q. Pratt, who became the ship's new skipper, but the partnership was short-lived and on 3 February 1874 *Mary Celeste* was sold to a consortium consisting of Frederick H. Harrison and David G. Cartwright, who owned four eighths, John B. Wilson, two eighths, John Birkbeck one eighth and Edward Crabb one eighth. They appointed a non-shareholder, E.M. Tuthill, as captain. The consortium remained owners of *Mary Celeste* from February 1874 until February 1880, when they sold her to a man named Wesley A. Grove, who appointed T.L. Fleming as the captain. Grove quickly went into partnership with four other men, Andrew W. Martin, Charles A. Grant, John S. Weeks and Sidney F. Whitehouse. T.L. Fleming remained in command until 25 June 1884, when he was replaced by Gilman C. Parker.

Gilman C. Parker hailed from Winthrop, a coastal town in Suffolk County, Massachusetts, and named after a remarkable English-born Puritan leader, John Winthrop, who became the state's first governor. Gilman C. Parker does not appear to have shared many characteristics with Winthrop. We don't know a great deal about his career before taking command of *Mary Celeste*, but his subsequent actions do not suggest that he was a man distinguished for his probity.

On 4 August 1884 *Mary Celeste* was registered at Boston and on 8 August she sailed for Haiti. She returned to Boston on 8 November and spent the rest of the month and early December loading for another voyage to the Greater Antilles. The shippers were local businessmen:

> *Knowles Freeman and Sullivan A. Freeman, fish dealers, of 388 Atlantic Avenue;*
> *Raphael and Emile Boris, commission merchants, of 176 Atlantic Avenue;*
> *George W. Miller, brewer's agent and bottler, of 362 Atlantic Avenue;*
> *Abraham Q. Wendell, commission merchant, also of 362 Atlantic Avenue.*

According to her manifest *Mary Celeste* was carrying 4,000 lbs of butter, 150 barrels of flour, 30 bales of dry goods, 975 barrels of pickled herring, 125 casks of ale, 54 cases of women's high button boots, and a quantity of hardware, all insured with five separate companies for $30,000.

Just before *Mary Celeste* was due to sail, Captain Parker dismissed the first mate, Jacob A. Knoph, allegedly for being drunk, but it was later thought suspicious that Knoph had supervised the loading, knew what had been loaded aboard and hadn't been fired until the loading had been completed. Knoph knew too much! He was replaced by Joseph E. Howe of East Boston.

On 16 December *Mary Celeste* sailed for Port-au-Prince, the chief port and capital of Haiti. Wildly exotic, colourful, and blessed with a perfect tropical climate, Haiti is the western one-third of the island of Hispaniola – the Dominican Republic make up the other two thirds – the second-largest island of the Antilles. Christopher Columbus landed there in 1492 and in 1493 he founded the first Spanish colony in the New World. A successful slave rebellion in 1802 led to Haiti declaring independence from France on 1 January 1804, although its independence was not recognised by France until 1825. Haiti's independence made it the world's first black republic and it announced that it was committed to ending slavery everywhere. In so doing it made itself a threat to slave-owning countries like the United States which implemented sanctions against Haiti. The country's financial fortunes suffered further in 1852 when France demanded that Haiti repay former slaveholders compensation for freed slaves, a sum well over 100 million gold Louis (equivalent to over $21 billion today). The United States lifted sanctions in 1863 and allowed trade with Haiti in 1868, but Haiti never managed to become prosperous, as did the Dominican Republic, and even today is noted for its extreme poverty.

The coastal city of Port-au-Prince, the capital of Haiti since 1770, stands almost at the centre of a deep triangular bay called the Gulf of Gonave (Goife de la Gonâve). In the centre of the Gulf, dividing the water into two arms, is the large Gonave Island. The northern arm is known as St Marc Channel and the southern as Gonave Channel. In the Gonave Channel, between Gonave Island and the mainland, is a large coral reef called Rochelois Bank. It was well known and marked on all the maritime charts, but it was to be where *Mary Celeste* ended her life, deliberately run aground on the rocks as part of an insurance scam.

Mary Celeste carried seven men and after she was run aground they came ashore at Miragoane, a small town and minor port on the North Jacmel Peninsula, 50 miles (80 km) west of Port-au-Prince. Captain Parker visited the US Consul's agent there, a man named Mitchell, and handed over the certificate of registry. In due course what was salvageable of the cargo was taken off the ship and purchased by Mitchell. A claim was then made against the insurers of *Mary Celeste*'s cargo. The insurance companies instituted a routine investigation to ensure the accuracy of the claim and asked a New York-based marine surveyor named Kingman N. Putnam to investigate the wreck of the vessel on their behalf. Kingman N. Putnam was one of the sons of George Palmer Putnam, founder of the famous publishing company G.P. Putnam. He was already in Port-au-Prince preparing to leave for Aux Cays on the south coast of the country to check the facts of the loss of a schooner called *Mary L. Phipps*, but he agreed to travel from Aux Cays to Miragoane, a journey he had to undertake by horse. At Miragoane he discovered that Captain Parker had sold the whole of *Mary Celeste*'s cargo to Consular Agent Mitchell for $500 and that Mitchell still had some of the cases salvaged from the wreck. For some reason Mitchell allowed Putnam to open them and examine the contents. Putnam found that a case supposed to contain cutlery insured for $1,000 in fact held dog collars worth no more than $50. Another case supposed to contain high quality ladies' shoes, turned out to hold poor quality rubber overshoes.

Putnam arranged for several of the cases of goods to be transported to Boston and got a consular certificate from Mitchell stating that the goods had been part of *Mary Celeste*'s cargo.

Unfortunately no indictment could be framed against the Boston-based shippers and crew of *Mary Celeste* unless documents could be presented in which the consignees described the goods being shipped. Putnam was asked to return to Haiti and secure copies of letters from the shippers. He was given some extra clout by being appointed a United States deputy marshal and provided with subpoenas to bring Mitchell back to the United States. He knew, and hoped that Mitchell didn't, that the subpoenas had no legal jurisdiction outside the United States.

Putnam then discovered that there was no passenger vessel leaving for Haiti for several weeks, and realising the urgency of his mission he took the extraordinary step of obtaining passage aboard the British steamship *Saxon* masquerading with the skipper's agreement as the ship's chaplain because *Saxon* wasn't allowed to carry passengers.

On arrival in Miragoane Putnam was met by a Haitian general who informed him that he had instructions from the Haitian president, Gen. President Louis-Félicité Lysius Salomon, to have Mitchell forcibly put aboard *Saxon* if necessary and that he had a squad of soldiers for that task. Gen. Salomon, the great black nationalist president who had returned to Haiti from exile to replace the provincial government formed in July 1879 following the departure of Pierre Théoma Boisrond-Canal, in 1883 let loose his poor black followers on the business district of Part-au-Prince in an orgy of destruction and indiscriminate murder that passed into history as Bloody Week. He would retain power until his death in 1888. Putnam thought it ill-advised to have Haitian troops act on subpoenas that had no legal jurisdiction outside the United States and forcibly put a United States consular official aboard a British vessel that wasn't allowed to carry passengers and on which he, a recently appointed deputy marshal, had falsely travelled as a chaplain. Instead he went to visit Mitchell himself and found that Mitchell had headed for the hills – probably literally.

It became clear that *Mary Celeste* had been filled with a cargo of rubbish that had been falsely insured for considerably more than it was worth, and that *Mary Celeste* had then been deliberately run aground, this being a crime called barratry (a term which encompasses damaging a vessel and or its cargo through desertion, illegal scuttling, or theft) which carried the death penalty. The insurance companies hired a Boston lawyer named Henry Munro Rogers to act on their behalf, and Rogers in turn hired detectives to hang around the Boston waterfront and frequent the bars popular with seamen to pick up what fragments of information they could. Years later in recollections of a distinguished life, *Memories of Ninety Years*, Rogers all too briefly recalled in passing his involvement with *Mary Celeste*. Looking back on days when a legal practice was robust and rugged, he described how he had sometimes assumed the role of detective himself or had hired detectives to assist his legal inquiries:

> *Every lawyer has had in his practise cases that have topped all others in their facts, or law, or otherwise, that have made them unforgettable in his memory. In my own experience, I can recall almost every incident in three or four cases at least, which made my life at the time of preparation and trial like a drama wherein I was unfolding, act by act, what things were to be exposed, as one would turn and expose the seeds of a fig. In some cases I have been my own detective here and abroad. In others I have had skilled assistance from others. Prominent among these was the case of the* Marie Celeste *– a case of barratry first, and a case of conspiracy to defraud insurance companies contemporaneously entered upon.*[1]

There was no doubt that *Mary Celeste* had carried goods different from and of considerably lesser value than they had been insured for and it seems to have been pretty much an open but unstated secret that *Mary Celeste* had deliberately been run aground. Proving it was a different matter and having pieced together fragments of conversation the detectives learned that Gilman C. Parker was confident that his men would say nothing against him. The exception seems to have been Mate Joseph E. Howe whom Parker had put on board *Mary Celeste* just before she sailed. Howe was at sea skippering a ship from Hamburg that was expected to arrive in Boston any day and in due course the ship came into port; Rogers tracked Howe down and Howe, urged by his wife, openly told him what he knew and what he suspected and afterwards signed and swore to an affidavit. According to Howe, he discovered what Captain Parker had planned to do and that he intended running *Mary Celeste* aground on Grand Turk in the Bahamas. Howe was horrified and also knew that running aground on Grand Turk would endanger the lives of the crew. He vehemently urged Parker to find an alternative and Parker selected Rochelois Bank. With Howe as a witness and with his signed affidavit, Gilman C. Parker and the rest of the crew could be and were arrested.

After various delays the trial began on 23 July 1885 and was immediately adjourned to mourn General Ulysses S. Grant who had died at 8.06 that morning. Grant's body would lie in state in the State Capitol, Albany, before being taken by an escort of thousands of Civil War veterans to a temporary vault. The funeral was one of the most impressive ever held in New York and was attended by the highest officials. After a day or two of mourning for the dead president and saviour of the Union the trial began. Gilman C. Parker along with the shippers Abraham Q. Wendell, George W. Miller, Raphael Boris, Emile Boris, Sullivan A. Freeman and Knowles Freeman were charged with wilfully and corruptly conspiring to misrepresent the cargo and its value with the purpose of defrauding the insurance companies, namely New York Mutual Insurance Company, Commercial Mutual Insurance Company, Phoenix Insurance Company, Boston Marine Insurance Company and the Switzerland Marine Insurance Company of Zurich (with New York offices). The Massachusetts Assistant District Attorney, Warren K. Blodgett, appeared for the Federal Government, Captain Parker was represented by Stephen H. Tyng, and the other defendants were variously represented by Nathan Morse, Halsey J. Boardman, Prentiss Cummings and Edward W. Hutchins.

The shippers, who the *Boston Evening Transcript* described as men 'of excellent standing, as was testified by numerous witnesses called for the defence', were only charged with misrepresenting the cargo in an attempt to defraud the insurance companies, for which they could be fined $10,000 or be imprisoned for ten years. Against Parker there was the additional charge of barratry, for which he could be executed. When Assistant District Attorney Blodgett laid out his case before the court, charging that Captain Parker had 'wilfully cast away the ship', which was official language to describe deliberately wrecking *Mary Celeste* by running her aground, he said that Parker had done so with the knowledge and agreement of the other defendants. It promised to be an interesting case.

Captain Gilman C. Parker claimed that *Mary Celeste* had run aground because of an accident. He claimed that a seaman named Ernest Berthold was at the wheel of *Mary Celeste* and that he, Parker, had ordered him to put the wheel hard aport, but that Berthold had mistakenly put it to starboard. The error was almost immediately recognised and Berthold had tried to return the ship to port but *Mary Celeste* had refused to answer the helm. Those aboard had been unable to do anything and *Mary Celeste* had run aground. Parker protested that it had been nothing more than an accident and claimed that he 'had no more intention of wrecking the vessel than I had of cutting my throat. If the vessel had been put to port when I ordered it, I have no doubt we should have gone around the reef.' Parker added that he had no direct knowledge of Rochelois Bank and knew nothing of it beyond it having been mentioned to him during a previous voyage to Haiti by some fishermen.

A different story began to emerge as evidence was supplied by various witnesses. Ernest Berthold said that he had been at the wheel of *Mary Celeste* and that Captain Parker did not tell him to put hard aport but had said to maintain the ship's course. It would have been impossible to decide for sure who was telling the truth had it not been for a sailor named Jacob English, who unfortunately for Captain Parker was standing nearby when Parker gave his order to Berthold and was able to support Berthold's statement. Assistant DA Blodgett also pointed out that no mention of Berthold had been made in the protest filed by Parker in Haiti – a protest being an official statement made by a captain on his arrival in port after a misadventure in which a full and accurate account of the circumstances as recorded in the log-book is given, the account being made a legal deposition by being provided before a notary, justice of the peace, consul, or any such authorised officer. In his signed protest Captain Parker did not mention that Ernest Berthold had misunderstood an order, but instead gave the impression that *Mary Celeste* had become waterlogged.

Blodgett would also point out that Captain Parker's claim to have known nothing about Rochelois Bank was barely credible, Parker having testified to making numerous voyages to Haiti over the last six years and it being unbelievable that he hadn't learned about the landmark in that time. On top of which, the reef had been plainly visible long before the *Mary Celeste* struck.

The cargo was examined more closely. The manifest claimed that *Mary Celeste* was shipping bottled beer, but it proved to be ullage ale (waste beer left at the bottom of an empty cask) and furthermore, more bottles had been listed per barrel than would fit in a barrel. The butter listed on the manifest proved to be 'slush', an extremely poor quality melted fat, and the quantity shipped was almost half that declared. The manifest also indicated that more flour had been shipped than had in fact been the case, and examination revealed it to be of the lowest grade. Perhaps worst of all, nearly 1,000 barrels of pickled herrings shipped by Raphael Boris and insured for $4,875, proved to be spoiled fish and gave off an odour that left no doubt of it. The cargo, said Assistant District Attorney Blodgett, was not what was described on the manifest, was not of the quantity described on the manifest, and was not of the value for which it had been insured. He also pointed out that the goods shipped were not the sort of goods usually shipped to Haiti.

Next Blodgett drew attention to the fact that the loading of the cargo had been supervised by Mate Knoph, who had been discharged as soon as the loading was completed. Captain Parker claimed that Mate Knoph had been dismissed for being drunk, or 'over the bay' as Parker euphemistically expressed it, but Blodgett threw doubt on this claim, saying that Knoph had not been fired until the cargo of rubbish had been loaded, and that Knoph was the only person apart from Parker who knew the true nature of the cargo. The inference was that Knoph would know that the manifest did not represent the actual cargo, which put him in the position of being able to alert the insurance companies of the scam and was accordingly fired so that he wouldn't see the manifest.

By midday on 14 August the evidence had been presented and the jury had retired to consider their verdict. The jury deliberated throughout the night and returned at 9.00 a.m. the following day and reported that they had been unable to reach an agreement. The reason given was that whilst Parker and the shippers had all been indicted for conspiracy to defraud, a separate indictment had been brought against Parker for barratry. The barratry case had yet to be heard and because they were aware of this, some of the jury were unwilling to prejudice Parker's case by finding against him under the conspiracy indictment. The judge then explained that there were legal reasons that meant that Captain Parker could not now be brought to trial under the barratry indictment, although the Federal Government could bring another indictment against him. He pointed out that the current trial had been long and expensive and asked the jurors to retire for further discussion. At midday the jury returned, again unable to agree. The judge thanked and discharged them.

The insurers immediately requested a new trial, but the judge suggested that instead of going through the process of another long and costly trial he was prepared to put the case on the suspended list if the policyholders abandoned their policies and if Raphael Boris, who had already received nearly $5,000 for his shipment of rotten fish, returned the money with interest and paid a further $1,000 towards the cost of the court case. All the shippers duly acknowledged their guilt, agreed to the terms and walked from the court free men, technically without a stain on their character. But if the court of man could not punish these men for causing the 'death' of *Mary Celeste*, the curse that had bedevilled the ship since her first skipper Robert McLellan had died on her maiden voyage could reach beyond the vessel's watery grave and exact its own terrible retribution. As lawyer Rogers would later write:

> *The accused were freed by the law; but if all that was told of the sequel be true, a* debacle *ensued resembling that in 'Hamlet,' of which Schlegel remarked that 'the criminals are at last punished, but, as it were, by an accidental blow, and not in the solemn way requisite to convey to the world a warning example of Justice, and that the less guilty and the innocent are equally involved in the general ruin.'*[2]

The sedate newspaper the *Transcript* reported that one of the defendants, Abraham Q. Wendell, while waiting for the jury to return its verdict, had overnight lost his reason and become a raving, violent madman who it took two men to restrain. 'Whether or not this is temporary, or whether he is hopelessly insane, cannot yet be determined,' reported the newspaper. According to Kingman Putnam, another of the conspirators committed suicide, Gilman C. Parker died within three months in poverty and disrepute, all the other conspirators went out of business within six months, the steamship *Saxon*, which had conveyed Putnam to Haiti, was wrecked on her next voyage with the loss of all aboard, and the schooner *Mary E. Douglas*, which had conveyed some of *Mary Celeste*'s cargo to the United States, was likewise lost.

It is perhaps unsurprising that the possible punishment of the court had placed a physical and mental strain on the defendants under which one might collapse, as Wendell had done, and it is equally unsurprising that their crime would have damaged their reputations and the social stigma associated with the charges would have caused their businesses to collapse. Less explicable was the fate of the *Saxon* and *Mary E. Douglas*. As the New York *Sun* observed, 'How the foundering of the *Saxon*, and the *Mary E. Douglas*, associated with the last sinister event in the *Mary Celeste*'s career, can be accounted for, may be left to the psychologists and the weavers of sea romances.'

Notes and references

1   It is interesting to note that the impact of Conan Doyle's story and its aftermath led even Mr Rogers, writing in 1928, to call the vessel *Marie Celeste*. *Memories of Ninety Years*, New York: Houghon Mifflin, 1928.

2   Ibid.

CHAPTER 13

Mary Celeste – found?

In August 2001 news services and newspapers around the world carried a story that *Mary Celeste* had been found. Earlier that year Clive Cussler, the best-selling author of a series of maritime adventure novels featuring Dirk Pitt and Al Giordino of the National Underwater and Marine Agency (NUMA), and John Davis and an enthusiastic team from ECO-NOVA Productions, a Halifax, Nova Scotia-based television company, set out to find the last resting place of *Mary Celeste*, the adventure to feature as a documentary in the National Geographic *Sea Hunters* television series.[1]

If one believed that *Mary Celeste* was cursed, one might gain the impression from reading Mr Cussler's account of the expedition in his book *Sea Hunters II* that the jinx, though weakened after more than a century, was nevertheless strong enough to reach through time and from the depths of the sea to touch those about to disturb her grave. A series of problems beset Cussler: a man sent to meet him at Fort Lauderdale airport missed him and he had to make his way to the hotel on the shuttle bus; he then discovered that he'd forgotten his passport and although his wife sent the passport via the airline's courier service, the aircraft bringing it was late and, almost uniquely among the world's airlines, the flight to Haiti left an hour ahead of time because all the passengers had checked in; and not calmed by repeated reassurances that the Haitian authorities wouldn't care that he hadn't got his passport, the anxieties Cussler felt at the prospect of arriving without proper documentation in a third world country where brooding violence was ever present and frequently broke out, made the flight a far from relaxing journey. Cussler eventually bumped down on the weed, infested airstrip of Cape Haitian on the northern coast. Cape Haitian is not as large or as densely populated as Port-au-Prince in the south, but is nevertheless the country's second largest city and exhibits the same extreme poverty for which Cussler, an experienced traveller who had met with poverty and squalor in third world countries, seems to have been completely unprepared and by which he appears to have been both horrified and not unsurprisingly scared. The return trip was equally fraught, consisting of having air tickets that gave departure time in US rather than Haitian time, causing Cussler to arrive at the airport too late to catch the plane home and forcing him to spend an extra night in Haiti. There was a worrying time the following day when he learned that not having a passport might cause Haitian airline pilots to refuse to carry him because US immigration might refuse to allow him back into the country. As it happened he received his passport and got out of Haiti, but was almost trapped on Caicos Island where he disembarked when the plane refuelled and walked through the wrong door into a part of the airport where he enjoyed a convivial beer before discovering he couldn't get back from there to the plane. It all worked out in the end.

The search for *Mary Celeste* was also troubled. The group from Eco Nova had chartered the 54-foot steel-hulled *Ella Warley III*, a vessel specially designed and fitted out for wreck hunting and which they joined on Wednesday, 28 March 2001 at Highland Beach, Florida. The following day they departed but the seas in the Gulf Stream were too rough and the vessel took the inter-coastal waterway to Biscayne Bay, but a member of the Eco-Nova crew was allowed to pilot the vessel and he ran her aground. He had to spend the night with Alan Gardener, the owner, replacing a damaged prop. As they did so a fierce thunderstorm raged overhead.

Clive Cussler had gone to stay at a luxury Cormier Plage Hotel to await the arrival of *Ella Warley III*, and had a pleasant time there. For a while the curse seems to have lifted, but it was back soon after *Ella Warley III* arrived on 2 April, when the seas turned very rough. Cussler went aboard, accompanied by Jean-Claude Diquemar, the Creole-speaking owner of the Cormier Plage Hotel, a long-time friend of Gardner and one of the main cameramen working with the great marine researcher Jacques Cousteau, who made many memorable films and TV programmes in the

1950s. The team also included Mike Fletcher, master diver, and under-water photographers Robert Guertin and Lawrence Taylor. It was not a very pleasant voyage to Rochelois Reef.

Today a mini-village has grown up on the reef. Apparently about eighty years ago two conch-hunting brothers began living on the reef and over the years more people moved there and the number of discarded conch shells have raised the height to more than four feet above the water. There are about fifty shacks built on the 'island' from assorted flotsam, home to maybe two hundred people who live under a merciless Caribbean sun, all their food, water and other necessities brought from the mainland twelve miles distant. These locals were curious about what Cussler and his team were up to, but were satisfied when told they were there to make a movie, an explanation supplemented by ten gallons of petrol and a case of Coca-Cola.

Discovering the wreckage – or the few scattered remains – of *Mary Celeste* was quickly achieved. Using a caesium marine magnetometer, the team began circling the reef in search of magnetic anomalies. These are caused by ferrous material such as steel and iron disturbing the local magnetic field, and a magnetometer is used to detect and measure the intensity of the fluctuations. Because even wooden ships like *Mary Celeste* had iron fittings, detecting these fluctuations or anomalies can indicate the presence of a wreck. There are different types of magnetometer, the caesium magnetometer used by the team being the most sensitive and proving the fastest response rate.

Fifty-yards offshore, dead centre of Rochelois Reef, precisely where a vessel coming from the east was likely to have struck, they got a single ten-gamma reading on the computer monitor. Fletcher and Guertin went into the water and half an hour later emerged with some old wood with brass spikes driven through, some copper sheathing and ballast rocks. It came from a shipwreck, but whether or not it came from *Mary Celeste* was altogether a different matter. The bulk of the wreck lay beyond mortal reach, now part of the beautiful coral growth, only a few pieces of wood and one or two other artefacts remaining to be salvaged. The site was excavated, the position of every artefact noted, even videotaped in its position, everything was tagged and catalogued, then the team sailed back through two days of choppy seas to the Cormier Plage Hotel, having spent seven days without setting foot on dry land.

The artefacts were given to Alan Ruffman, President and Director of Geomarine Associates Limited, based in Halifax, Nova Scotia, a geoscience consulting firm specialising in marine and petroleum geology and geophysics, who coordinated the scientific testing of the wood and ballast stones to see if it could be determined what they were and whether they were likely to have come from the area where *Mary Celeste* was constructed. A noted marine archaeologist James Delgado, who had participated in expeditions to the wreck of RMS *Titanic*, the *Carpathia* and USS *Arizona*, and who co-hosted the television series *The Sea Hunters*, and is otherwise Director of the Vancouver Maritime Museum, examined the copper sheathing. The rock ballast appeared to be basalt, a hard, black volcanic rock – the most common rock type on Earth – that had a texture and mineralogy characteristic of the North Mountains of Nova Scotia. The wood was identified as yellow birch, common to the Maritimes, white pine, common to the northeast United States and Canada, and southern pine, a wood used extensively by New York shipbuilders such as those who would have been responsible for the enlargements to *Mary Celeste* before Captain Briggs set sail. The copper sheathing was Muntz metal, used in the 1860s and after to protect hulls from shipworms. The most remarkable – and surprising – piece of evidence, however, was research undertaken on Clive Cussler's behalf that showed that *Mary Celeste* was the only vessel recorded as having run aground on Rochelois Reef and not been pulled off.

It seemed there could be no doubt that the remains of *Mary Celeste* had been found.

But had they?

At the GeoDaze Conference hosted by the Department of Geosciences, University of Arizona, between 1–3 April 2004, Scott St George delivered a paper entitled 'Tree-ring dating and the mystery of the *Mary Celeste*' in which he claimed that two of the three species of wood (*Quercus alba* L. and *Betula alleghaniensis* Britt.) claimed by the NUMA team to be from species of tree native to Northern New England and the Canadian Maritime provinces, were not in fact endemic to Nova Scotia and were widespread over much of north eastern North America. Perhaps more significantly, the *Pinus palustris* (Mill.) timbers, the largest recovered from the wreck, came from the Longleaf Pine, a species not native to Canada, but common to the south eastern US. This was the wood it is supposed that was used when *Mary Celeste* was refitted in New York before sailing with Captain Briggs in command. According to Scott St George, however, dendrochronological dating indicates that this wood was from trees still living, probably somewhere near south-western Georgia, at least 10 years after the *Mary Celeste* sank!

Perhaps, then, *Mary Celeste* has had the last laugh.

Notes and references

1   I appeared on the programme when it was broadcast in the United Kingdom on Channel 5.

J. Habakuk Jephson's Statement

'J. Habakuk Jephson's Statement' by Arthur Conan Doyle is probably the most influential tale ever written about *Mary Celeste*. It not only caused the ship's name to become popularly known as '*Marie Celeste*', but it also gave us the foundation for many of the common misconceptions about the ship, and whilst 'J. Habakuk Jephson's Statement' may not rank as great literature, it does have the distinction of being an early work by one of popular literature's greatest names. It is therefore a story that deserves to be read and enjoyed, and no apology is given or needed for including it here.

'J. Habakuk Jephson's Statement', by Arthur Conan Doyle

In the month of December in the year 1873, the British ship Dei Gratia steered into Gibraltar, having in tow the derelict brigantine Marie Celeste, which had been picked up in latitude 38 degrees 40', longitude 17 degrees 15' W. There were several circumstances in connection with the condition and appearance of this abandoned vessel which excited considerable comment at the time, and aroused a curiosity which has never been satisfied. What these circumstances were was summed up in an able article which appeared in the *Gibraltar Gazette*. The curious can find it in the issue for January 4, 1874, unless my memory deceives me. For the benefit of those, however, who may be unable to refer to the paper in question, I shall subjoin a few extracts which touch upon the leading features of the case.

'We have ourselves,' says the anonymous writer in the *Gazette*, 'been over the derelict Marie Celeste, and have closely questioned the officers of the Dei Gratia on every point which might throw light on the affair. They are of opinion that she had been abandoned several days, or perhaps weeks, before being picked up. The official log, which was found in the cabin, states that the vessel sailed from Boston to Lisbon, starting upon October 16. It is, however, most imperfectly kept, and affords little information. There is no reference to rough weather, and, indeed, the state of the vessel's paint and rigging excludes the idea that she was abandoned for any such reason. She is perfectly watertight. No signs of a struggle or of violence are to be detected, and there is absolutely nothing to account for the disappearance of the crew. There are several indications that a lady was present on board, a sewing-machine being found in the cabin and some articles of female attire. These probably belonged to the captain's wife, who is mentioned in the log as having accompanied her husband. As an instance of the mildness of the weather, it may be remarked that a bobbin of silk was found standing upon the sewing-machine, though the least roll of the vessel would have precipitated it to the floor. The boats were intact and slung upon the davits; and the cargo, consisting of tallow and American clocks, was untouched. An old-fashioned sword of curious workmanship was discovered among some lumber in the forecastle, and this weapon is said to exhibit a longitudinal striation on the steel, as if it had been recently wiped. It has been placed in the hands of the police, and submitted to Dr Monaghan, the analyst, for inspection. The result of his examination has not yet been published. We may remark, in conclusion, that Captain Dalton, of the Dei Gratia, an able and intelligent seaman, is of opinion that the Marie Celeste may have been abandoned a considerable distance from the spot at which she was picked up, since a powerful current runs up in that latitude from the African coast. He confesses his inability, however, to advance any hypothesis which can reconcile all the facts of the case. In the utter absence of a clue or grain of evidence, it is to be feared that the fate of the crew of the Marie Celeste will be added to those numerous mysteries of the deep which will never be solved until the great day when the sea shall give up its dead. If crime has been committed, as is much to be suspected, there is little hope of bringing the perpetrators to justice.'

I shall supplement this extract from the *Gibraltar Gazette* by quoting a telegram from Boston, which went the round of the English papers, and represented the total amount of information which had been collected about the *Marie Celeste*. 'She was,' it said, 'a brigantine of 170 tons burden, and belonged to White, Russell & White, wine importers, of this city. Captain J.W. Tibbs was an old servant of the firm, and was a man of known ability and tried probity. He was accompanied by his wife, aged thirty-one, and their youngest child, five years old. The crew consisted of seven hands, including two coloured seamen, and a boy. There were three passengers, one of whom was the well-known Brooklyn specialist on consumption, Dr. Habakuk Jephson, who was a distinguished advocate for Abolition in the early days of the movement, and whose pamphlet, entitled "Where is thy Brother?" exercised a strong influence on public opinion before the war. The other passengers were Mr. J. Harton, a writer in the employ of the firm, and Mr. Septimius Goring, a half-caste gentleman, from New Orleans. All investigations have failed to throw any light upon the fate of these fourteen human beings. The loss of Dr. Jephson will be felt both in political and scientific circles.'

I have here epitomised, for the benefit of the public, all that has been hitherto known concerning the *Marie Celeste* and her crew, for the past ten years have not in any way helped to elucidate the mystery. I have now taken up my pen with the intention of telling all that I know of the ill-fated voyage. I consider that it is a duty which I owe to society, for symptoms which I am familiar with in others lead me to believe that before many months my tongue and hand may be alike incapable of conveying information. Let me remark, as a preface to my narrative, that I am Joseph Habakuk Jephson, Doctor of Medicine of the University of Harvard, and ex-Consulting Physician of the Samaritan Hospital of Brooklyn.

Many will doubtless wonder why I have not proclaimed myself before, and why I have suffered so many conjectures and surmises to pass unchallenged. Could the ends of justice have been served in any way by my revealing the facts in my possession I should unhesitatingly have done so. It seemed to me, however, that there was no possibility of such a result; and when I attempted, after the occurrence, to state my case to an

English official, I was met with such offensive incredulity that I determined never again to expose myself to the chance of such an indignity. I can excuse the discourtesy of the Liverpool magistrate, however, when I reflect upon the treatment which I received at the hands of my own relatives, who, though they knew my unimpeachable character, listened to my statement with an indulgent smile as if humouring the delusion of a monomaniac. This slur upon my veracity led to a quarrel between myself and John Vanburger, the brother of my wife, and confirmed me in my resolution to let the matter sink into oblivion – a determination which I have only altered through my son's solicitations. In order to make my narrative intelligible, I must run lightly over one or two incidents in my former life which throw light upon subsequent events.

My father, William K. Jephson, was a preacher of the sect called Plymouth Brethren, and was one of the most respected citizens of Lowell. Like most of the other Puritans of New England, he was a determined opponent to slavery, and it was from his lips that I received those lessons which tinged every action of my life. While I was studying medicine at Harvard University, I had already made a mark as an advanced Abolitionist; and when, after taking my degree, I bought a third share of the practice of Dr. Willis, of Brooklyn, I managed, in spite of my professional duties, to devote a considerable time to the cause which I had at heart, my pamphlet, 'Where is thy Brother?' (Swarburgh, Lister & Co., 1859) attracting considerable attention.

When the war broke out I left Brooklyn and accompanied the 113th New York Regiment through the campaign. I was present at the second battle of Bull's Run and at the battle of Gettysburg. Finally, I was severely wounded at Antietam, and would probably have perished on the field had it not been for the kindness of a gentleman named Murray, who had me carried to his house and provided me with every comfort. Thanks to his charity, and to the nursing which I received from his black domestics, I was soon able to get about the plantation with the help of a stick. It was during this period of convalescence that an incident occurred which is closely connected with my story.

Among the most assiduous of the negresses who had watched my couch during my illness there was one old crone who appeared to exert considerable authority over the others. She was exceedingly attentive to me, and I gathered from the few words that passed between us that she had heard of me, and that she was grateful to me for championing her oppressed race.

One day as I was sitting alone in the verandah, basking in the sun, and debating whether I should rejoin Grant's army, I was surprised to see this old creature hobbling towards me. After looking cautiously around to see that we were alone, she fumbled in the front of her dress and produced a small chamois leather bag which was hung round her neck by a white cord.

'Massa,' she said, bending down and croaking the words into my ear, 'Me die soon. Me very old woman. Not stay long on Massa Murray's plantation.'

'You may live a long time yet, Martha,' I answered. 'You know I am a doctor. If you feel ill let me know about it, and I will try to cure you.'

'No wish to live – wish to die. I'm gwine to join the heavenly host.' Here she relapsed into one of those half-heathenish rhapsodies in which negroes indulge. 'But, massa, me have one thing must leave behind me when I go. No able to take it with me across the Jordan. That one thing very precious, more precious and more holy than all thing else in the world. Me, a poor old black woman, have this because my people, very great people, 'spose they was back in the old country. But you cannot understand this same as black folk could. My fader give it me, and his fader give it him, but now who shall I give it to? Poor Martha hab no child, no relation, nobody. All round I see black man very bad man. Black woman very stupid woman. Nobody worthy of the stone. And so I say, Here is Massa Jephson who write books and fight for coloured folk – he must be good man, and he shall have it though he is white man, and nebber can know what it mean or where it came from.' Here the old woman fumbled in the chamois leather bag and pulled out a flattish black stone with a hole through the middle of it. 'Here, take it,' she said, pressing it into my hand; 'take it. No harm nebber come from anything good. Keep it safe – nebber lose it!' and with a warning gesture the old crone hobbled away in the same cautious way as she had come, looking from side to side to see if we had been observed.

I was more amused than impressed by the old woman's earnestness, and was only prevented from laughing during her oration by the fear of hurting her feelings. When she was gone I took a good look at the stone which she had given me. It was intensely black, of extreme hardness, and oval in shape – just such a flat stone as one would pick up on the seashore if one wished to throw a long way.

It was about three inches long, and an inch and a half broad at the middle, but rounded off at the extremities. The most curious part about it were several well-marked ridges which ran in semicircles over its surface, and gave it exactly the appearance of a human ear. Altogether I was rather interested in my new possession, and determined to submit it, as a geological specimen, to my friend Professor Shroeder of the New York Institute, upon the earliest opportunity. In the meantime I thrust it into my pocket, and rising from my chair started off for a short stroll in the shrubbery, dismissing the incident from my mind.

As my wound had nearly healed by this time, I took my leave of Mr. Murray shortly afterwards. The Union armies were everywhere victorious and converging on Richmond, so that my assistance seemed unnecessary, and I returned to Brooklyn. There I resumed my practice, and married the second daughter of Josiah Vanburger, the well-known wood engraver. In the course of a few years I built up a good connection and acquired considerable reputation in the treatment of pulmonary complaints. I still kept the old black stone in my pocket, and frequently told the story of the dramatic way in which I had become possessed of it. I also kept my resolution of showing it to Professor Shroeder, who was much interested both by the anecdote and the specimen. He pronounced it to be a piece of meteoric stone, and drew my attention to the fact that its resemblance to an ear was not accidental, but that it was most carefully worked into that shape. A dozen little anatomical points showed that the worker had been as accurate as he was skilful. 'I should not wonder,' said the Professor, 'if it were broken off from some larger statue, though how such hard material could be so perfectly worked is more than I can understand. If there is a statue to correspond I should like to see it!' So I thought at the time, but I have changed my opinion since.

The next seven or eight years of my life were quiet and uneventful. Summer followed spring, and spring followed winter, without any variation in my duties. As the practice increased I admitted J.S. Jackson as partner, he to have one-fourth of the profits. The continued strain had told upon my constitution, however, and I became at last so unwell that my wife insisted upon my consulting Dr. Kavanagh Smith, who was my colleague at the Samaritan Hospital.

That gentleman examined me, and pronounced the apex of my left lung to be in a state of consolidation, recommending me at the same time to go through a course of medical treatment and to take a long sea-voyage. My own disposition, which is naturally restless, predisposed me strongly in favour of the latter piece of advice, and the matter was clinched by my meeting young Russell, of the firm of White, Russell & White, who offered me a passage in one of his father's ships, the *Marie Celeste*, which was just starting from Boston. 'She is a snug little ship,' he said, 'and Tibbs, the captain, is an excellent fellow. There is nothing like a sailing ship for an invalid.' I was very much of the same opinion myself, so I closed with the offer on the spot.

My original plan was that my wife should accompany me on my travels. She has always been a very poor sailor, however, and there were strong family reasons against her exposing herself to any risk at the time, so we determined that she should remain at home. I am not a religious or an effusive man; but oh, thank God for that! As to leaving my practice, I was easily reconciled to it, as Jackson, my partner, was a reliable and hard-working man.

I arrived in Boston on October 12, 1873, and proceeded immediately to the office of the firm in order to thank them for their courtesy. As I was sitting in the counting-house waiting until they should be at liberty to see me, the words *Marie Celeste* suddenly attracted my attention. I looked round and saw a very tall, gaunt man, who was leaning across the polished mahogany counter asking some questions of the clerk at the other side.

His face was turned half towards me, and I could see that he had a strong dash of negro blood in him, being probably a quadroon or even nearer akin to the black. His curved aquiline nose and straight lank hair showed the white strain; but the dark restless eye, sensuous mouth, and gleaming teeth all told of his African origin. His complexion was of a sickly, unhealthy yellow, and as his face was deeply pitted with small-pox, the general impression was so unfavourable as to be almost revolting. When he spoke, however, it was in a soft, melodious voice, and in well-chosen words, and he was evidently a man of some education. 'I wished to ask a few questions about the *Marie Celeste*,' he repeated, leaning across to the clerk. 'She sails the day after to-morrow, does she not?'

'Yes, sir,' said the young clerk, awed into unusual politeness by the glimmer of a large diamond in the stranger's shirt front.

'Where is she bound for?'

'Lisbon.'

'How many of a crew?'

'Seven, sir.'

'Passengers?'

'Yes, two. One of our young gentlemen, and a doctor from New York.'

'No gentleman from the South?' asked the stranger eagerly.

'No, none, sir.'

'Is there room for another passenger?'

'Accommodation for three more,' answered the clerk.

'I'll go,' said the quadroon decisively; 'I'll go, I'll engage my passage at once. Put it down, will you – Mr. Septimius Goring, of New Orleans.'

The clerk filled up a form and handed it over to the stranger, pointing to a blank space at the bottom. As Mr. Goring stooped over to sign it I was horrified to observe that the fingers of his right hand had been lopped off, and that he was holding the pen between his thumb and the palm. I have seen thousands slain in battle, and assisted at every conceivable surgical operation, but cannot recall any sight which gave me such a thrill of disgust as that great brown sponge-like hand with the single member protruding from it. He used it skilfully enough, however, for, dashing off his signature, he nodded to the clerk and strolled out of the office just as Mr. White sent out word that he was ready to receive me.

I went down to the *Marie Celeste* that evening, and looked over my berth, which was extremely comfortable considering the small size of the vessel. Mr. Goring, whom I had seen in the morning, was to have the one next mine. Opposite was the captain's cabin and a small berth for Mr. John Harton, a gentleman who was going out in the interests of the firm. These little rooms were arranged on each side of the passage which led from the main-deck to the saloon. The latter was a comfortable room, the panelling tastefully done in oak and mahogany, with a rich Brussels carpet and luxurious settees. I was very much pleased with the accommodation, and also with Tibbs the captain, a bluff, sailor-like fellow, with a loud voice and hearty manner, who welcomed me to the ship with effusion, and insisted upon our splitting a bottle of wine in his cabin. He told me that he intended to take his wife and youngest child with him on the voyage, and that he hoped with good luck to make Lisbon in three weeks. We had a pleasant chat and parted the best of friends, he warning me to make the last of my preparations next morning, as he intended to make a start by the midday tide, having now shipped all his cargo. I went back to my hotel, where I found a letter from my wife awaiting me, and, after a refreshing night's sleep, returned to the boat in the morning.

From this point I am able to quote from the journal which I kept in order to vary the monotony of the long sea-voyage. If it is somewhat bald in places I can at least rely upon its accuracy in details, as it was written conscientiously from day to day.

October 16.—Cast off our warps at half-past two and were towed out into the bay, where the tug left us, and with all sail set we bowled along at about nine knots an hour. I stood upon the poop watching the low land of America sinking gradually upon the horizon until the evening haze hid it from my sight. A single red light, however, continued to blaze balefully behind us, throwing a long track like a trail of blood upon the water, and it is still visible as I write, though reduced to a mere speck. The Captain is in a bad humour, for two of his hands disappointed him at the last moment, and he was compelled to ship a couple of negroes who happened to be on the quay. The missing men were steady, reliable fellows, who had been with him several voyages, and their non-appearance puzzled as well as irritated him. Where a crew of seven men have to work a fair-sized ship the loss of two experienced seamen is a serious one, for though the negroes may take a spell at the wheel or swab the decks, they are of little or no use in rough weather. Our cook is also a black man, and Mr. Septimius Goring has a little darkie servant, so that we are rather a piebald community. The accountant, John Harton, promises to be an acquisition, for he is a cheery, amusing young fellow. Strange how little wealth has to do with happiness! He has all the world before him and is seeking his fortune in a far land, yet he is as transparently happy as a man can be. Goring is rich, if I am not mistaken, and so am I; but I know that I have a lung, and Goring has some deeper trouble still, to judge by his features. How poorly do we both contrast with the careless, penniless clerk!

October 17.—Mrs. Tibbs appeared upon deck for the first time this morning – a cheerful, energetic woman, with a dear little child just able to walk and prattle. Young Harton pounced on it at once, and carried it away to his cabin, where no doubt he will lay the seeds of future dyspepsia in the child's stomach. Thus medicine doth make cynics of us all! The weather is still all that could be desired, with a fine fresh breeze from the west-sou'-west. The vessel goes so steadily that you would hardly know that she was moving were it not for the creaking of the cordage, the bellying of the sails, and the long white furrow in our wake. Walked the quarter-deck all morning with the Captain, and I think the keen fresh air has already done my breathing good, for the exercise did not fatigue me in any way. Tibbs is a remarkably intelligent man, and we had an interesting argument about Maury's observations on ocean currents, which we terminated by going down into his cabin to consult the original work. There we found Goring, rather to the Captain's surprise, as it is not usual for passengers to enter that sanctum unless specially invited. He apologised for his intrusion, however, pleading his ignorance of the usages of ship life; and the good-natured sailor simply laughed at the incident, begging him to remain and favour us with his company. Goring pointed to the chronometers, the case of which he had opened, and remarked that he had been admiring them. He has evidently some practical knowledge of mathematical instruments, as he told at a glance which was the most trustworthy of the three, and also named their price within a few dollars. He had a discussion with the Captain too upon the variation of the compass, and when we came back to the ocean currents he showed a thorough grasp of the subject. Altogether he rather improves upon acquaintance, and is a man of decided culture and refinement. His voice harmonises with his conversation, and both are the very antithesis of his face and figure. The noonday observation shows that we have run two hundred and twenty miles. Towards evening the breeze freshened up, and the first mate ordered reefs to be taken in the topsails and top-gallant sails in expectation of a windy night. I observe that the barometer has fallen to twenty-nine. I trust our voyage will not be a rough one, as I am a poor sailor, and my health would probably derive more harm than good from a stormy trip, though I have the greatest confidence in the Captain's seamanship and in the soundness of the vessel. Played cribbage with Mrs. Tibbs after supper, and Harton gave us a couple of tunes on the violin.

October 18.—The gloomy prognostications of last night were not fulfilled, as the wind died away again, and we are lying now in a long greasy swell, ruffled here and there by a fleeting catspaw which is insufficient to fill the sails. The air is colder than it was yesterday, and I have put on one of the thick woollen jerseys which my wife knitted for me. Harton came into my cabin in the morning, and we had a cigar together. He says that he remembers having seen Goring in Cleveland, Ohio, in '69. He was, it appears, a mystery then as now, wandering about without any visible employment, and extremely reticent on his own affairs. The man interests me as a psychological study. At breakfast this morning I suddenly had that vague feeling of uneasiness which comes over some people when closely stared at, and, looking quickly up, I met his eyes bent upon me with an intensity which amounted to ferocity, though their expression instantly softened as he made some conventional remark upon the weather. Curiously enough, Harton says that he had a very similar experience yesterday upon deck. I observe that Goring frequently talks to the coloured seamen as he strolls about – a trait which I rather admire, as it is common to find half-breeds ignore their dark strain and treat their black kinsfolk with greater intolerance than a white man would do. His little page is devoted to him, apparently, which speaks well for his treatment of him. Altogether, the man is a curious mixture of incongruous qualities, and unless I am deceived in him will give me food for observation during the voyage.

The Captain is grumbling about his chronometers, which do not register exactly the same time. He says it is the first time that they have ever disagreed. We were unable to get a noonday observation on account of the haze. By dead reckoning, we have done about a hundred and seventy miles in the twenty-four hours. The dark seamen have proved, as the skipper prophesied, to be very inferior hands, but as they can both manage the wheel well they are kept steering, and so leave the more experienced men to work the ship. These details are trivial enough, but a small thing serves as food for gossip aboard ship. The appearance of a whale in the evening caused quite a flutter among us. From its sharp back and forked tail, I should pronounce it to have been a rorqual, or 'finner,' as they are called by the fishermen.

October 19.—Wind was cold, so I prudently remained in my cabin all day, only creeping out for dinner. Lying in my bunk I can, without moving, reach my books, pipes, or anything else I may want, which is one advantage of a small apartment. My old wound began to ache a little to-day, probably from the cold. Read 'Montaigne's Essays' and nursed myself. Harton came in in the afternoon with Doddy, the Captain's child, and the skipper himself followed, so that I held quite a reception.

October 20 and 21.—Still cold, with a continual drizzle of rain, and I have not been able to leave the cabin. This confinement makes me feel weak and depressed. Goring came in to see me, but his company did not tend to cheer me up much, as he hardly uttered a word, but contented himself with staring at me in a peculiar and rather irritating manner. He then got up and stole out of the cabin without saying anything. I am beginning to suspect that the man is a lunatic. I think I mentioned that his cabin is next to mine. The two are simply divided by a thin wooden partition which is cracked in many places, some of the cracks being so large that I can hardly avoid, as I lie in my bunk, observing his motions in the adjoining room. Without any wish to play the spy, I see him continually stooping over what appears to be a chart and working with a pencil and compasses. I have remarked the interest he displays in matters connected with navigation, but I am surprised that he should take the trouble to work out the course of the ship. However, it is a harmless amusement enough, and no doubt he verifies his results by those of the Captain.

I wish the man did not run in my thoughts so much. I had a nightmare on the night of the 20th, in which I thought my bunk was a coffin, that I was laid out in it, and that Goring was endeavouring to nail up the lid, which I was frantically pushing away. Even when I woke up, I could hardly persuade myself that I was not in a coffin. As a medical man, I know that a nightmare is simply a vascular derangement of the cerebral hemispheres, and yet in my weak state I cannot shake off the morbid impression which it produces.

October 22.—A fine day, with hardly a cloud in the sky, and a fresh breeze from the sou'-west which wafts us gaily on our way. There has evidently been some heavy weather near us, as there is a tremendous swell on, and the ship lurches until the end of the fore-yard nearly touches the water. Had a refreshing walk up and down the quarter-deck, though I have hardly found my sea-legs yet. Several small birds – chaffinches, I think – perched in the rigging.

4.40 P.M.—While I was on deck this morning I heard a sudden explosion from the direction of my cabin, and, hurrying down, found that I had very nearly met with a serious accident. Goring was cleaning a revolver, it seems, in his cabin, when one of the barrels which he thought was unloaded went off. The ball passed through the side partition and embedded itself in the bulwarks in the exact place where my head usually rests.

I have been under fire too often to magnify trifles, but there is no doubt that if I had been in the bunk it must have killed me. Goring, poor fellow, did not know that I had gone on deck that day, and must therefore have felt terribly frightened. I never saw such emotion in a man's face as when, on rushing out of his cabin with the smoking pistol in his hand, he met me face to face as I came down from deck. Of course, he was profuse in his apologies, though I simply laughed at the incident.

11 P.M.—A misfortune has occurred so unexpected and so horrible that my little escape of the morning dwindles into insignificance. Mrs. Tibbs and her child have disappeared – utterly and entirely disappeared. I can hardly compose myself to write the sad details. About half-past eight Tibbs rushed into my cabin with a very white face and asked me if I had seen his wife. I answered that I had not. He then ran wildly into the saloon and began groping about for any trace of her, while I followed him, endeavouring vainly to persuade him that his fears were ridiculous. We hunted over the ship for an hour and a half without coming on any sign of the missing woman or child. Poor Tibbs lost his voice completely from calling her name. Even the sailors, who are generally stolid enough, were deeply affected by the sight of him as he roamed bareheaded and dishevelled about the deck, searching with feverish anxiety the most impossible places, and returning to them again and again with a piteous pertinacity. The last time she was seen was about seven o'clock, when she took Doddy on to the poop to give him a breath of fresh air before putting him to bed. There was no one there at the time except the black seaman at the wheel, who denies having seen her at all. The whole affair is wrapped in mystery. My own theory is that while Mrs. Tibbs was holding the child and standing near the bulwarks it gave a spring and fell overboard, and that in her convulsive attempt to catch or save it, she followed it. I cannot account for the double disappearance in any other way. It is quite feasible that such a tragedy should be enacted without the knowledge of the man at the wheel, since it was dark at the time, and the peaked skylights of the saloon screen the greater part of the quarter-deck. Whatever the truth may be it is a terrible catastrophe, and has cast the darkest gloom upon our voyage. The mate has put the ship about, but of course there is not the slightest hope of picking them up. The Captain is lying in a state of stupor in his cabin. I gave him a powerful dose of opium in his coffee that for a few hours at least his anguish may be deadened.

October 23.—Woke with a vague feeling of heaviness and misfortune, but it was not until a few moments' reflection that I was able to recall our loss of the night before. When I came on deck I saw the poor skipper standing gazing back at the waste of waters behind us which contains everything dear to him upon earth. I attempted to speak to him, but he turned brusquely away, and began pacing the deck with his head sunk upon his breast. Even now, when the truth is so clear, he cannot pass a boat or an unbent sail without peering under it. He looks ten years older than he did yesterday morning. Harton is terribly cut up, for he was fond of little Doddy, and Goring seems sorry too. At least he has shut himself up in his cabin all day, and when I got a casual glance at him his head was resting on his two hands as if in a melancholic reverie. I fear we are about as dismal a crew as ever sailed. How shocked my wife will be to hear of our disaster! The swell has gone down now, and we are doing about eight knots with all sail set and a nice little breeze. Hyson is practically in command of the ship, as Tibbs, though he does his best to bear up and keep a brave front, is incapable of applying himself to serious work.

October 24.—Is the ship accursed? Was there ever a voyage which began so fairly and which changed so disastrously? Tibbs shot himself through the head during the night. I was awakened about three o'clock in the morning by an explosion, and immediately sprang out of bed and rushed into the Captain's cabin to find out the cause, though with a terrible presentiment in my heart. Quickly as I went, Goring went more quickly still, for he was already in the cabin stooping over the dead body of the Captain. It was a hideous sight, for the whole front of his face was blown in, and the little room was swimming in blood. The pistol was lying beside him on the floor, just as it had dropped from his hand. He had evidently put it to his mouth before pulling the trigger. Goring and I picked him reverently up and laid him on his bed. The crew had all clustered into his cabin, and the six white men were deeply grieved, for they were old hands who had sailed with him many years. There were dark looks and murmurs among them too, and one of them openly declared that the ship was haunted. Harton helped to lay the poor skipper out, and we did him up in canvas between us. At twelve o'clock the foreyard was hauled aback, and we committed his body to the deep, Goring reading the Church of England burial service. The breeze has freshened up, and we have done ten knots all day and sometimes twelve.

The sooner we reach Lisbon and get away from this accursed ship the better pleased shall I be. I feel as though we were in a floating coffin.

Little wonder that the poor sailors are superstitious when I, an educated man, feel it so strongly.

October 25.—Made a good run all day. Feel listless and depressed.

October 26.—Goring, Harton, and I had a chat together on deck in the morning. Harton tried to draw Goring out as to his profession, and his object in going to Europe, but the quadroon parried all his questions and gave us no information. Indeed, he seemed to be slightly offended by Harton's pertinacity, and went down into his cabin. I wonder why we should both take such an interest in this man! I suppose it is his striking appearance, coupled with his apparent wealth, which piques our curiosity. Harton has a theory that he is really a detective, that he is after some criminal who has got away to Portugal, and that he chooses this peculiar way of travelling that he may arrive unnoticed and pounce upon his quarry unawares. I think the supposition is rather a far-fetched one, but Harton bases it upon a book which Goring left on deck, and which he picked up and glanced over. It was a sort of scrap-book it seems, and contained a large number of newspaper cuttings. All these cuttings related to murders which had been committed at various times in the States during the last twenty years or so. The curious thing which Harton observed about them, however, was that they were invariably murders the authors of which had never been brought to justice. They varied in every detail, he says, as to the manner of execution and the social status of the victim, but they uniformly wound up with the same formula that the murderer was still at large, though, of course, the police had every reason to expect his speedy capture. Certainly the incident seems to support Harton's theory, though it may be a mere whim of Goring's, or, as I suggested to Harton, he may be collecting materials for a book which shall outvie De Quincey. In any case it is no business of ours.

October 27, 28.—Wind still fair, and we are making good progress. Strange how easily a human unit may drop out of its place and be forgotten! Tibbs is hardly ever mentioned now; Hyson has taken possession of his cabin, and all goes on as before. Were it not for Mrs. Tibbs's sewing-machine upon a side-table we might forget that the unfortunate family had ever existed. Another accident occurred on board to-day, though fortunately not a very serious one. One of our white hands had gone down the afterhold to fetch up a spare coil of rope, when one of the hatches which he had removed came crashing down on the top of him. He saved his life by springing out of the way, but one of his feet was terribly crushed, and he will be of little use for the remainder of the voyage. He attributes the accident to the carelessness of his negro companion, who had helped him to shift the hatches. The latter, however, puts it down to the roll of the ship. Whatever be the cause, it reduces our shorthanded crew still further. This run of ill-luck seems to be depressing Harton, for he has lost his usual good spirits and joviality. Goring is the only one who preserves his cheerfulness. I see him still working at his chart in his own cabin. His nautical knowledge would be useful should anything happen to Hyson – which God forbid!

October 29, 30.—Still bowling along with a fresh breeze. All quiet and nothing of note to chronicle.

October 31.—My weak lungs, combined with the exciting episodes of the voyage, have shaken my nervous system so much that the most trivial incident affects me. I can hardly believe that I am the same man who tied the external iliac artery, an operation requiring the nicest precision, under a heavy rifle fire at Antietam. I am as nervous as a child. I was lying half dozing last night about four bells in the middle watch trying in vain to drop into a refreshing sleep. There was no light inside my cabin, but a single ray of moonlight streamed in through the port hole, throwing a silvery flickering circle upon the door. As I lay I kept my drowsy eyes upon this circle, and was conscious that it was gradually becoming less well-defined as my senses left me, when I was suddenly recalled to full wakefulness by the appearance of a small dark object in the very centre of the luminous disc. I lay quietly and breathlessly watching it. Gradually it grew larger and plainer, and then I perceived that it was a human hand which had been cautiously inserted through the chink of the half-closed door – a hand which, as I observed with a thrill of horror, was not provided with fingers. The door swung cautiously backwards, and Goring's head followed his hand. It appeared in the centre of the moonlight, and was framed as it were in a ghastly uncertain halo, against which his features showed out plainly. It seemed to me that I had never seen such an utterly fiendish and merciless expression upon a human face. His eyes were dilated and glaring, his lips drawn back so as to show his white fangs, and his straight black hair appeared to bristle over his low forehead like the hood of a cobra. The sudden and noiseless apparition had such an effect upon me that I sprang up in bed trembling in every limb, and held out my hand towards my revolver. I was heartily ashamed of my hastiness when he explained the object of his intrusion, as he immediately did in the most courteous language. He had been suffering from toothache, poor fellow! and had come in to beg some laudanum, knowing that I possessed a medicine chest. As to a sinister expression he is never a beauty, and what with my state of nervous tension and the effect of the shifting moonlight it was easy to conjure up something horrible. I gave him twenty drops, and he went off again with many expressions of gratitude. I can hardly say how much this trivial incident affected me. I have felt unstrung all day.

A week's record of our voyage is here omitted, as nothing eventful occurred during the time, and my log consists merely of a few pages of unimportant gossip.

November 7.—Harton and I sat on the poop all the morning, for the weather is becoming very warm as we come into southern latitudes. We reckon that we have done two-thirds of our voyage. How glad we shall be to see the green banks of the Tagus, and leave this unlucky ship for ever! I was endeavouring to amuse Harton today and to while away the time by telling him some of the experiences of my past life. Among others I related to him how I came into the possession of my black stone, and as a finale I rummaged in the side pocket of my old shooting coat and produced the identical object in question. He and I were bending over it together, I pointing out to him the curious ridges upon its surface, when we were conscious of a shadow falling between us and the sun, and looking round saw Goring standing behind us glaring over our shoulders at the stone. For some reason or other he appeared to be powerfully excited, though he was evidently trying to control himself and to conceal his emotion. He pointed once or twice at my relic with his stubby thumb before he could recover himself sufficiently to ask what it was and how I obtained it – a question put in such a brusque manner that I should have been offended had I not known the man to be an eccentric. I told him the story very much as I had told it to Harton. He listened with the deepest interest, and then asked me if I had any idea what the stone was. I said I had not, beyond that it was meteoric. He asked me if I had ever tried its effect upon a negro. I said I had not. 'Come,' said he, 'we'll see what our black friend at the wheel thinks of it.' He took the stone in his hand and went across to the sailor, and the two examined it carefully. I could see the man gesticulating and nodding his head excitedly as if making some assertion, while his face betrayed the utmost astonishment, mixed I think with some reverence. Goring came across the deck to us presently, still holding the stone in his hand. 'He says it is a worthless, useless thing,' he said, 'and fit only to be chucked overboard,' with which he raised his hand and would most certainly have made an end of my relic, had the black sailor behind him not rushed forward and seized him by the wrist. Finding himself secured Goring dropped the stone and turned away with a very bad grace to avoid my angry remonstrances at his breach of faith. The black picked up the stone and handed it to me with a low bow and every sign of profound respect. The whole affair is inexplicable.

I am rapidly coming to the conclusion that Goring is a maniac or something very near one. When I compare the effect produced by the stone upon the sailor, however, with the respect shown to Martha on the plantation, and the surprise of Goring on its first production, I cannot but come to the conclusion that I have really got hold of some powerful talisman which appeals to the whole dark race. I must not trust it in Goring's hands again.

November 8, 9.—What splendid weather we are having! Beyond one little blow, we have had nothing but fresh breezes the whole voyage. These two days we have made better runs than any hitherto.

It is a pretty thing to watch the spray fly up from our prow as it cuts through the waves. The sun shines through it and breaks it up into a number of miniature rainbows – 'sun-dogs,' the sailors call them. I stood on the fo'csle-head for several hours today watching the effect, and surrounded by a halo of prismatic colours.

The steersman has evidently told the other blacks about my wonderful stone, for I am treated by them all with the greatest respect. Talking about optical phenomena, we had a curious one yesterday evening which was pointed out to me by Hyson. This was the appearance of a triangular well-defined object high up in the heavens to the north of us. He explained that it was exactly like the Peak of Teneriffe as seen from a great distance – the peak was, however, at that moment at least five hundred miles to the south.

It may have been a cloud, or it may have been one of those strange reflections of which one reads. The weather is very warm. The mate says that he never knew it so warm in these latitudes. Played chess with Harton in the evening.

November 10.—It is getting warmer and warmer. Some land birds came and perched in the rigging today, though we are still a considerable way from our destination. The heat is so great that we are too lazy to do anything but lounge about the decks and smoke. Goring came over to me today and asked me some more questions about my stone; but I answered him rather shortly, for I have not quite forgiven him yet for the cool way in which he attempted to deprive me of it.

November 11, 12.—Still making good progress. I had no idea Portugal was ever as hot as this, but no doubt it is cooler on land. Hyson himself seemed surprised at it, and so do the men.

November 13.—A most extraordinary event has happened, so extraordinary as to be almost inexplicable. Either Hyson has blundered wonderfully, or some magnetic influence has disturbed our instruments. Just about daybreak the watch on the fo'csle-head shouted out that he heard the sound of surf ahead, and Hyson thought he saw the loom of land. The ship was put about, and, though no lights were seen, none of us doubted that we had struck the Portuguese coast a little sooner than we had expected. What was our surprise to see the scene which was revealed to us at break of day! As far as we could look on either side was one long line of surf, great, green billows rolling in and breaking into a cloud of foam. But behind the surf what was there! Not the green banks nor the high cliffs of the shores of Portugal, but a great sandy waste which stretched away and away until it blended with the skyline. To right and left, look where you would, there was nothing but yellow sand, heaped in some places into fantastic mounds, some of them several hundred feet high, while in other parts were long stretches as level apparently as a billiard board.

Harton and I, who had come on deck together, looked at each other in astonishment, and Harton burst out laughing. Hyson is exceedingly mortified at the occurrence, and protests that the instruments have been tampered with. There is no doubt that this is the mainland of Africa, and that it was really the Peak of Teneriffe which we saw some days ago upon the northern horizon. At the time when we saw the land birds we must have been passing some of the Canary Islands. If we continued on the same course, we are now to the north of Cape Blanco, near the unexplored country which skirts the great Sahara. All we can do is to rectify our instruments as far as possible and start afresh for our destination.

8.30 P.M.—Have been lying in a calm all day. The coast is now about a mile and a half from us. Hyson has examined the instruments, but cannot find any reason for their extraordinary deviation.

This is the end of my private journal, and I must make the remainder of my statement from memory. There is little chance of my being mistaken about facts which have seared themselves into my recollection. That very night the storm which had been brewing so long burst over us, and I came to learn whither all those little incidents were tending which I had recorded so aimlessly. Blind fool that I was not to have seen it sooner! I shall tell what occurred as precisely as I can.

I had gone into my cabin about half-past eleven, and was preparing to go to bed, when a tap came at my door. On opening it I saw Goring's little black page, who told me that his master would like to have a word with me on deck. I was rather surprised that he should want me at such a late hour, but I went up without hesitation. I had hardly put my foot on the quarter-deck before I was seized from behind, dragged down upon my back, and a handkerchief slipped round my mouth. I struggled as hard as I could, but a coil of rope was rapidly and firmly wound round me, and I found myself lashed to the davit of one of the boats, utterly powerless to do or say anything, while the point of a knife pressed to my throat warned me to cease my struggles. The night was so dark that I had been unable hitherto to recognise my assailants, but as my eyes became accustomed to the gloom, and the moon broke out through the clouds that obscured it, I made out that I was surrounded by the two negro sailors, the black cook, and my fellow-passenger Goring. Another man was crouching on the deck at my feet, but he was in the shadow and I could not recognise him.

All this occurred so rapidly that a minute could hardly have elapsed from the time I mounted the companion until I found myself gagged and powerless. It was so sudden that I could scarce bring myself to realise it, or to comprehend what it all meant. I heard the gang round me speaking in short, fierce whispers to each other, and some instinct told me that my life was the question at issue. Goring spoke authoritatively and angrily —

the others doggedly and all together, as if disputing his commands. Then they moved away in a body to the opposite side of the deck, where I could still hear them whispering, though they were concealed from my view by the saloon skylights. All this time the voices of the watch on deck chatting and laughing at the other end of the ship were distinctly audible, and I could see them gathered in a group, little dreaming of the dark doings which were going on within thirty yards of them. Oh! that I could have given them one word of warning, even though I had lost my life in doing it I but it was impossible. The moon was shining fitfully through the scattered clouds, and I could see the silvery gleam of the surge, and beyond it the vast weird desert with its fantastic sand-hills. Glancing down, I saw that the man who had been crouching on the deck was still lying there, and as I gazed at him, a flickering ray of moonlight fell full upon his upturned face. Great Heaven! even now, when more than twelve years have elapsed, my hand trembles as I write that, in spite of distorted features and projecting eyes, I recognised the face of Harton, the cheery young clerk who had been my companion during the voyage. It needed no medical eye to see that he was quite dead, while the twisted handkerchief round the neck, and the gag in his mouth, showed the silent way in which the hell-hounds had done their work. The clue which explained every event of our voyage came upon me like a flash of light as I gazed on poor Harton's corpse. Much was dark and unexplained, but I felt a great dim perception of the truth. I heard the striking of a match at the other side of the skylights, and then I saw the tall, gaunt figure of Goring standing up on the bulwarks and holding in his hands what appeared to be a dark lantern. He lowered this for a moment over the side of the ship, and, to my inexpressible astonishment, I saw it answered instantaneously by a flash among the sand-hills on shore, which came and went so rapidly, that unless I had been following the direction of Goring's gaze, I should never have detected it. Again he lowered the lantern, and again it was answered from the shore.

He then stepped down from the bulwarks, and in doing so slipped, making such a noise, that for a moment my heart bounded with the thought that the attention of the watch would be directed to his proceedings. It was a vain hope. The night was calm and the ship motionless, so that no idea of duty kept them vigilant. Hyson, who after the death of Tibbs was in command of both watches, had gone below to snatch a few hours' sleep, and the boatswain who was left in charge was standing with the other two men at the foot of the foremast. Powerless, speechless, with the cords cutting into my flesh and the murdered man at my feet, I awaited the next act in the tragedy.

The four ruffians were standing up now at the other side of the deck. The cook was armed with some sort of a cleaver, the others had knives, and Goring had a revolver. They were all leaning against the rail and looking out over the water as if watching for something. I saw one of them grasp another's arm and point as if at some object, and following the direction I made out the loom of a large moving mass making towards the ship. As it emerged from the gloom I saw that it was a great canoe crammed with men and propelled by at least a score of paddles. As it shot under our stern the watch caught sight of it also, and raising a cry hurried aft. They were too late, however. A swarm of gigantic negroes clambered over the quarter, and led by Goring swept down the deck in an irresistible torrent. All opposition was overpowered in a moment, the unarmed watch were knocked over and bound, and the sleepers dragged out of their bunks and secured in the same manner.

Hyson made an attempt to defend the narrow passage leading to his cabin, and I heard a scuffle, and his voice shouting for assistance. There was none to assist, however, and he was brought on to the poop with the blood streaming from a deep cut in his forehead. He was gagged like the others, and a council was held upon our fate by the negroes. I saw our black seamen pointing towards me and making some statement, which was received with murmurs of astonishment and incredulity by the savages. One of them then came over to me, and plunging his hand into my pocket took out my black stone and held it up. He then handed it to a man who appeared to be a chief, who examined it as minutely as the light would permit, and muttering a few words passed it on to the warrior beside him, who also scrutinised it and passed it on until it had gone from hand to hand round the whole circle. The chief then said a few words to Goring in the native tongue, on which the quadroon addressed me in English. At this moment I seem to see the scene. The tall masts of the ship with the moonlight streaming down, silvering the yards and bringing the network of cordage Into hard relief; the group of dusky warriors leaning on their spears; the dead man at my feet; the line of white-faced prisoners, and in front of me the loathsome half-breed, looking in his white linen and elegant clothes a strange contrast to his associates.

'You will bear me witness,' he said in his softest accents, 'that I am no party to sparing your life. If it rested with me you would die as these other men are about to do. I have no personal grudge against either you or them, but I have devoted my life to the destruction of the white race, and you are the first that has ever been in my power and has escaped me. You may thank that stone of yours for your life. These poor fellows reverence it, and indeed if it really be what they think it is they have cause. Should it prove when we get ashore that they are mistaken, and that its shape and material is a mere chance, nothing can save your life. In the meantime we wish to treat you well, so if there are any of your possessions which you would like to take with you, you are at liberty to get them.' As he finished he gave a sign, and a couple of the negroes unbound me, though without removing the gag. I was led down into the cabin, where I put a few valuables into my pockets, together with a pocket-compass and my journal of the voyage. They then pushed me over the side into a small canoe, which was lying beside the large one, and my guards followed me, and shoving off began paddling for the shore. We had got about a hundred yards or so from the ship when our steersman held up his hand, and the paddlers paused for a moment and listened. Then on the silence of the night I heard a sort of dull, moaning sound, followed by a succession of splashes in the water. That is all I know of the fate of my poor shipmates. Almost immediately afterwards the large canoe followed us, and the deserted ship was left drifting about – a dreary, spectre-like hulk. Nothing was taken from her by the savages. The whole fiendish transaction was carried through as decorously and temperately as though it were a religious rite.

The first grey of daylight was visible in the east as we passed through the surge and reached the shore. Leaving half-a-dozen men with the canoes, the rest of the negroes set off through the sand-hills, leading me with them, but treating me very gently and respectfully. It was difficult walking, as we sank over our ankles into the loose, shifting sand at every step, and I was nearly dead beat by the time we reached the native village, or town rather, for it was a place of considerable dimensions. The houses were conical structures not unlike bee-hives, and were made of compressed seaweed cemented over with a rude form of mortar, there being neither stick nor stone upon the coast nor anywhere within many hundreds of miles. As we entered the town an enormous crowd of both sexes came swarming out to meet us, beating tom-toms and howling and screaming. On seeing me they redoubled their yells and assumed a threatening attitude, which was instantly quelled by a few words shouted by my escort. A buzz of wonder succeeded the war-cries and yells of the moment before, and the whole dense mass proceeded down the broad central street of the town, having my escort and myself in the centre.

My statement hitherto may seem so strange as to excite doubt in the minds of those who do not know me, but it was the fact which I am now about to relate which caused my own brother-in-law to insult me by disbelief. I can but relate the occurrence in the simplest words, and trust to chance and time to prove their truth. In the centre of this main street there was a large building, formed in the same primitive way as the others, but towering high above them; a stockade of beautifully polished ebony rails was planted all round it, the framework of the door was formed by two magnificent elephant's tusks sunk in the ground on each side and meeting at the top, and the aperture was closed by a screen of native cloth richly embroidered with gold. We made our way to this imposing-looking structure, but, on reaching the opening in the stockade, the multitude stopped and squatted down upon their hams, while I was led through into the enclosure by a few of the chiefs and elders of the tribe, Goring accompanying us, and in fact directing the proceedings. On reaching the screen which closed the temple – for such it evidently was – my hat and my shoes were removed, and I was then led in, a venerable old negro leading the way carrying in his hand my stone, which had been taken from my pocket. The building was only lit up by a few long slits in the roof, through which the tropical sun poured, throwing broad golden bars upon the clay floor, alternating with intervals of darkness.

The interior was even larger than one would have imagined from the outside appearance. The walls were hung with native mats, shells, and other ornaments, but the remainder of the great space was quite empty, with the exception of a single object in the centre. This was the figure of a colossal negro, which I at first thought to be some real king or high priest of titanic size, but as I approached it I saw by the way in which the light was reflected from it that it was a statue admirably cut in jet-black stone. I was led up to this idol, for such it seemed to be, and looking at it closer I saw that though it was perfect in every other respect, one of its ears had been broken short off. The grey-haired negro who held my relic mounted upon a small stool, and stretching up his arm fitted Martha's black stone on to the jagged surface on the side of the statue's head. There could not be a doubt that the one had been broken off from the other. The parts dovetailed together so accurately that when the old man removed his hand the ear stuck in its place for a few seconds before dropping into his open palm.

The group round me prostrated themselves upon the ground at the sight with a cry of reverence, while the crowd outside, to whom the result was communicated, set up a wild whooping and cheering. In a moment I found myself converted from a prisoner into a demi-god. I was escorted back through the town in triumph, the people pressing forward to touch my clothing and to gather up the dust on which my foot had trod. One of the largest huts was put at my disposal, and a banquet of every native delicacy was served me. I still felt, however, that I was not a free man, as several spearmen were placed as a guard at the entrance of my hut. All day my mind was occupied with plans of escape, but none seemed in any way feasible. On the one side was the great arid desert stretching away to Timbuctoo, on the other was a sea untraversed by vessels. The more I pondered over the problem the more hopeless did it seem. I little dreamed how near I was to its solution.

Night had fallen, and the clamour of the negroes had died gradually away. I was stretched on the couch of skins which had been provided for me, and was still meditating over my future, when Goring walked stealthily into the hut. My first idea was that he had come to complete his murderous holocaust by making away with me, the last survivor, and I sprang up upon my feet, determined to defend myself to the last. He smiled when he saw the action, and motioned me down again while he seated himself upon the other end of the couch.

'What do you think of me?' was the astonishing question with which he commenced our conversation.

'Think of you!' I almost yelled. 'I think you the vilest, most unnatural renegade that ever polluted the earth. If we were away from these black devils of yours I would strangle you with my hands!'

'Don't speak so loud,' he said, without the slightest appearance of irritation. 'I don't want our chat to be cut short. So you would strangle me, would you!' he went on, with an amused smile. 'I suppose I am returning good for evil, for I have come to help you to escape.'

'You!' I gasped incredulously.

'Yes, I,' he continued.

'Oh, there is no credit to me in the matter. I am quite consistent. There is no reason why I should not be perfectly candid with you. I wish to be king over these fellows – not a very high ambition, certainly, but you know what Caesar said about being first in a village in Gaul. Well, this unlucky stone of yours has not only saved your life, but has turned all their heads so that they think you are come down from heaven, and my influence will be gone until you are out of the way. That is why I am going to help you to escape, since I cannot kill you' – this in the most natural and dulcet voice, as if the desire to do so were a matter of course.

'You would give the world to ask me a few questions,' he went on, after a pause; 'but you are too proud to do it. Never mind, I'll tell you one or two things, because I want your fellow white men to know them when you go back – if you are lucky enough to get back. About that cursed stone of yours, for instance. These negroes, or at least so the legend goes, were Mahometans originally. While Mahomet himself was still alive, there was a schism among his followers, and the smaller party moved away from Arabia, and eventually crossed Africa. They took away with them, in their exile, a valuable relic of their old faith in the shape of a large piece of the black stone of Mecca. The stone was a meteoric one, as you may have heard, and in its fall upon the earth it broke into two pieces. One of these pieces is still at Mecca. The larger piece was carried away to Barbary, where a skilful worker modelled it into the fashion which you saw to-day. These men are the descendants of the original seceders from Mahomet, and they have brought their relic safely through all their wanderings until they settled in this strange place, where the desert protects them from their enemies.'

'And the ear?' I asked, almost involuntarily.

'Oh, that was the same story over again. Some of the tribe wandered away to the south a few hundred years ago, and one of them, wishing to have good luck for the enterprise, got into the temple at night and carried off one of the ears. There has been a tradition among the negroes ever since that the ear would come back some day. The fellow who carried it was caught by some slaver, no doubt, and that was how it got into

America, and so into your hands – and you have had the honour of fulfilling the prophecy.'

He paused for a few minutes, resting his head upon his hands, waiting apparently for me to speak. When he looked up again, the whole expression of his face had changed. His features were firm and set, and he changed the air of half levity with which he had spoken before for one of sternness and almost ferocity. 'I wish you to carry a message back,' he said, 'to the white race, the great dominating race whom I hate and defy. Tell them that I have battened on their blood for twenty years, that I have slain them until even I became tired of what had once been a joy, that I did this unnoticed and unsuspected in the face of every precaution which their civilisation could suggest. There is no satisfaction in revenge when your enemy does not know who has struck him. I am not sorry, therefore, to have you as a messenger. There is no need why I should tell you how this great hate became born in me. See this,' and he held up his mutilated hand; 'that was done by a white man's knife. My father was white, my mother was a slave. When he died she was sold again, and I, a child then, saw her lashed to death to break her of some of the little airs and graces which her late master had encouraged in her. My young wife, too, oh, my young wife!' a shudder ran through his whole frame. 'No matter! I swore my oath, and I kept it. From Maine to Florida, and from Boston to San Francisco, you could track my steps by sudden deaths which baffled the police. I warred against the whole white race as they for centuries had warred against the black one. At last, as I tell you, I sickened of blood. Still, the sight of a white face was abhorrent to me, and I determined to find some bold free black people and to throw in my lot with them, to cultivate their latent powers, and to form a nucleus for a great coloured nation. This idea possessed me, and I travelled over the world for two years seeking for what I desired. At last I almost despaired of finding it. There was no hope of regeneration in the slave-dealing Soudanese, the debased Fantee, or the Americanised negroes of Liberia. I was returning from my quest when chance brought me in contact with this magnificent tribe of dwellers in the desert, and I threw in my lot with them. Before doing so, however, my old instinct of revenge prompted me to make one last visit to the United States, and I returned from it in the Marie Celeste.

'As to the voyage itself, your intelligence will have told you by this time that, thanks to my manipulation, both compasses and chronometers were entirely untrustworthy. I alone worked out the course with correct instruments of my own, while the steering was done by my black friends under my guidance. I pushed Tibbs's wife overboard. What! You look surprised and shrink away. Surely you had guessed that by this time. I would have shot you that day through the partition, but unfortunately you were not there. I tried again afterwards, but you were awake. I shot Tibbs. I think the idea of suicide was carried out rather neatly. Of course when once we got on the coast the rest was simple. I had bargained that all on board should die; but that stone of yours upset my plans. I also bargained that there should be no plunder. No one can say we are pirates. We have acted from principle, not from any sordid motive.'

I listened in amazement to the summary of his crimes which this strange man gave me, all in the quietest and most composed of voices, as though detailing incidents of everyday occurrence. I still seem to see him sitting like a hideous nightmare at the end of my couch, with the single rude lamp flickering over his cadaverous features.

'And now,' he continued, 'there is no difficulty about your escape. These stupid adopted children of mine will say that you have gone back to heaven from whence you came. The wind blows off the land. I have a boat all ready for you, well stored with provisions and water. I am anxious to be rid of you, so you may rely that nothing is neglected. Rise up and follow me.'

I did what he commanded, and he led me through the door of the hut.

The guards had either been withdrawn, or Goring had arranged matters with them. We passed unchallenged through the town and across the sandy plain. Once more I heard the roar of the sea, and saw the long white line of the surge. Two figures were standing upon the shore arranging the gear of a small boat. They were the two sailors who had been with us on the voyage.

'See him safely through the surf,' said Goring. The two men sprang in and pushed off, pulling me in after them. With mainsail and jib we ran out from the land and passed safely over the bar. Then my two companions without a word of farewell sprang overboard, and I saw their heads like black dots on the white foam as they made their way back to the shore, while I scudded away into the blackness of the night. Looking back I caught my last glimpse of Goring. He was standing upon the summit of a sand hill, and the rising moon behind him threw his gaunt angular figure into hard relief. He was waving his arms frantically to and fro; it may have been to encourage me on my way, but the gestures seemed to me at the time to be threatening ones, and I have often thought that it was more likely that his old savage instinct had returned when he realised that I was out of his power. Be that as it may, it was the last that I ever saw or ever shall see of Septimius Goring. There is no need for me to dwell upon my solitary voyage. I steered as well as I could for the Canaries, but was picked up upon the fifth day by the British and African Steam Navigation Company's boat Monrovia. Let me take this opportunity of tendering my sincerest thanks to Captain Stornoway and his officers for the great kindness which they showed me from that time till they landed me in Liverpool, where I was enabled to take one of the Guion boats to New York.

From the day on which I found myself once more in the bosom of my family I have said little of what I have undergone. The subject is still an intensely painful one to me, and the little which I have dropped has been discredited. I now put the facts before the public as they occurred, careless how far they may be believed, and simply writing them down because my lung is growing weaker, and I feel the responsibility of holding my peace longer. I make no vague statement. Turn to your map of Africa. There above Cape Blanco, where the land trends away north and south from the westernmost point of the continent, there it is that Septimius Goring still reigns over his dark subjects, unless retribution has overtaken him; and there, where the long green ridges run swiftly in to roar and hiss upon the hot yellow sand, it is there that Harton lies with Hyson and the other poor fellows who were done to death in the Marie Celeste.

Transcript of the Gibraltar Proceedings

Note: This legal document is copied exactly from the original available to the author.

In the Vice Admiralty Court of Gibraltar

Wednesday the 18th day of December 1872

Before the Worshipful Sir James Cochraine Knight Judge and commissary of the Vice Admiralty Court of Gibraltar at a court held by adjournment from Tuesday the 17th day of December. Present Edward Joscelyn Baumgartner, Registrar The Queen in her Offices of Admiralty against the ship or vessel supposed to be Called *Mary Celeste* and her cargo proceeded against as derelict. Frederick Solly Flood Esquire – Advocate and Proctor for the Queen in her Office of Admiralty. Henry Peter Pisani Esquire – Advocate and Proctor for David Reed Morehouse Master of the British Brigantine *Dei Gratia* and for the owners Officers and Crew of the Brigantine claiming as salvors.

This being the day assigned by the Judge to take the evidence on their examination Viva voce in open court of Oliver Deveau, John Wright, John Johnson, Charles Lund and Augustus Anderson witnesses produced by Pisani as necessary for the Proof of the claims of his parties and now about to leave the jurisdiction of the Vice Admiralty Court of Gibraltar in the prosecution of their voyage.

The following witnesses were duly sworn and examined Oliver Deveau – duly sworn who on his examination deposed as follows.

Corrections

I am the Chief Mate of the British Vessel *Dei Gratia* I left New York on the 15th November bound for Gibraltar for Orders Captain Morehouse, On the 5th December Sea time, being my watch below the Captain called me and said there was a strange sail on the windward bow apparently in distress requiring assistance that was about 3.p.m. sea time.

probably about 1 p.m.

I came on deck and saw a vessel thro' the glass. She appeared about 4 or 5 miles off. The Master proposed to speak to the vessel in order to render assistance if necessary and to haul wind for that purpose which we did. By my reckoning we were 38° 20 N. Lat 17° 15 West Longitude by dead reckoning of our own ship. We hauled up, hailed the vessel, found no one on board. I cannot say whether the Master or I proposed to lower the boat, but one of us did so and a boat was Lowered and I and two men with me went in her to board the vessel. The sea was running high the weather having been stormy though then the wind was moderating I boarded the vessel and the first thing I did was to sound the pumps which were in good order I found no one on board the vessel. I found three feet and a half of water in the pumps on sounding them.

launched

Evidence of this Witness given on The 20th December But inserted here by Direction of Court as Connected with the state of the pumps

The pump gear was good but one of the pumps was drawn to let the sounding rod down. There was no place to let the rod down without drawing The box as is often the case in a small vessel. I cannot say how long it would take to draw the pump it depends upon circumstances. I only used the other pump on my way here and the first pump I left in the same state as I found it. I found the forehatch and the lazaret hatch both off, the binnacle stove in a great deal of water between the decks, the forward house full of water up to the combing the forward house is on the upper deck. I found everything wet in the cabin in which there had been a great deal of water, the clock was spoilt by the water, the sky light of the cabin was open and raised, the compass in the binnacle was destroyed. I found all the Captains effects had been left. I mean his clothing furniture &c the bed was just as they had left it. The bed and other clothes were wet. I judged that there had been a woman on board, I found the Captain's Charts and Books a number of them, in the Cabin, some were in two bags under the bed and some (two or three) loose charts over the bed. I found no charts on the table. I found the log book and the log slate. I found the log book in the mate's cabin on his desk, the log slate I found on the Cabin table. I found an entry in the log book up to the 24th November and an entry on the log slate dated 25th November showing that they had made the Island of Saint Mary. I did not observe the entry on the slate the first day and made some entries of my own on it and unintentionally rubbed out the entry when I came to use the slate at least I thought so. I did not find the ship' Register or other papers concerning the ship but only some letters and account books.

explanation
given

Exhibit A

I found the mate's book in which were entered receipts for Cargo &c. The book now shown me is the book I found also the Mate's Chart in his cabin hanging over the mate's bed showing the track of the vessel up to the 24th there were two charts in the mate's cabin, one under the mate's bed and as I have said hanging over it. I am not positive whether the chart with the ship's track marked on it was found above or below the mate's bed. There seemed to be everything left behind in the cabin as if left in a great hurry but everything in its place. I noticed the impression in the Captain's bed as of a child having lain there. The hull of the vessel appeared in good condition and nearly new. There were a great many other things in the cabin but impossible for me to mention all, the things were all wet, the sky light was not off but open, the hatches were off, the cabin was wet but had no water in it the water had naturally run out of it, the hull of the ship was apparently new, the masts were good, the spars all right, the rigging in very bad order, some of the running rigging carried away gone, the standing rigging was all right, the upper foretopsail and foresail gone apparently blown away from the yards. Lower foretopsail hanging by the four corners. Main stay sail hauled down and laying on the forward house loose as if it had been let run down, jib and foretop stay sail set, all the rest of the sails being furled.

To Judge

The vessel is a Brigantine rigged I should say was sea worthy and almost a new vessel. Anchors and chains all right, there were not boats and no davits at the side. I don't think she used davits. It appeared as if she carried her boat on deck, there was a spar lashed across the stern davits so that no boat had been there. I went back to my own vessel and reported the state of the Brigantine to the Captain. I proposed taking her in, he told me well to consider the matter as there was great risk and danger to our lives and also to our own vessel. We consulted amongst ourselves and crew and resolved to bring her in a distance I estimate at six to seven hundred miles, but have not made out the exact distance. The Captain gave me two men a small boat a barometer compass and watch. I took with me my own nautical instruments and whatever food our steward had prepared and I went on board the same afternoon the 5th about an hour afterwards perhaps, hoisted the boat on deck, pumped her out and took charge of the vessel. Augustus Anderson and Charles Land are the names of the two men I took with me when I first boarded the Brigantine. Their names are John Wright and John Johnson. We arrived in Gibraltar on the morning of the 13th December. When we first went on board we had a good deal to do to get the ship into order. I found a spare trysail which I used as a foresail. It took me two days to set things to rights so as to proceed on the voyage to make any headway. We had fine weather at first until we got into the straits when it came on a storm so that I dare not make the Bay but laid under Ceuta and afterwards on the Spanish Coast to the East. When I arrived at Gibraltar I found the

Dei Gratia already here. I had seen her almost every day during the voyage and spoke her three or four times. We kept company with her until the night of the storm when I lost sight of her. I saw between decks the nature of the cargo-barrels marked alcohol on the head of them and likewise in the note book of a mate of the *Celeste* whereby it appeared he had given receipts for so many barrels of alcohol at a time. I forgot to state that the cabin which was a deck cabin had all its windows battened up. I also found the sounding rod on deck alongside the pump.

Cross examined by the Queen's Advocate and Proctor

I left New York on the 15th November. I examined the log of the vessel found to see when she left New York and believe she had left 8 days before us or 11 days before us more or less. I cannot say what number of days she left before us. I found the vessel a fair sailor. I could not call her more than a fair sailor. I call the *Dei Gratia* a fair sailor. Supposing both vessels to have been equally well found manned and sailed she would have been faster than our own ship. We spoke one other Brigantine on our voyage bound to Boston, but we did not pass nor see any other vessel of a similar class on our outward voyage. Therefore the first time we could have seen this vessel was the day we found her as we did deserted. I cannot say without referring to my log where our ship was on the 24th or 25th. I do know we were to the North of the other vessel. I know that we were between Latitudes 40 and 42. I only know that they were North of the vessel from seeing her track traced on her chart. We did not sight St. Mary's Isle during any part of our voyage. I do not know the latitude or longitude of St. Mary without seeing a chart. I have made only one voyage from New York to Gibraltar before and did not sight St. Mary's then, I never was at St. Mary's, never saw it. I think I could enter St. Mary's by help of the Charts and sailing directions as well as any other port to which I have not been without reference to a chart or sailing direction. I do not know what sort of harbour St. Mary was. From 15th November to 24th November we had stormy weather most time of our passage, most time very heavy weather. During that time we never took off our forehatch since we sailed, the main hatch was off for one hour perhaps we have four hatches fore main aft and lazaret. The *Mary Celeste* has only two hatches fore and main besides the lazarets. The Cabin of the *Mary Celeste* is lightly raised above the upper deck about 2 feet above and the windows are in those two feet, there were five windows, 2 in the Captains, 1 in Mate, 1 in W.C. and one in pantry they were all battened up with canvas and boards. I knocked one off in the Mate's room all the others remained the same as I found them, the topgallant and foreyards and topgallant royal yards, the Royal and topgallant sails were furled the running rigging of those sails was all in the proper place. The rigging out of order was forebraces on port side broken. Starboard lower topsail brace broken. Main peak halyards broken, the Gear of the foresail all broken lashings and buntings gone, her head was westward when we first saw her, she was on the starboard tack, the wheel was not lashed, the wheel gear was good with her foresails set she would not come up to the wind and fall off again, the wind was North not much then though blowing heavily in the morning I am not acquainted with the currents but we allow for a current running Easterly the currents there depend very much on the winds, the first point I made when I could take bearings by sight was Cape St. Vincent which I know from my latitude. I compared my dead reckoning with the place I supposed St. Vincent and of course found myself out of my reckoning but I cannot say how much I was out perhaps 10 miles or so, I was in advance of my reckoning but cannot say how much. There were no spare spars on the decks of the *Mary Celeste* whatever. When there is no boat on the davits in the stern there is often a spar lashed to keep the davits steady. In this case the spar was lashed thro' the sheave holes which showed there had been no boat there.

One window omitted a sixth facing the bow of the ship

The following additions were made by the witness when the depositions were read over to him.

With the sails she had set when I first saw her she might come up and fall away a little but not such she would always keep those sails full

The sheet was fast on the Port Side. She was found on the Starboard tack. The wind would entirely govern the tack on which she was at the time. Both vessels going one way one might be on Port tack the other on Starboard tack on the same day. Wind would be blowing from S.E. if the vessel was bound to Gibraltar

We had two boats, the *Celeste* had not accommodation on deck for two boats. One could see where the boat had been lashed across the main hatch but that was not the right place for her there were no lashings visible therefore I cannot swear that the *Mary Celeste* had any boat at all but there were two fenders where the boat would be lashed. Assuming that there was a boat there was nothing to show how the boat was launched there were no signs of any tackles to launch her. We launched our boat that way from the rail of the vessel without tackle or hoisting her up with a tow rope only to secure her, the way down into the hold is through the hatchways which is quite different from the Cabin. Into the cabin the entrance is thro' the companion way down steps. I went into the cabin within a few minutes of sounding the pumps. On the table there was the log slate but I cannot state what else there might be on the table. I do not know whether there were any knives. I saw no preparation made for eating in the Cabin, there was plenty to eat, but all the knives and forks were in the pantry the rack was on the table but no eatables there was nothing to eat or drink in the cabin on the table, but pre-served meats in the pantry. I examined the state of the ship's galley. It was in the corner of the forward house and all the things pots kettle &c were washed up, water in the house a foot or so deep. I cannot say how the water got in but the door was open and the scuttle hatch off, the win-dows were shut, there were no cooked provisions in the galley. I never saw the water come over the top of the mast of the vessel. There was a barrel of flour in the galley one third gone. We used the provisions found on board the *Mary Celeste* we used potatoes and meat, she had I should say six months provisions on board, I fixed it and used it on our way here. The glass was broken the binnacle was washed away from its place and I set it back again. It is lashed on the top of the cabin above the deck being a wooden one the lashing had given away one of the cleats was gone. I found a compass on board afterwards, the

Cabin compass in the mate's room I did not find until I went on board a second time. It is usual for the vessel to carry two or three compasses. I found quadrants, one in the second Mate's room. I made no further examination of the cargo than what I have already stated, the cargo seemed to be in good condition and well stowed and had not shifted, as far as I could judge the cargo was not injured. I found no wine beer or spirits whatever in the ship.

By Judge

The vessel was perfectly upright whilst I was on board and I saw no signs whatever to induce me to believe that she had been on her beam ends at anytime. If she had been thrown on her beam ends her hatches would have been washed off. Suppose the vessel had been thrown on her beam ends and her hatches had been all close she might have righted again without her cargo shifting or without showing any indication. My idea is that the crew got alarmed and by the sounding rod being found lying alongside the pumps that they had sounded the pumps and found perhaps a quantity of water in the pumps at the moment and thinking she would go down abandoned her. The pumps would be sounded perhaps every two hours or four hours in order to make entry in the log of "pumps carefully attended to" the pumps should be sounded every watch or every four hours. If the vessel were leaky more often, the fact of finding the vessel with only four feet of water when I boarded her shows that she made little or no water about 1 inch in 24 hours and therefore I conclude that all the water found in her went down her hatches and through the cabin.

Exhibit

The log now produced is the one I found on board the *Mary Celeste* and which I continued in my journey to Gibraltar. It is in my writing from the 5th day of December to the 13th December day of arrival including the marginal notes of latitude and longitude, the figures showing the figure of speed are only a guess. I had no log on board to heave and no log line. When I made the land I omitted the entry of supposed speed, the weather came on to blow hard after we had made Cape Spartel on the 11th Ceuta light.

I say we must have run up the Spanish Coast 30 miles after leaving Cape Ceuta or 40 miles that was after leaving Ceuta at 6 a.m. in the sight of land.

Exhibit

The Slate.

The Attorney General reads the entry on the slate log 26th November.

I never used the side of the slate upon which this entry now appears. I left the Charts on board the *Mary Celeste*.

To Judge   I have been Master of a Brig myself. I kept the log on board the *Dei Gratia* I have no Master's Certificate but a Mate's Certificate.

The judge Adjourned the Vice Admiralty Court to Friday next.

2nd day

Friday 20th December 1872

Mary Celeste

The further examination of the witnesses was proceeded with this day.

The witness Oliver Deveau recalled

I wish to correct a statement I made on Wednesday namely that the hour at which the Captain called me was half past one and not 3 p.m. as I have stated. It was 3 p.m. when I boarded the vessel we found abandoned.

To the Judge   The tonnage of my ship is about 295 tons. Our crew members eight hands all told, the *Dei Gratia* is also a Brigantine.

The Queen's Proctor and Advocate

We passed North of the whole group of the Azores. Some vessels go to the South and some to the North. I myself have only passed to the North of the Group of the Azores. I have said that there was the appearance on the bed in the Captain's Cabin as if a child had slept in it, there was room in berth for a child and a woman and also for the Captain. I saw articles of Child's wearing apparel also Child's toys. The bed was as it had been left being slept in not made. I noticed female clothing an old dress hanging near the bed, also India rubber over shoes, the dress was dirty as if worn not wet, the bedding was wet. I should say that the water had got through the windows near the bed or probably it might have got through the sky light, the windows were battened up. There had been rain and squalls the morning we found the *Mary Celeste* but I don't think it was that which had wetted the bed. There were two boxes of clothing. In one box male and female clothing mixed together the box was shut but not locked the clothing was not wet, the other box had only remnants of cloth in it, both boxes were open. I afterwards found some clothing in the drawers, which I also afterwards took out and put into the second box which was nearly empty, the clothing found under the bed place were mostly men's clothing and some of it was wet, that found in the lower drawer, the clothing was of the usual sort worn by men and women, there was also work bags with needles threads buttons books and case of instruments a dressing case and other things in the drawers, the two boxes were in the cabin there was also a valise which I could open, there was also a writing desk there was a bag of dirty clothing man's woman's and child's hanging up in the water closet, they were damp I cannot say how they got damp, there was a stove in the forecabin but I made no fire in it, there were a few old coats and a pair of boots also the clothes were not those of a passenger but of a seafaring man the stove was in the forecabin not in the Captains Cabin, there was a swinging lamp on the side of the cabin, one in each cabin, they were paraffin lamps there was no appearance of damage by fire nor any appearance of fire or smoke in any part of the ship the stay sail which had fallen down was of the stove pipe of the galley there was plenty of provisions and plenty of water on board the vessel. There was a harmonium or melodium in the cabin.

The chart now produced is the chart I found on board the *Mary Celeste* with the ship's course marked on it. I used it afterwards myself for our track here. The words written *Mary Celeste* abandoned 5th December 1872 are in my writing. I put it down merely by guess as the place where I supposed we found the vessel as nearly as I could, the arrows thrown on the chart show the way the currents are supposed to run but they often particularly run just in a contrary direction. That chart is the chart found in the Mate's cabin.

We passed in the North of the group the *Mary Celeste* passed to the South. I should say that from the spot marked on the Chart as the last position of the *Mary Celeste* on the 24th up to the place where we found her I should say would be from five to six hundred miles. The wind was blowing from the N. to S.W. in the interval between 24th November and 5th December as near as I can tell which will more correctly appear in the log of the *Dei Gratia*. The only explanation of the abandonment which I can give is that there was a panic from the belief that the vessel had more water in her than she had as afterwards proved. I cannot give an opinion as to whether the derelict could have run the distance where we found her in the interval with the sails she had set. She was going steadily from 1&½ to 2 knots when we saw her with the wind on her beam. She might have had more sails set at first, she would not run steadily before the wind with her rudder unleashed. She had two head sails set Gib and foretop stay sail set on starboard tack, her yards were square her lower foretop sail was hanging by four corners the wind was to the Northward her head Westward. She was then going in opposite direction to ourselves when we met her. She probably had changed her course more than once. She was going backwards. It is impossible to say therefore how long or how often she had changed her course. There were four berths in the forecastle with bedding in the *Celeste* but only three sea chests. Often two sailors chum for one chest, the bedding was damp as if it had been used. There was one berth in the Mate's cabin and one berth in the galley also a berth in the second mate's room or boatswain's room all apparently had been occupied with the Captain making eight all told besides the woman and child. She was sheeted on the starboard tack when we found her. The wind during the last four days before we found the vessel was North Westerly the men's clothing was all left behind their oilskins boots and even their pipes as if they had left in a great hurry or haste. My reason for saying they to have left in haste is that a sailor would generally take such things especially his pipe if not in great haste. The Chronometer the Sextant and Navigation book were all absent the ship's Register and papers also not found. There was no log line ready for use, the Carpenters tools were in the mate's room the water casks were on chocks the chocks had been moved as if struck by a heavy sea the provision casks were below in their proper place they were not thrown over. If the vessel had been capsized they would have been thrown over.

The evidence having been read over to the witness by the Registrar in Open Court and corrected as it now appears, he stated that it was all correct to the best of his belief.

Edward J. Baumgartner
Registrar

20th December 1872
Evidence read at the hearing of the Cause in the 3rd March 1873

Edward J. Baumgartner
Registrar

John Wright   Sworn examined by Pisani
I am Second Mate of *Dei Gratia* I remember on the 5th December Being on watch on the deck from 12 to 4. I remember sighting a vessel about 1 o'clock on that day p.m. sea time. The vessel was about 6 miles distant on our

port bow. We were steering S.E. by N. I boarded the vessel with the mate Deveau and a man named Jon Johnson to see what was the matter with her. We found no one on board that vessel. I sounded the pump well and found about 3½ feet of water. I went into the cabin and saw no charts. I had no time or did not take time to look I did not see anything in the cabin more than in any other cabin. The Hull and Spars of the vessel were in good order the standing rigging was old it was not broken, but wanted repairing the sails were furled except lower topsail gib and foretop stay sail, those things three were set to foresail and upper foretopsail were gone there was water in the cabin between decks and in the forehouse the forward hatch and the lazaret hatches were off the skylight was in a good state. It was not open Johnson remained in the boat alongside and did not come on board. I returned on board my own vessel and did not again return to the *Celeste* after I returned to my own ship and we were ship and stood down to the other ship until she the other ship got under way. The mate Deveau returned to the other ship with two men Johnny and James. The crew of the *Dei Gratia* numbered 8 all told there was a tolerably heavy sea running when we launched our boat to go to the *Celeste*. We had had heavy weather before that but was then moderating. We were bound to Gibraltar. We sailed keeping sight of the other vessel until 3 o'clock in the night, about the time when we lost sight of her. We got to Gibraltar on Tuesday morning. I am sure it was not Thursday afternoon I had lost sight of the other vessel for three days previously. The Derelict arrived at Gibraltar the next day after we did.

Cross-examined by Queen's Proctor
We came to an anchor in Gibraltar between 11 and 12 o'clock one morning and the other vessel arrived the following morning. It was as I have said during my watch that we sighted the derelict the man at the wheel named Johnson first sighted her and he called to me and showed

me the vessel. Our head was then S.E. by E. the head of the other vessel was N.W. by N. as far as I could judge. She was on our port bow, when I first saw the vessel it was the state of the vessel's sails that caught my attention. I am sure she had her lower top foresail set. She had no after sail on. I should say it was about 2 hours from time of first seeing her to lowering boat to board her. She yawed some but not much, that also attracted my attention. I did not particularly notice the state of her masts and yards they were all standing the Royal was bent and furled. I saw the rigging was out of order, the standing rigging wanted getting up and rattling down, the running rigging I did not notice. I did not notice the state of the peak Halyards I went into the Cabin. Before I went I assisted sounding the pumps the pumps were in a good state there was no sounding rod but a piece of iron with a piece of line attached to it. I found no proper sounding rod. I was able to sound with the piece of iron and line attached to it. It was found lying on the deck near the cabin but could only guess from the line being wet the water in the pump. The line as wetted showed about 3 feet and a half. There was no box in one of the pumps and I let the rod down through the box and pipe where the pump should have been. It would take about 15 minutes to remove the box &c from the pump so as to be able to sound thro' it, there is a door to the companion stairs the door was open, the top of the cabin is above the deck. I should say about 10 inches above the deck the only way of lighting the cabin is by the skylight and the windows three on each side of the cabin and by the companion when the door is open, the windows were nailed up on the starboard side with plank, they were not nailed up on port side, the windows were shut on port side and would let the light in I could not say whether the windows were fastened up for the voyage, or had been fastened during the voyage. On the starboard side the planking was nailed outside the glass on the port side the windows were shut with glass only and were not broken. When below in the cabin there was plenty of light to see what was on the table. I did not see any of the skylight glass broken. I saw that the Binnacle was knocked off it's stand it was lying on deck alongside the wheel, the wheel was not lashed nothing was the matter with the wheel the Binnacle had been fastened by two cleats on each side but I cannot say how it had been fastened to the cleats the binnacle was knocked out of his place but had nothing the matter with it, it was not destroyed, there were only two cleats, neither of them was drawn. I examined the place where the binnacle stood it had slipped in under the cleats and the cleats themselves were not drawn, the compass the glass cover of the compass was knocked off. I left it where it was. I did nothing to it, there were davits to hang a boat to a stern they were in a good state. I could not tell one way or the other whether a boat had been launched from them. I could not tell whether any boat or had not been there at all. There were no davits on the quarter of the vessel. I saw nothing from which I could judge whether a boat had been on deck. I saw no lashing outs loose. I saw no ropes on either side showing that a boat had been launched from the ship at all. I observed no remains of any towline. I saw no spare spars on deck, the ship's anchors and chains were all right and on board so that there was nothing to show that she had been moored and parted her cable. If she had done so we should have seen it and did not see it. I went to the galley the door was open. It was in a bad state, the stove was knocked out of it's place, that could have been done by a sea striking the galley and the stove through the door, it would knock the stove out of it's place, the sea could come in anywhere besides from coming from the head could come in from the stern but I never was in a vessel that was pooped. I have been onboard a ship where the galley had been carried away on two or three occasion the stove was on the starboard side of the door. The cooking utensils were knocked about strewn about a good deal of water in the galley. I did not go in and could not see what provisions there were, the door still is about 9 inches high and would prevent the water running out of the galley there was no place for it to run out and I don't know how long the water had been there the water couldn't come down the galley funnel there was nothing lying on the funnel the sail was lying alongside it, the forehatch was laying portside, three feet from the hatch itself. A sea which would fill the galley would send a lot of water down the hatchway, the lazaret hatch was open and a good deal of water would have gone down had she been struck by a beam sea, the door of the companion faces forward. If a heavy sea were shipped it would down companion some of it. I did not notice anything on the cabin's table. I saw nothing particular in the cabin to claim attention I did not go inside the Captain's cabin. I stood at the door I stayed on board about half an hour and about ten minutes near the cabin door, the main hatch was closed, fastened down, the spars were lashed they were rough spars, I do not know why they were out there.

The evidence of the witness was read over to him in open court and he says it is correct to the best of his belief.

Edward Baumgartner

Registrar

Read in open court at the hearing of the Cause 4th March 1873.

Edward Baumgartner

Registrar

Charles Lund   Sworn examined by Pisani

I am one of the crew of the *Dei Gratia* A.B. I remember On the 5th December sighting the *Mary Celeste* I was not on watch. I was called up from below and came on deck. I was ordered to board the vessel the second time with the Chief Mate and Anderson. When I went on board it was about 4 o'clock p.m. or afternoon and came with that vessel to Gibraltar. We arrived at Gibraltar on the morning of the 13th and found my own vessel *Dei Gratia* here.

During the voyage we kept sight of the *Dei Gratia* until we arrived in the straits when we lost sight of her. We had a stiff breeze and fair wind all the way until we got into the straits when it blew hard with rain.

Cross examined by Queen's Proctor
We lost sight of our own ship about two days before we reached Gibraltar. I think so perhaps three. It was not ten or five days, to the best of my recollection it was two or three days that we lost sight of the *Dei Gratia* I am sure it was two days, it was bad weather. We did not lose any sails or carry away any of our running rigging or standing rigging nor any sails the weather was not so bad as to carry away our binnacle. When I went on board first the binnacle was lying on the deck close to the wheel. We put it into its place again. It may have taken 5 to 10 minutes to put it back again, the binnacle was not again carried away by bad weather whilst we were on board. If a sea had come over it might have again struck and carried away the binnacle. I never saw any sea that would do so we got no water into the galley during the bad weather we were in but we had to come and close the doors and to keep the hatches on. It would not have been prudent to keep the forehatch open in such weather as we had encountered. If we had kept it open some water would have come in during the rough weather we had in the straits. The sea never came over our bow end as far off as the Lazaret hatch whilst we were on the *Celeste* the binnacle is in a box. It has no glass cover to it. It is a wooden box without any glass over it, the compass has a glass over it and also the lights, the sea whilst I was on board never came so far aft as to do any damage to the binnacle. The cabin is flush with a lower deck floor. The top of the cabin is a foot and a half or two feet above the deck. There are I think two windows on each side of the cabin. There was wooden canvas nailed over the glass of the windows on the starboard side. I cannot say whether the windows on the port side were or were not covered

over. With wood and canvas or not. I cannot speak to what I am not sure about. I cannot say not being sure. I did not see any glass broken in the windows or in the sky light. The sky light was open, one pair of glass in sky light was split down, the cabin door was open, I went down into the cabin perhaps in a quarter of an hour or ten minutes after I was on board. I did not see anything on the table. I did not go into the pantry. I did not see any bread or food in

Sounding rod

the cabin. The first time I went into the cabin was for the sounding line. I sounded the well of the *Celeste*. I sounded it with an iron bolt and a piece of line tied to it, the bold was 6 inches to one foot long. I found it and the line in the cabin. I saw no sounding rod. I had no time to look after such things. The chief mate sounded the pump with my assistance, there were 3 feet and a half. It had been sounded before the first time he went on board. The chief mate sounded it before and sounded again the second time. We made it 3 feet and a half. I did not sound it. It was sounded through the pump pipe where the box should be there was 3 feet 6. The first thing I did was to pump her dry. It took three hours or more to do so, there was only one pump going, the *Celeste* made a little water afterwards I cannot say how much about 20 to 25 strokes. I cannot say how much water she made in the day. I pumped her out morning and evening and 25 strokes each time sucked the pipe. The *Dei Gratia* made more water than the *Celeste*. We found no boats on board I cannot say how many boats there had been. I am sure there had been a boat at the Main hatch from the fixing there. I cannot say whether there had been any boat at the davits, the standing rigging was old but was taut, she had a lower topsail. Gib and foretop stay sail. I think on the starboard tack some of the running rigging was broken the lea brace of the foretop stay sail, the peak halyards were broken and gone, the main sail was furled perhaps the sail had been furled afterwards there were no spare spars on deck, the wheel was not damaged in any way. I saw no other damage to the vessel than I have stated except that two of the sails had gone, I saw davits in the stern of the *Celeste* I could not see any tackle to them the boat had lain across the main hatch, there was a spar lashed across the stern davits from one side to the other. I cannot say whether there could have been a boat as well as a spar lashed to the stern davits.

The evidence given by the witness was read over to him and he stated to be correct

Edward J. Baumgartner
Registrar

The Vice Admiralty Court is adjourned till tomorrow Saturday 21st December instant.

The evidence of the last witness is read at the hearing of the Salvage Cause on the 4th March 1873.

Edward J. Baumgartner
Registrar V.A. Court

3rd Day

The further examination of the witnesses on behalf of the *Dei Gratia* Salvors is proceeded with this day *Augustus Anderson* – sworn –

I am an A.B. Seaman and one of the crew of the *Dei Gratia*. On the 5th December the Captain of my vessel sighted a vessel and he ordered a boat to be lowered and the Mate Deveau, myself and John Johnson got into the boat. I had the watch on deck at the time when we sighted her. We got into the boat and went on board the other vessel. We found no one on board the vessel (The witness it appears did not go to the vessel first trip) I went on board only after the boat had been to the vessel and had returned again to our vessel. I went with the boat the second time only and sounded the pumps on board the abandoned vessel. I did not go into the cabin I was holding on aft I went to the abandoned vessel in the second boat. I came to Gibraltar in the vessel with Johnson. It was Lund and not Johnson who came with me to Gibraltar in the vessel with the first Mate. We three went in the boat the 2nd trip she made to the vessel, the first thing I did was to sound the pumps. I did not go into the cabin until I had been on board half an hour I did not notice anything on the cabin table I had not time to do so. I did not take any notice of anything particular in the cabin the cabin was wet everything was wet in it the clothes and all, there was three feet and a half of water in the hold, there was a good deal of water between decks and also in the forward house (up to the combings. Judge.) the foresail and upper top sail were gone the lower top sail hanging by the four corners, the Gib and the foretop mast stay sail were wet. I came with this vessel to Gibraltar and arrived on the 13th of this month. We kept company with the *Dei Gratia* until we got to the straits when we lost sight of her that was two days before we reached Gibraltar. We had fine weather until we got into the straits when we had a storm and weather became thick with rain.

Cross examined by the Queen's Proctor
The Captain first sighted the strange sail. I was on deck at the time. I do not recollect whereabouts on deck. I was not at the wheel Johnson was at the wheel I was nigh to the wheel at the time the vessel was sighted I saw the vessel as soon as Captain drew my attention to it. The vessel was under very short canvass, there was no signal of distress up I do not recollect how we were standing, we were steering towards Gibraltar, the vessel was on our port bow on the starboard bow heading towards us. She was going pretty steady but she was then too far off for me to tell whether she yawed or not. I do not know whether the wheel was lashed when the first boat went on board I do not know whether the wheel was lashed or not when we boarded the vessel. I went up second from boat immediately after the first Mate. Her masts and spars were all right the topgallant and royal yards bent, the standing rigging was all to pieces the ratlines were all to pieces the back stays and fore stays were all right the door of the forward house was open the forehatch was off, all open, the cover was all in one and

was off the lazaret hatch was in one piece there was big hole in one pane of glass on one corner of the skylight except that there were three windows on starboard side 2 windows on the port side and 1 window in the fore part facing the bow. All the windows were covered with plank they are all covered yet, except the one into the Mate's room which was also covered but he opened it, the cabin window facing the bow was covered also I am sure, the companion door was open. Examined it there was nothing then the matter with it. I took notice of the Binnacle it was knocked down lying near the wheel and lazaret hatch, the compass was broken the cleats which fastened the Binnacle were also broken, the Binnacle had been fastened on the cabin house, on the roof of the cabin house. It had been fastened by being lashed to the cleats the cleats are kind of hooks, there were two, one each side, the cleats has been torn from the deck and also from the box on one side and one of the cleats was lying on the decks, the compass was still in the box but broken all to pieces, the glass cover was broken. I did not notice whether the metal of the compass was broken or not. I did not see any needle the Binnacle itself had sustained no injury there were no spars on deck, there were water casks 4 or 5 on deck all in their proper places, there were no ropes coiled on the deck the ropes of the running gear were coiled, there was all kind of running gear hanging over her side, cleats and braces, hanging over both sides, the anchors and chains were all in their proper places, the anchor made fast to the cathead.

To Judge   I was present when the pump was sounded it was sounded with a piece of line and a bolt six or seven inches long, the line and bolt were found in the cabin, the bolt was about 1½ inch thick, the line was fastened to the bolt round the end there was no hole in it, it had no head to it, it was a piece of iron fastened by having the cord tied round it. We used the same bolt end line to sound during the voyage to Gibraltar. The mate found a sounding rod on deck but I did not see him find it. It was all wet and could not be used. I did not see it, the mate saw it. I never took notice of the sounding rod myself. I did not see it when I first went on board. I never saw any other sounding rod than the iron bolt and string, the mate told me there was a sounding rod lying on the deck but that it was all wet and could not be used, he did not tell me what he did with it, there was nothing wrong with the vessel. We had hard work to get her into good order to get the gear into order and the sails right. It took us two or three days to set her to rights, on her voyage to Gibraltar, the vessel herself was sounded and made little or no water. We got the vessel under sail the same night, but it took us two or three days before we got her all right. We had to pump her out first.

Queen's Proctor reads from the log.

She was pumped dry between 8 and 9 o'clock same evening and then sail was set on her.

Memo

The witness is questioned as to what was done on board the *Mary Celeste* from the entries in the log.

The vessel was in a fit state to go round the world with a good crew and good sails. We made Cape Spartel 3 p.m. of the 11th there was then a fresh breeze. I saw our own ship when we were off Cape Spartel, there was a good many lights I don't know the name of and I do not know Ceuta light I was never in the straits of Gibraltar before I shipped on board my Vessel at New York but never made this voyage before.

The depositions of the witness were read over to him and he stated that they are correct.

Edward J. Baumgartner
Registrar

The evidence of the above witness is read in court at the hearing of the Cause of Salvage the 4th March 1875.

Edward J. Baumgartner
Registrar

John Johnson   called sworn examined by Pisani a Russian Lutheran sworn on the New Testament.

My name is John Johnson. I am an able bodied seaman on board *Dei Gratia*. I do not know what day it was but I do remember meeting or seeing at sea a vessel which is now in Gibraltar. I went in the first boat with John Wright and 2nd Mate and the first Mate of *Dei Gratia* on board this vessel, we went on her deck.

The witness does not understand English except in slight degree. Mr Pisani proposes that one of the other crew who understands more English should interpret but the Queen's Advocate objects because he can admit nothing. I did not go on deck I remained in the boat alongside. I returned back to my own vessel. Yes. And the boat returned a second time from our vessel. *Dei Gratia* to this derelict.

The Queens Proctor declines to cross examine the witness as not understanding English.

The Judge to the Queens Proctor

You have the opportunity of seeing the log of the *Dei Gratia* now if you please and therefore if you do not choose to avail yourself of it is your own fault.

The Queen's Proctor

I have asked for the log 20 times a day and have not been able to procure it

Pisani   The log is here in Court and has always been accessible to the Queen's Proctor

Pisani   The Mate is here and if the Queen's Proctor or your lordship would like to ask him further question about the sounding rod here he is.

The Judge   I don't wish to ask him anything if the Queen's Proctor chooses to do so he may do it. I understand in the first instance that the Captain of the "*Dei Gratia*" was not to be examined and I cannot understand what objection there could be made to its production.

Mr Pisani hands in a copy of the ship's (*Dei Gratia*) Register produced yesterday.

N.B. Certified copy of the Register also certified copy of the log of the *Dei Gratia* to be deposited in Registry.

Oliver Deveau recalled by Queen's Proctor. This book now produced is my ship's log and is in my handwriting up to the 5th the day I left the ship. On the 24th November the latitude was 41.49 Long by Chronometer 50. 56.

25th   (Latitude 41. 52

      (

      (Longitude 46. 52

Edward J. Baumgartner

Registrar

The evidence as above and Notes are read in Court the 4th March 1873.

Edward J. Baumgartner

Registrar

Wednesday the 29th day of January 1873
Before the worshipful Sir James Cochraine Night Judge and Commissary Of the Vice Admiralty Court of Gibraltar.

At a Court held by adjournment from Tuesday the 28th day of January Instant.

Present – Edward Joscelyn Baumgartner. Registrar The Queen in her Office of Admiralty against the ship or vessel supposed to be called the

Mary Celeste

And her Cargo proceeded against as derelict.

Frederick Solly Flood Advocate and Proctor for the Queen in Her Office of Admiralty, for the Queen.

Stokes.   Proctor for the Claimants of Cargo

Pisani.   Proctor for the Salvors

This being the day assigned Stokes to hear the claim of his parties as owners of the Cargo. Stokes appeared and having read the Petition claim and affidavits duly filed called James Henry Winchester Sworn and examined viva voce by Stokes. I am a ship owner. Ship Broker and Commission Merchant at New York City United States of America my residence is at Brockland.

I have come to Gibraltar to look after my interests in the vessel *Mary Celeste* of New York of which I was the owner of twelve 24th parts or one half of the whole. I heard that the vessel *Mary Celeste* was at Gibraltar through telegraphic despatch received from Captain Moorhouse Commander of the vessel *Dei Gratia*, sent to New York brought to me by the President of the Great Western Insurance Company who received the despatch stated 'Brig *Mary Celeste* found 4th brought to Gibraltar'. Admiralty Court in possession 'Telegraph offer of salvage'.

At the request of the underwriters who refused to receive the abandonment of the vessel I came to Gibraltar having left New York on Christmas Day 25th December, 1872.

The telegram was received at New York on the 14th December I left by the Abyainia Steamer for Liverpool having previously telegraphed to Gibraltar to protect the interests of owners.

I arrived at Liverpool in about ten days voyage. I left Liverpool at 4 o'clock Tuesday morning for Gibraltar and arrived here on the 15th instant.

I have seen the vessel now in this Bay in the custody of the Marshal supposed to be the *Mary Celeste* and she is *Mary Celeste* of New York that I swear to.

I was at New York when the *Mary Celeste* sailed on her last voyage. I know what cargo she had on board. It consisted of 1701 barrels of alcohol. One barrel in dispute with thirty tons of stone ballast beneath the cargo. To my knowledge she had no other cargo. She is a chartered ship by Meisner Ackerman and Company Merchants of New York a very respectable German House known to me personally. I saw the Bills of Lading and should know them if I saw them again.

The two bills of Lading now shown me marked A and A2 respectively, the first is in the writing of Meisners

Ackerman. The second is in the hand writing of my clerk are the Bills of Lading. That cargo was shipped on board the *Mary Celeste* at New York which is the same vessel now in the Bay of Gibraltar.

I saw the signature "Benj. S. Brigg" to those Bills signed in my office in my presence.

That is the whole of the cargo I saw it going on board several times and no other cargo.

I know Benj. S. Brigg the Master of the *Mary Celeste*. I had known him for many years previously and saw him write his name to the bills of Lading. I was acting as ship's husband on this occasion and had there been any other cargo I should have most likely have known of it. I have no doubt whatever of the vessel being the *Mary Celeste* and positively swear she is the same vessel as *Mary Celeste* New York.

Cross Examined by the Queen's Advocate

I do not know whether or not the *Mary Celeste* had a ship's manifest when she left New York.

When she sailed from New York she had a chronometer on board. It was a shared one found by the Master himself who sailed the vessel on shares.

I do not know whether she had on board a Sextant or quadrant.

I think that she was 15 to 20 days getting the Cargo on board there was a good deal of trouble getting it out of bond I believe it was of American Manufacture as it came from Hudson River Railway, there is a great deal of Alcohol shipped at New York and also manufactured in the Country. There is a draw back of 2 per gallon on the export of alcohol from America.

The vessel loaded at 44 East River about one mile from my office. I used to go there once a day three different days during the time she took in her cargo.

I think I was there about three times and that she took in about 300 barrels on board as part of her Cargo. Albert G.

Richardson the Mate was previously and up to that time in charge of the *Mary Celeste*. She came with a cargo of coal from the Cow Bay to New York before she took in the alcohol.

I have a Certified Copy of the Charter Party of the Vessel but not the Charter Party itself, the original Charter party is in my office in New York. I do not think it is possible that there was any other cargo or bullion or other valuables on board without my knowing it, but still such a thing is possible. Briggs was in charge ten or twelve days before the *Mary Celeste* sailed. I do not know that he took any valuables on board without my knowledge. Briggs was a married man and his wife was with him on board the *Mary Celeste*. She went with him I believe as I saw a trunk belonging to her onboard with herself and her child but I did not see the ship sail.

I believe he had been married ten or twelve years, one a boy seven years old left at home at school so the Captain told me, the other child was about two years old and was the one I saw on board.

The Lady played a melodium or musical instrument as I once heard her play on a melodium on his own vessel not the *Mary Celeste* but ten years before I saw a melodium put on board the *Mary Celeste* but I cannot say whether it was the same that she had played previously.

I know or think I should know a photograph of Benj. Briggs.

The photograph now shown me is that of Captain Oliver Briggs his brother. So is the second photograph, the photograph now shown me is that of Captain Benj. Briggs the Master of the *Mary Celeste*.

I do not know the maiden name of Mrs. Briggs, wife of Benj. Briggs but he told me she was a minister's daughter. I did not see a photograph of Mrs. Benj Briggs in this book.

Captain. B. Briggs bore a high character, the character of a courageous officer and good seaman who would not I think desert his ship except to save his life. I also knew the

Mate Richardson. I had done so for two years, he was an experienced and courageous officer in whom I had great confidence I believe he had presence of mind, his three previous Captains spoke of him as fit to command any ship and I believe he would not leave his ship except for life or death. He was a married man his wife was my wife's niece her name was Frances before her marriage her maiden name was Spates.

The Captain provided the log. I had not seen it. I knew the Mate's handwriting. I don't think that either Richardson or the Captain had any venture on their own onboard the Celeste as they had not private funds, but they might have had a venture on behalf of someone else. Richardson was in charge until Briggs's came on board, perhaps for three weeks before Briggs came.

The Log The entry in the Log now shown me dated 10th September, is not in the handwriting of either Richardson or Briggs. I should think it is the handwriting of the other mate who had charge of her in Cow Bay. The entry made in the log on the 16th October which is the next entry in the log is handwriting of Richardson the Mate and the whole of the writing in the Log to the 24th November inclusive is in the same writing. I cannot say whether he was skilful in taking observation other than his general character for being skilful and good sailor and I should believe any entry made by him in the Log as to the position of the vessel to be correct and correctly indicate the position of the vessel. The last entry in the log is 36.56.N. Lat. by observation at noon on the 24th November. Long. 29.20 West. I think the Lat. is 36.36.N. not 56, it may be 56. The wind as shown on Log is N.c. West and ends S.W. – No that appears to be the current.

Slate Log The writing shown to me on the Slate purporting to be a continuation of the Log or the Slate Log I believe not to be in the handwriting of Richardson. The Slate Log shows the vessel to have gone 162 miles in twenty hours. I do not think that any of the entries written in upon this slate are in Richardson's handwriting except the last line on the left hand side engraved or scratched on the Slate 'Frances my own dear wife Frances N.R'. In the Lat. 36.56 the length of a degree of Longitude would be 50. I Think. If there is a difference of 109 instead of 159 an error of 50 per cent on the Log calculated that would confirm my belief that the entry was not made by Richardson.

I know nothing of the crew myself whatever except their names from the shipping agent or Commissioner at New York who shipped the men, he is a Government appointment.

The names are:–

Albert C. Richardson – mate. Andrew Gilling 2nd ditto. Ed. W. Head Stewd & Cook. Valkert Lorenson Seaman. Arian Hardenn-Boy-Lorenson. Gotlieb Gondschall. Benj. S. Briggs Captain.

The vessel was staunch and strong when she left New York. She has a forward house and the main cabin raised above deck.

I do not think that any of the windows of the Cabin were fastened up before she left New York, to the best of my belief they were all open, but when the repairs were made to the ship some of the cabin windows were filled up entirely and fresh windows made. There was spare canvass on board the *Celeste* besides her sails and spare sails. I did not notice whether there was a clock on board or not I suppose there was a clock on board as there always was one. I cannot account for the clock being found upside down, especially in a vessel navigated by Captain Briggs. I have examined the outside of the vessel and her bows and the bows are not now in the same condition that they were at New York.

I do not know anything if the Captain or Mate having a sword nor of a sword being on board at all. I never saw such a sword as the sword now shown me in their possession. I do not know whether either of them carried a revolver or gun which would be a much more likely weapon for them to have.

The vessel had six months provision on board with the exception of flour, which was four months only, there was plenty of water on board. She was well found in everything The Captain was a teetotaller and a Christian man or religious man and I should expect to find religious books on board rather than any other.

The ship had no bulwarks but a topgallant rail round the ship. It was painted before it left New York. The cut of the rail of the ship now shown me was not made when she left New York. I am satisfied it was not then there and has been done by a severe blow with a sharp instrument. I am owner of one half of this ship. The vessel was chartered and Feel almost certain that there was no other cargo put into her besides the spirit or alcohol.

If there had been more than one charter I must have known it, moreover the cargo she carries is large cargo for her tonnage and as much as she can carry.

I don't think the vessel with such a cargo could have sunk and I don't think that unless she had struck upon the rocks any prudent man would have abandoned a vessel at sea with such a cargo.

My explanation of the long splints or marks in her bow is that they spauled off the wood having been steamed and bent to fit it on.

I know that the Captain's wife had some jewellery used to wear earrings and chains and finger rings.

I have been a Sea Captain myself but have not been at the Azores.

I think there was a proper sounding rod on board the *Mary Celeste*. I have no doubts about it as she was well found in everything.

Edward J. Baumgarter

Registrar

This concludes the examination and cross examination of the witness James Henry Winchester.

Edward J Baumgartner
Registrar

At the prayer of Stokes with the consent of the Queen's advocate and Procurator General in her office of Admiralty the Judge admitted the claim of Stokes parties as the true and lawful owners of the Cargo of Alcohol laden on board the *Mary Celeste*. By interlocutory Decree pronounced the same to belong as claimed and decreed the said cargo of alcohol to be restored to the said claimants upon payment of salvage and salvage expenses and the expenses on behalf of Our Lady the Queen in her offices of Admiralty.

The judge adjourned the Vice Admiralty Court to Friday next the thirty first day of January instant.

Edward Baumgartner
Registrar

Friday the 31st day of January 1873

Before the Worshipful Sir James Cochraine Knight. Judge and commissary of the Vice Admiralty Court of Gibraltar.

Wednesday the twenty ninth day of January instant.

Present Edward Joscelyn Baumgartner Registrar.

The Queen in her Office of Admiralty against the ship or vessel supposed to be called the

Mary Celeste

Derelict

Frederick Solly Flood esquire Advocate and Procurator General for the Queen in her office of Admiralty.

George Fredrick Cornwell Advocate and Proctor for the claimants of the vessel.

Martin W. Stokes Advocate and Proctor for the owners of the cargo.

Henry Peter Pisano Advocate and Proctor for the asserted Salvors.

This being the day assigned Cornwell to bring in the proofs of his parties claiming to be the lawful owners of the ship or vessel supposed to be the *Mary Celeste*. Cornwell appearing for James Henry Winchester of New York in the United States of America part owner of the Brig or vessel *Mary Celeste* of New York aforesaid to the extent of twelve twenty fourth parts of shares in the said vessel and holding Powers of Attorney from the owners and mortgages of the remaining twelve twenty fourth parts of shares in the said vessel read the petition affidavit and claim of the said James Henry Winchester filed in the Registry of the Vice Admiralty Court of Gibraltar on the twenty eights day of January instant and called the said James Henry Winchester who being already sworn was examined on his former oath and viva voce by Cornwell and deponed as follows. I have already stated on my former examination in this court on Wednesday last that I had no doubt whatever having seen the vessel now in the Bay of Gibraltar supposed to be the *Mary Celeste* as to the identity of that vessel with the Brig *Mary Celeste* of New York and that they are one and the same vessel.

I am owner of the *Mary Celeste* of New York to the extent of twelve twenty fourth parts or one half of her whole and I hold powers of Attorney from Sylvester Goodwin of New York owner of two twenty fourth parts of the said Brig from Daniel Sampson of New York also holder of two twenty fourth parts of the said Brig and from Sampson Hart of New Bedford Massachusetts U.S. Mortgages of one third or eight twenty fourth parts of the said Brig *Mary Celeste* giving me full powers to act as their agent and in their place and steed for them as fully in this matter as they could have done so themselves. I know the handwriting of Sylvester Goodwin having often seen it before and I believe that the signature S. Goodwin to the power of Attorney now shown me marked A is the signature and handwriting of D. Sylvester Goodwin shareholder

Exhibit A

Exhibit B

Exhibit C

of the Brig *Mary Celeste* to the extent of two twenty fourths as named and described in the ship's register an official copy of which I procured from New York. I also know the handwriting of Daniel L Samson to the Power of Attorney now shown me marked B is the proper signature and handwriting of the said Daniel L. Samson shareholder of the Brig *Mary Celeste* to the extent of two twenty fourth parts or shares as named and described in the ship's register. I also know the handwriting of Simpson Hart to the Power of Attorney now shown me marked C is the proper signature and handwriting of the said Simpson Hart the mortgage executed to him by Benjamin S. Briggs part share owner and Master of the said Brig *Mary Celeste* also named and described in the ship's register as owner of eight twenty fourth parts of the said vessel and who is the same Benjamin S. Briggs who sailed in command of the vessel *Mary Celeste* from New York bound to Genoa with a cargo of alcohol.

Cross examined by the Queen's Advocate
I am still in total in total ignorance of what has become of the Master B. S. Briggs his wife and the crew of the *Mary Celeste*. I have received no intelligence of them whatever since my examination in this court on Wednesday last I have been on board the Brig *Mary Celeste* now lying in this bay and have examined her thoroughly and am perfectly certain she is the *Mary Celeste* of New York. From what I have seen of the state and condition of the vessel I cannot believe she was abandoned by her Master Officers and Crew in consequence of stress of weather only. I had plenty of time to examine her thoroughly and feel very certain that she was not abandoned through perils of sea. I have already stated that I knew Benjamin S. Briggs and also the mate Richardson and that they bore high characters as able seaman and I add to here what I have previously stated respecting their characters and that I am very

certain both men would remain by their ship to the last and that neither would have deserted the ship unless forced to do so or in fear of their lives.

The Queen's Advocate states that he regrets that there is no copy of the mortgaged annexe to the power of Attorney from Simpson Hart to James H. Winchester to the ownership of the vessel and to the Decree for restitution and suggests that a remedy to this objection may be found by Bail being given by him to answer all latent claims for salvage and salvage expenses &c.

Cornwell

We are quite willing to meet the suggestion of her Majesty's Advocate and to give any reasonable bail for latent claims which may be required as well as the usual bail to answer salvage and expenses for the value of the vessel.

Cornwell then prayed the Judge to admit the claims of his party James H. Winchester as the lawful owner of the said Brig *Mary Celeste* and to decree restitution thereto as also Pisani Proctor for the Salvors.

The Judge There are certain matters which have been brought to my notice respecting this vessel my opinion about which I have already very decidedly expressed and which make it desirable and even very necessary that further investigations should take place before the release of the vessel can be sanctioned or before she can quit this port. The conduct of the Salvors in going away as they have done has in my view been most reprehensible and may probably influence the decision as to their claim for remuneration for their services and it appears very strange why the Captain of the *Dei Gratia* who knows little or nothing to help the investigation should have remained here whilst the first mate and the crew who boarded the *Celeste* and brought her here should have been allowed to go away as they have done. The Court will take time to consider the Decree for restitution.

Pisani For the Salvors having consulted the Master of *Dei Gratia* who is in court states that although the *Dei Gratia* the mate and crew will probably be on their return voyage from Genoa shortly that there will be no difficulty in procuring the more prompt attendance of the mate if required by telegraphing to Genoa for him, that the only desire of the Captain of the *Dei Gratia* was to do what he considered most to the interest of his owners deeming it probable that the salvage claims might be settled by mutual consent and without having to come to the Court.

Thes. J.
Vacchio

The Judge adjourned the Vice Admiralty Court to Monday third day of February next.

Edward J. Bamgartner
Registrar

Monday the 3rd day of March 1873

Before the worshipful Sir James Cochrane Knight Judge

Marshal

and Commissary of the Vice Admiralty Court of Gibraltar a Court held by adjournment from Saturday 1st day of March instant.

Present Edward Joscelyn Baumgartner. Registrar.

The Queen in her Office of Admiralty against the ship or vessel

Mary Celeste

And her cargo proceeded against derelict.

Cause of Salvage
Frederick Solly Flood Advocate and Procurator General for the Queen

H.P. Pisani   For the Salvors
N.W. Stokes   For the owners of the Cargo and also representing
S.P. Cornwell For the owners of the vessel

This being the day assigned by the Judge to hear Pisani's proofs in support of the claim of his parties to salvage and the Advocates and Proctors generally in this cause.

Pisani – read his act on Petition.

The Queen's Advocate here interrupts the reading of the pleadings stating that he wishes before the hearing of the Salvage Cause is proceeded with to examine the Marshal respecting the personal effects of the Master Officers and crew of the *Mary Celeste* found by him on board the vessel.

The Marshal is sworn and examined by the Queen's Advocate. The Registrar having previously read the minutes of the order of the court of the 24th February ordering the marshal to restore the personal effects of the crew of the *Mary Celeste* found on board to H.J. Spragues, American Consul at Gibraltar for the use of the said crew &c or their relatives.

The effects now produced in the court are part of the personal effects of the Captain and Crew which I found on board the *Mary Celeste* and which the order of the court directed should be given up to the American Consul.

The pocket book and the letters now produced by you are some that were found on board the *Mary Celeste* on my first arresting her in December. Also the two yellow envelopes addressed to Captain Briggs by Captain Winchester. I found the letters in the bottom drawer in the Captain's cabin they were wet and damp when first found but I dried them as they now appear. I also found a sword which is the sword now produced in Court. I also found some photographs in the Captain's private chest which are those now produced. I also found a paper in the foreward cabin house next the cook galley having the entrance facing the stern, which paper is now shown me. I found it in a chest in the cabin. In the envelope are eight photographs and a post office order for thirty five dollars currency equal to twenty five dollars 50 centimes gold currency.

The several effects are pointed out by the Marshal &c Stokes reads his answer to Pisani's Act of Petition Stokes appearing for Cornwell's answer to Pisani's Act on Petition.

Pisani reads the concluding Act.

Pisani proposed to read the evidence of the Mate Deveau taken on the 18th day of December last viva voce in the Court.

The Queen's Proctor – as the witness Oliver Deveau has returned to the jurisdiction of the Court he should be called and re-sworn before the evidence he has given is read if it is to be re-read.

Stokes – Mr Pisani should first address the Court on the Merits of his case.

Pisani addressed the Court on the merit of the services rendered by his parties the Salvors reads Handy Book of Law of Salvors by James page 125 relies on the risk run to the Salvage vessel parting with three of her crew out of 8 all told leaving only five men and boys on board the *Dei Gratia*, again the vessel *Celeste* was found abandoned with her hatches left open and therefore in imminent danger of being lost or water logged.

Pritchard Digest 2 Vol. 776. The *Monkwearmonth*.

The danger to the ship salving is an equal impediment for remuneration as the danger to the ship salved.

Pisani calls.

David Reed Morehouse Captain or Master of the Brigantine *Dei Gratia* duly sworn – I am the Master of the vessel *Dei Gratia*, on the 15th Nov. 1872 at 8 o'clock a.m. Civil time I left New York in the *Dei Gratia* bound to Gibraltar for orders.

My cargo was refined petroleum 1735 round barrels and 499 cases of petroleum and one in dispute.

We had heavy weather but with nothing extraordinary till 5th December sea time at nine o'clock p.m. when I came on deck and saw a sail on the weather bow bearing E.N.E. wind about N. we were then steering S.E. ½ N. by Compass. 38° 20 North Lat. 1737 Long by chronometer.

When I first saw the vessel I judged she was 6 miles distant.

I looked at her through my glass and saw something amiss with her judged so from her having so little sail set on her and I bore up towards her 2 points.

I could make out nothing else the matter with her just then and fifteen or twenty minutes later I saw from her yawing what I supposed to be a flag floating from her port yardarm that something was the matter and judged she was in distress.

I immediately called the Mate and told him that there was a vessel which I thought was in distress and required assistance.

As soon as he came on deck he agreed with me and we braced up the yards at once and hauled for the vessel.

We were then I should say from 4 to 5 miles distance from the vessel. We came alongside the vessel about 3 o'clock p.m. I mean passed alongside her 300 or 400 yards off. We hailed her but got no answer and saw no one on deck

We lowered a small boat and the mate and two men went on board of her. The weather had been blowing very hard for seven or eight days previous but had on that morning, morning of the 4th commenced to moderate.

In ³/₄'s or half an hour or it may have been an hour the mate returned in the boat to my ship which was lying about one quarter of a mile off and he reported the vessel to be in apparently good condition, but that there was no one on board he reported three feet and a half of water in the hold but proposed that we should take her in which he thought could be done under favourable circumstances.

I told him I was willing that he should do so but that he must consider the risk we were running I meant by the risk we were running the risk to our own ship or our lives and property that if anything happened I should have to bear all the blame and loss, and that we had hitherto had very heavy weather. He said that he would attempt it and I then called all hands aft. I pointed out the risk that I was running and that they would be running on going on board a vessel which we knew nothing about, and I asked them whether they would be willing to share the extra risk and extra labour that would fall upon them in both vessels. And they all agreed to do so.

The result was the mate took men and proceeded on board the vessel.

They were not the same men that went with him the first time. I do not remember their names. I gave him the pick, of our crew and he chose the two best men.

I think their names were as you now say Augustus Anderson and Charles Lund.

I gave them the boat a compass a barometer and my watch the mate having reported to me that he had found a compass on board but that it was destroyed in the binnacle and useless.

They took with them also all the food that the steward had cooked, also the small boat.

We then made sail but the wind fell very light and we kept in company of each other and saw each other every day until the night before we got into Gibraltar.

That night we had a very rough night thick and foggy the night of the 11th December we had to run through the straits.

We lost sight of each other about 3 o'clock a.m.

I arrived at Gibraltar 4 p.m. of the 12th December civil time.

The other vessel *Mary Celeste* arrived at about 9 a.m. next morning the 13th December.

I went on board the *Mary Celeste* almost as soon as she arrived but I met him first on board our own vessel the *Dei Gratia* the mate having got pratique and come on board our own vessel.

I saw the Mate first on our vessel having whilst on my way to the *Mary Celeste* from shore seen him on the deck of my vessel as I was passing.

I remarked to him that I congratulated him on his having succeeded in bringing in the ship and he answered, 'Yes, but I don't know that I could attempt it again'. He appeared very fatigued and sleepy. If a storm had come on there would have been great risks to both of us and that was what I had told them to consider.

He would perhaps have had to run even as far as the West Indies, as I don't know of any safe ports in the Western Isles. I consider that there was considerable I must say great danger to our lives and property.

Cross examined by Stokes

The head of the *M. Celeste* was bearing W.S.W. when I first saw her as near as I can judge my own ship S.E. As soon as the mate went on board the *Celeste* he wore her round but made no sail.

The vessel *M. Celeste* was manageable her helm was all right. After she wore round she followed after me. I think she did not make sail till nearly midnight. I saw them at the pumps till dark.

When I first saw her she had set lower topsail and fore topmast stay sail. He hauled the gib round before he wore her round there was something the matter with it.

I think he set the main staysail soon after he wore round. She followed my vessel at the rate of 1 an a $\frac{1}{2}$ to 2 knots an hour during the night, the wind died away but still there was a moderate breeze and a heavy swell or sea running. The sea was on our quarter neither for nor against us. My ship was also making from one and a half to two knots an hour. About 10 o'clock p.m. I wore my ship round and under his stern to note whether he felt safe and had got his vessel pumped dry, and answered both questions yes.

He said he had just finished pumping her out and he thought he was all right but asked me not to leave him that night and I said I would not do so. I also told him to show a flash if at any time during the night he felt any danger. At one time I thought he did so, but he did not.

The next morning about 9 a.m. I spoke to him and asked him how he was getting along he said pretty well but hard work. He was then shifting his fore topgallant sail to a foretopsail. During the forenoon he also set the tow gibs and all three stay sails were I think also set that day.

The two vessels kept in sight of each other during the following days losing sight of each other, at night. We had moderate weather generally speaking a few little squalls.

After he got up his canvas the speed of the two vessels was nearly equal. We spoke to each other two or three times afterwards on our way to Gibraltar.

My vessel sustained no damage whatever to herself only loss of time perhaps four days loss of time or even more by meeting with the vessel.

It was something over 600 miles away from Gibraltar that we brought the vessel. Being short hauled I was obliged to take in sail much sooner than I otherwise should have done and I was driven through the Straits nearly to Malaga and had to back again making a loss of two days also together a loss of four days.

I am not aware that the *Mary Celeste* sustained any damage during her run to Gibraltar.

The loss of the four days I do not give as a matter of positive fact but as a matter of opinion.

My vessel is a heavy vessel to handle so much that the Mate and his two men handled the *Mary Celeste* with as much ease as I and my four men could handle the *Dei Gratia*. Whenever the weather looked doubtful I was forced to prepare for taking in sail longer than I should have done had I had my full complement of men and took longer to make sail and therefore a loss of time. The work with a short handed crew is also much harder than with a full crew.

Cross examined by the Queen's Proctor

The wind fell light and died away after we fell in with *Mary Celeste*. The mate kept the Log till he left and I then kept it – reads from the Log.

Friday the 6th – fine throughout, light breeze forming – clouds.

Saturday 7th – light breeze light clouds passing shower of small rain.

Sunday 8th – light breeze fine clear weather without.

Monday 9th – F. Moderate breeze hazy, light breeze and very hazy.

Tuesday 10th – fresh mod. Breeze and hazy. Midnight – light breeze and fine.

Noon fresh gale and cloudy.

All that is I believe correct as stated in the Log. With such as that I do not think 80 miles too much to put down. I should say the breeze may have been four knots breeze.

I have stated the Long. In which we picked up the vessel. The Long. Of Gibraltar is I believe 5° 21, supposing that to be so the distance would be 630 miles. Therefore supposing 96 miles a day at seven days would be 672.

I do not know of a safe port in the Western Isles. I know of the port you name but I also know of vessels going on shore there. I have not been there and simply stated and state that I do not know of any safe port.

The Queen's Proctor reads.

Account of the Anchorage ground in the roadsteads.

Witness – I do not consider that a safe Port of anchorage from which you have to run in certain winds. The spot where we picked the *Mary Celeste* is in the track of vessels between several places you name and read from all the charts now produced, rather to the west of the track. I did not go on board the *Mary Celeste* at all until she came into the Port of Gibraltar.

I could see with my glass that both gangways or topgallant sails of the *Mary Celeste* were off and were unshipped when we found the vessel. I am sure of that. I made the remark to my Mate that they had probably removed the sails to launch their boat. I also saw the marks or spalls on the bow's of the *Mary Celeste*. As we were steering we should have left the *Mary Celeste* on the port hand. We were on the port tack, she was on the starboard tack. We should have passed to southward of her. The wind of the 5th was then N.N.E. The vessel would have passed us to windward. The log shows the wind to have been blowing from N. for some days previously, previous twenty four hours 12 N.N.E. the first 12 N. It would have been possible for the vessel under the canvas she had on to have gone on the other tack.

I think the gib was trimmed on the port side when we first met her although she was on the opposite tack. I have seen vessels behave so strangely that it is impossible to say how or what they will do. She was yawing coming into the wind and then falling off again I watched her for two hours doing that. It is possible that she may have been further to the East than she was when I first saw her.

My opinion is that the vessel had worn round before I picked her up. By the yard being left square I should say that when she was abandoned she was running before the wind. I cannot give any opinion as to whether she had been further to the east and if so how far the squall I met with in my own vessel at 4 o'clock that same morning from N.N.E. would have been very likely to have sent her round had she also met it.

Log Book

Log and log slate of the *Mary Celeste* produced by Queen's Proctor and the witness examined thereon.

Monday 25th – 1 o'clock, 8 knots and 9 knots show to be speed of vessel all day 162 total.

Witness.

The only way you can discover the error of the chronometer is when you sight the land and therefore when St. Mary's was sighted as mentioned in the log may have been the first opportunity of discovering any error in reckoning.

When Deveau returned from the *Celeste* after his first visit to it he said nothing particular about the state of the deck except that things were all in confusion the hatch's off, ropes about. He said nothing about any marks of violence or distress. The flag or what I thought was a flag from the port yardarm we found when we got up to it part of the upper topsail hanging down torn.

I think the torn sail now showed me in court is part of the foretop sail. I think it has been cut across with a knife although I have seen sails torn by the wind in every sort of way, across and against the grain.

Oliver Deveau – mate resworn.

The evidence given by the witness before the court of the 18th and 20th December 1872 and read over to him by the Registrar and he certifies the same to be correct. There was no regular sounding rod found onboard the *Mary Celeste* it was only a bolt attached to a line.

We have on board the *Dei Gratia* no regular sounding rod. We use an line with marks made on it.

The sounding apparatus I left on board is not the same line that I found onboard the other day when I went onboard the *Mary Celeste*.

The whole of the evidence having been read over to him. Her Majesties Advocate and the other Advocates and Proctors defer their further examination it being 5.12 p.m.

The judge adjourns Vice Admiralty Court until tomorrow, Tuesday 4th March and assign to hear council further in this cause on that day.

Tuesday 4th March 1873

Oliver Deveau cross examined by the Queens Advocate and Proctor in her office of Admiralty.

I have stated that I found the peak halyards on the *Mary Celeste* broken when I went on board. I had a fresh rope put in its place but not a new rope and that will account for the Surveyor's not finding the rope spliced or mended. I cannot say how the halyard had been broken it was a very old one and had been spliced.

When the wind is right dead aft we often do not carry the main sail though sometimes it may be, looking at the log of the *Mary Celeste* as now shown me by you, the wind appears to have been aft and such as therefore would not require the main sail to be set.

There is an entry in the log of the main sail having been again set. We found both the topgallant sails moved lashed at one end and cast off at the other end so that it would open on being lifted up.

In port there is no occasion to keep them lashed but at sea it would be necessary to do so. When I went on board I found the rails on both sides lying on the deck lashed or fastened at one end. I cannot say whether my men replaced it with lashings or took off the lashing or took off the lashing from the ends of the rails that were lashed. The rails fits in tight in the socket and it takes some force to remove or raise it and also to replace it, the lashing was a temporary rope lashing not a regular type lashing.

There was only the appearance as of one boat having been on board. I could not see any means or tackle for hoisting the boat on or off deck therefore conclude the boat must have been launched. I saw no remains or pieces of a painter or boats rope fastened to the rail. I did not notice any mark of an axe on the rail or cut. I did not see this cut in the rail now shown me to notice it.

I cannot say how the cut came in the rail it appears to have been done with a sharp axe and I do not think it would have been done by my men whilst we were in possession of the vessel. I did not see any new axes on board the *Celeste* there was an old axe found on board. I did not replace the rails of the ship found on the deck before I returned to the *Dei Gratia* the first time.

I can form no opinion about the cause of the axe cut on the rail. I observed no marks of blood on the deck I noticed no marks or traces of blood upon the deck. I cannot say whether there were any or not. We never washed the decks of the *Mary Celeste* nor scraped them. We had not men enough for that. The sea washed over the decks. The Queen's Proctor explains that salt water contains chloric acid which dissolves the particles of the blood. If there are some parts of the deck or sail scraped I did not notice them and they were not done whilst we were on board.

I saw a sword on board the *Mary Celeste*. I found that sword under the Captain's berth. I took it out from there. I looked at it drew it from it's sheath there was nothing remarkable on it. I do not think there is anything remarkable about it now it seems rusty. I think I put it back where I found it or somewhere near there. I did not see it at the foot of the ladder perhaps some of my men have put it there. I was not on board the *Celeste* when the Marshal came on the *Celeste* to arrest the vessel and therefore I did not see him find the sword.

The Queen's Proctor goes on to explain that the sword has been cleaned with lemon which has covered it with a citrate of iron which has destroyed the marks of the supposed blood which therefore is not blood at all as at first supposed but another substance put there to destroy and disguise the original marks of the blood which were once there.

It did not occur to me that there had been any act of violence there was nothing whatever to enduce one to believe or to show that there had been any violence. I used often when at the wheel to think how and why the vessel had been abandoned by her crew and came to the conclusion that she had been left in panic that being also strengthened by the sounding rod found near the pump and her sails being rather injured.

She was so sound and stout that I cannot think that if I had been on board I should have abandoned her. I should have considered her safer than an open boat unless she was on the rocks.

The sewing machine produced was in the cabin I think under the sofa certainly not on the harmonium when we first went on board the *Celeste* I may have put it there myself as I looked at it and it was free from rust damp and water as it appears now. I cannot say whether it would or would not be rusty if the skylight had been left open for ten days previously.

My men were in possession of the *Mary Celeste* for about four hours after I left and before the Marshal arrested the vessel.

I had great many of the things found in the Captain's cabin taken out to dry. Some were dry and some were wet, there were so many that it took two of us several hours to take them all out and we did not try to put them back again. Everything in the Mate's desk were dry some of his clothes were wet not damp but regularly wet and he had them out to dry there were many things dry and many things wet both in the Captain's Cabin and in the Mate's Cabin we had the wet things out and dried them. I saw some new shoes or boots I think in the forward cabin but cannot say whether the boots now shown were the same or whether I have seen them before.

The clothes on the Captain's bed and the bed itself were so wet that I could not sleep upon it I had them all out to dry them and did dry them before I slept in the bed myself which I did.

I cannot say anything about the chests which were in the forward house, but I know that the forward house itself was full of water because I ordered holes to be bored in it to let out the water. Probably the dry things in the Seaman's chest remained dry because the chest was watertight my own chest is watertight. I did not examine the contents of the chest particularly but they were all had up on deck and laid out to dry more than once. I know the quadrant in the box it was brought to me by one of the men it was quite dry and I took the sun with it, there were two quadrants the other quadrant was damp I think it came out of the forecastle, it was different from the quadrant now shown to me.

The Queen's Proctor contends that this story is not consistent with the first told in which it was stated that everything was wet.

The water in the forecastle was not so deep as it was in the Galley where it washed the pots and pans about and the water slushed out of the door when the ship rolled.

All the boxes had been moved by the rolling of the vessel and the swash of the water, the boxes did not float. I do not know how deep the water was in the forecabin. In the galley there must have been a foot of water it was over the tops of my shoes. After boring the holes the water run out of the cabin but it not all run out until the next day. The water in the forecabin I should say would be perhaps six inches deep.

I myself do not think that the water found by us in the galley and cabins had been there ten days. There had been rain and squals only a morning or two before we found the vessel and the hatches were all off and the cabin skylight and windows open the rain would necessarily get in.

I found a barrel of flour which was three parts full of water the barrel had been standing near the open hatchway. I threw it overboard it appeared to me as if there had been bread in it. I did not notice any barrel of Stockholm tar on the ship or in the cabin.

The Queen's Advocate states the all these questions are necessary in the ends of justice in order to endeavour to solve the mystery of the abandonment of the ship by her master and crew. Also that he alone represents the interests of the master Briggs the owner of the equity of redemption of some of the shares of the *Mary Celeste*.

As to the topsail I know nothing about it being cut, my men if they had wanted a piece of old canvass would probably cut it but I do not know that they did cut it nor have I seen any pieces of canvass about the ship. I kept the log of the *Mary Celeste* after I got on board that is to say I wrote it by memory after we got in to Gibraltar. I did not write it down at the time but the Captain of the *Dei Gratia* having come on board and said he wished I had done so I said I thought I still could do it from memory with the help of my chart on which was the ship's course and the latitude and longitude and from that I entered the log up as it now appears.

The entry made on Friday the sixth is not correct. I see there that it stated that the Captain on the *Dei Gratia* came on board the *Mary Celeste* that was not so. The Entry Captain Moorehouse came on board 'with a letter of instructions' is not correct. In point of fact Captain Moorehouse did not come on board he had stated that he should come on board but he sent the letter of instructions in a boat by two men without himself coming I cannot explain otherwise how I made the error. The Captain has not seen the entry nor spoke to me about it and my attention is now called for the first time, to the error by you. I cannot say positively whether the letter of instruction was brought to me on that day or on the day before, it was on the first or on the second day.

Re examined by Pisani

I was obliged to leave one of the two men in hospital at Genoa in consequence of his having strained or injured himself from over exertion whilst bringing the *Mary Celeste* to Gibraltar. His name is Charles Dund he is still in hospital in Genoa.

Pisani Calls

Thomas Joseph Vecchio Marshal of the Court already sworn when I first went on board the *Mary Celeste* to arrest the vessel the things in the bottom of the Captain's trunk and of the Mate's trunk were very wet. It took many days to Dry them and some of them I have not been able to dry which induces me to believe they were wetted by salt water and not by fresh water. The things belonging to the lady were only damp they were not wet nor stained which they would have been as some of them were silk dresses. The things were handed to me by Captain Moorehouse in the Captain's cabin the things in the lower drawers were all wet and damaged the things in the upper drawers were quite dry.

I have kept on board the *Mary Celeste* since she has been in my arrest no less than five men by advice of the Port Authorities and two anchors in the water and one ready to drop.

By Queen's Proctor There were four drawers in the Captain's cabin. In one of the lower drawers only were the things wet the things were dry in the three upper drawers. There was or had been more water on one side of the cabin on the starboard side than on the port side owing it is supposed to the inclination of the vessel. All the articles or almost all the articles had been removed from the *Mary Celeste*, the particular position therefore in which my article was found by me is not to be relied upon as indicating where it was when the vessel was abandoned.

The skylight extends over the two cabins the water closet opens into the Captain's cabin the pantry opens into the other cabin. The chart in use was found in the mate's cabin it was high up over his bed and was quite dry. The Harmonium was exactly under the skylight when I found it but it was quite dry and uninjured. It was made of rosewood. This musical instrument and the articles of her dress and ornaments found in the cabin lead to the belief that she was a lady of refined taste and habits her child's thing likewise pointed to the same belief.

With the exception of one box which contained the Captain's white summer clothing all the other boxes were open when I received them in charge. I found a silver watch and some gold money.

The mate explained to me the mystery of the clock being found upside down he himself had taken it down to dry and clean and try and make it go but not succeeding had put it up as found it.

The evidence of John Wright able seaman of the vessel *Dei Gratia* and one of the crew placed on board the *Mary Celeste* to bring her into the port of Gibraltar taken before the court on his examination viva voce on the 20th December 1872 is read in open court by the Registrar.

The evidence of Charles Dund taken on the 20th December 1872 the evidence of Augustus Anderson and of John Johnson taken and examined on the 29th day of January and the 31st day of January 1873 were read in court by the Registrar.

The Judge assigned to hear council further tomorrow and adjourned the Vice Admiralty Court to that day.

Edward J. Baumgartner

Registrar

Wednesday 5th March 1873

Mary Celeste

-derelict-

Cause of Salvage

The further hearing of this cause was proceeded with this day

Her Majesty's Advocate and Proctor in her office of Admiralty read the affidavit and survey of John Austen sworn and filed on the 8th day of January last – prepared by himself the Advocate for H. M. mentions that Colonel Laffan and others had seen the cuts in the bow of the vessel called the spalls and that if necessary he was prepared to prove that they had been made by a sharp cutting instrument also affidavit of Ricardo Fortune to the diver sworn and filed 7th January.

Stokes Advocate and Proctor for the owners of the cargo laden on board the *Mary Celeste* and appearing for Cornwell Proctor for the owners of the vessel, addressed the court on the question of amount of salvage admits salvage services rendered Posini's parties to be meritorious but not to entitle them to their claim of one half. The value of cargo is 36943 0 0. nett. And of the vessel 5700 together 42643 or 8528 Doblonces de Isabel and 60 reels vellon. Reads the cases. The true Blue 1.2. Rep Ad.Cases.

The *Charles* MAR. Law cases p. 296 October 1872 showing principles of remuneration to which salving vessels are entitled there are several elements or ingredients which influence reports in it's award, one element of danger in rendering services, element of season of the year which is connected with the first element, of value of vessel or cargo salved, element of value of vessel and cargo salving element that a vessel is derelict &c

Stokes reads the case of the *Charles*.

Stokes contends that the owners of the cargo should be charged with the heavy expenses which have been incurred since she was brought in but that they should fall upon the vessel herself the expenses having been occasioned by the abandonment of the ship by her Master and crew either Improperly or for some cause unknown.

The Queen's Advocate replies to Stokes argument or does not propose to do so only some strictures made by Stokes upon the owners of the vessel now unrepresented through absence of Cornwell, moreover, Captain Briggs the Master of the *Mary Celeste* is entirely unrepresented by anyone except by himself, the Queen's Proctor Briggs will be ruined if the whole expense is thrown on the ship as his mortgage will go scot free and escape contributing anything to salvage expenses.

The Queen's Advocate addressed the Court for some time on the salvage question taking place of Cornwell and of Briggs as counsel for them and against the claim of Salvors.

Mr Pisani replies and reads handbook on salvage p. 119 contends that the care of a derelict is quite different to that of a vessel with a crew on board and that each case should be judged on it's own merits and the merits of this case were very great.

The vessel was entirely abandoned found drifting in the middle of the ocean in the winter, the stormy season of the year, with her hatches and sky lights open with the chances of her going down and being absolutely lost or the chances of her being run into by some other vessel perhaps to the loss of both.

There was great courage and risk to both vessels in dividing the crew of the *Dei Gratia* as was done and great skill in bringing the two vessels into the port of Gibraltar as has been done — reads his book on salvage of derelicts. Principal seldom more than one half or less than one thirds avoided.

The *Fortune* 4 Robinson p. 193

The *George Dean* 1 Swabey p. 219.

The Judge assigned to give judgment at a future day And adjourned the Vice Admiralty Court to Tuesday next the eleventh day of March instant.

Edward J. Baumgartner
Registrar

Bibliography

Baldwin, Hanson. W. *Sea Fights and Shipwrecks*. New York: Hanover House, 1956.

Bradford, Gershom. *The Secret of Mary Celeste and Other Sea Fare*. London: Foulsham, 1967.

Bryan, George S. *Mystery Ship, the Mary Celeste in Fancy and in Fact*. Philadelphia: J.B. Lippincott, 1942.

Cobb, Oliver W. *Rose Cottage*. New Bedford, Massachusetts: Reynolds-DeWalt Publishers, 1968.

Cohen, Daniel. *Missing! Stories of Strange Disappearances*. New York: Dodd Mead, 1979.

Dennis, Clara. *More About Nova Scotia. My Own, My Native Land*. Toronto: The Ryerson Press, 1937.

Fay, Charles Edey. *Mary Celeste: The Odyssey of an Abandoned Ship*. Salem, Mass.: Peabody Museum, 1942.

Fay, Charles Edey. *The Story of the 'Mary Celeste'*. New York: Dover Publications, 1988.

Furneaux, Rupert. *What Happened on the Mary Celeste*. London: M. Parrish, 1964.

Gould, Rupert Thomas. *The Stargazer Talks*. London: Geoffrey Bles, 1946.

Hastings, Macdonald. *Mary Celeste: A Centenary Record*. London: Michael Joseph, 1972.

Hoehling, A.A. *Lost at Sea*. Harrisburgh, Pennsylvania: Stackpole Books, 1984.

Keating, Laurence J. *The Great Mary Celeste Hoax, a Famous Sea Mystery Exposed*. London: Heath Cranton, 1929.

Lockhart, J.G. *A Great Sea Mystery: The True Story of the 'Mary Celeste'*. London: Phillip Allen and Co, 1927.

Lockhart, John Gilbert. *The 'Mary Celeste' and Other Strange Tales of the Sea*. London: Rupert Hart-Davis, 1952.

Peach, Lawrence du Garde. *Radio Plays*. London: G. Newnes Ltd, 1932.

Spicer, Stanley. *The Saga of the Mary Celeste*. Hantsport, Nova Scotia: Lancelot Press, 1993.

Spicer, Stanley T. *Masters of Sail*. Toronto: Ryerson Press, 1968.

Index